T0305389

SUSTAINABLE OPERATIONS AND SUPPLY CHAIN MANAGEMENT

Wiley Series in
Operations Research and Management Science

A complete list of the titles in this series appears at the end of this volume.

SUSTAINABLE OPERATIONS AND SUPPLY CHAIN MANAGEMENT

VALERIA BELVEDERE
Catholic University of the Sacred Heart, Milan, Italy

ALBERTO GRANDO
Bocconi University – SDA Bocconi School of Management, Milan, Italy

This edition first published 2017
© 2017 John Wiley & Sons Ltd

Registered office
John Wiley & Sons Ltd, The Atrium, Southern Gate, Chichester, West Sussex, PO19 8SQ,
United Kingdom

For details of our global editorial offices, for customer services and for information about how to apply
for permission to reuse the copyright material in this book please see our website at www.wiley.com.

Library of Congress Cataloging-in-Publication Data

Names: Belvedere, Valeria, 1973– author. I Grando, Alberto, 1957– author.
Title: Sustainable operations and supply chain management / Valeria Belvedere, Alberto Grando.
Description: Hoboken : Wiley, 2017. I Series: Wiley series in operations research
   and management science I Includes bibliographical references and index.
Identifiers: LCCN 2016036070 (print) I LCCN 2016037822 (ebook) I ISBN 9781119284956 (cloth) I
   ISBN 9781119285366 (pdf) I ISBN 9781119285373 (epub)
Subjects: LCSH: Sustainable development. I Business logistics.
Classification: LCC HC79.E5 B4455 2017 (print) I LCC HC79.E5 (ebook) I DDC 658.5–dc23
LC record available at https://lccn.loc.gov/2016036070

A catalogue record for this book is available from the British Library.

Set in 10/12pt Times by SPi Global, Pondicherry, India

10 9 8 7 6 5 4 3 2 1

DEDICATION

'We have only one planet. There is no plan B because there is no planet B'.
Ban Ki Moon, 2015

To our daughters
Giulia and Carla,
Margherita and Chiara,
who will live in the planet we will be able to give them.

DEDICATION

CONTENTS

PREFACE

The increasing relevance of the debate on the future of our planet is witnessed by the high number of claims and speeches recently pronounced, among which the following seem to be particularly meaningful:

In rising to the climate challenge, we can set the world on a sustainable footing for generations to come, and lay the foundation for prosperity and security for all... We have only one planet. There is no Plan B because there is no planet B.

Ban Ki Moon, United Nations General Secretary, on the first day of the final week of the 21st UN Climate Summit, December 7, 2015.

I urgently appeal, then, for a new dialogue about how we are shaping the future of our planet. We need a conversation which includes everyone, since the environmental challenge we are undergoing, and its human roots, concern and affect us all.... Some forms of pollution are part of people's daily experience. Exposure to atmospheric pollutants produces a broad spectrum of health hazards, especially for the poor, and causes millions of premature deaths.... Technology, which, linked to business interests, is presented as the only way of solving these problems, in fact proves incapable of seeing the mysterious network of relations between things and so sometimes solves one problem only to create others.

Pope Francis, encyclical letter "Laudato Si'" On Care for our Common Home, May 24, 2015.

Unsafe and poor working conditions lead to significant social and economic losses and are linked to environmental damage. Given our prominent share in the globalisation process, G7 countries have an important role to play in promoting labour rights, decent working conditions and environmental protection in global supply chains. We will strive for better application of internationally recognised labour, social and environmental standards, principles and commitments (in particular UN, OECD, ILO and applicable environmental agreements) in global supply chains. We will engage with other countries, for example within the G20, to that end.

G7 Leaders' Declaration on Responsible Global Supply Chains, G7 Summit at Schloss Elmau, Germany, June 7–8, 2015.

We have a moral obligation to leave our children a planet that's not polluted or damaged. The effects of climate change are already being felt across the nation.... Extreme weather events – from more severe droughts and wildfires in the West to record heat waves – and sea level rise are hitting communities across the country. In fact, 14 of the 15 warmest years on record have all occurred in the first 15 years of this century and last year was the warmest year ever. The most vulnerable among us – including children, older adults, people with heart or lung disease, and people living in poverty – are most at risk from the impacts of climate change. Taking action now is critical.

President Obama's announcement on the Clean Power Plan, August 3, 2015.

...We will unwaveringly pursue a strategy of sustainable development and stay committed to green, low-carbon and circular development and China's fundamental policy of conserving resources and protecting the environment. In promoting green development, we also aim to address climate change and over-capacity. .... We will meet the people's aspirations for a better life, raise their living standards and the quality of their lives, improve the public services system and enlarge the middle-income group.... With more attention paid to equity and fairness, we will make the pie bigger and ensure that people get a fair share of it. We will resolve the most pressing problems affecting the immediate interests of the people to their satisfaction.

H.E. Xi Jinping, President of the People's Republic of China at the Opening Ceremony of the B20 Summit, Hangzhou, China, September 3, 2016.

As demonstrated by these quotes, the topic of sustainability is crucial for the well-being of populations and of their future generations but is complex to address. It can be analysed from several perspectives, as those of policymakers, companies and even individuals willing to undertake appropriate actions in this regard. Focusing on the enterprises, such a complexity is made even higher due to the numerous processes that can affect the sustainability of an organisation and to the wide range of choices to be made in each of them.

The perimeter of investigation of this book refers to operations and supply chain management processes carried out within companies, with the aim of identifying the principles, frameworks and managerial tools that can be adopted along the life cycle of the product to achieve a satisfactory overall performance, in accordance with the triple bottom line approach.

This book is the final output of an intense research effort, whose purpose was to provide a wide range of readers (entrepreneurs, managers, students) with a systematic and updated review of this topic, grounding it into the most consolidated knowledge in the field of operations and supply chain management.

We want to thank all those who supported us in this project: colleagues, managers, guest speakers from public and private institutions and, most of all, our students, who let us understand the relevance of sustainability in the perspective of the young generations.

This work has been conceived through a strong cooperation between the authors. However, Chapters 1, 2, 3 and 7 have been written by Alberto Grando and Chapters 4, 5, 6 and 8 by Valeria Belvedere.

We hope that this book can determine a higher degree of awareness towards these challenges and contribute to the dissemination of a managerial culture rooted in the principles of sustainability, especially for younger generations, who are going to lead and change the world in the near future.

Valeria Belvedere
Alberto Grando
Milan
January, 2017

ACKNOWLEDGEMENTS

Except where acknowledged in the text, all illustrations in this book are the property of copyright holders. The authors and publisher are grateful to all who gave their permission for the use of copyright material. They apologise if they have inadvertently failed to acknowledge any copyright holder and will be glad to correct any omissions that are drawn to their attention in future reprints or editions.

We are indebted to the anonymous reviewers for their valuable suggestions that helped us improve our work.

We are grateful to the following publishing companies and societies for permitting us to include parts of their papers and reports in this book: Emerald Group Publishing Ltd. for Figures 2.4 and 2.5; McGraw-Hill for Figures 3.5 and 3.6 and for Table 3.1; Taylor & Francis for Figures 5.7, 6.2 and 6.4 and for Tables 4.1 and 4.2; Elsevier for Figure 6.3 and for Table 6.6; Barilla Center for Food & Nutrition for Table 1.1; the Chartered Institute of Procurement & Supply for Figure 4.2 and for Table 4.3; Ellen MacArthur Foundation for Figure 3.2 and for Box 3.1; California Management Review for Figures 7.4 and 7.7; RobecoSAM for Figures 8.2 and 8.3; Oxford University Press for Figure 3.1; The British Standards Institution for Figure 3.3; the Lean Enterprise Institute for Figure 5.1; the European Union Road Federation for Figure 6.1; Business Expert Press for Figure 7.5; the Global Footprint Network for Figure 8.1; the United Nations for Table 8.1; and Corbett (2009), http://www.jiem.org/index.php/jiem/article/viewArticle/15, used under CC BY 3.0 http://creativecommons.org/licenses/by/3.0/, for Figures 2.6 and 2.7.

1

SUSTAINABILITY AND FUTURE TRENDS

1.1 INTRODUCTION

The 70th session of the General Assembly has opened with a towering achievement: the adoption of the 2030 Agenda, including 17 inspiring Sustainable Development Goals, the SDGs.

Our aim is clear. Our mission is possible. And our destination is in our sights: an end to extreme poverty by 2030; a life of peace and dignity for all.

What counts now is translating promises on paper into change on the ground.

We owe this and much more to the vulnerable, the oppressed, the displaced and the forgotten people in our world.

We owe this to a world where inequality is growing, trust is fading, and impatience with leadership can be seen and felt far and wide.

We owe this to 'succeeding generations', in the memorable words the Charter.

In this year in which we mark the 70th anniversary of the United Nations, we must heed the call of the Charter, and hear the voices of 'we the peoples.' That is how we can overcome the grim realities of the present and seize the remarkable opportunities of our era.

The Millennium Development Goals made poverty history for hundreds of millions of people.

Now we are poised to continue the job while reaching higher, broader and deeper.

Sustainable Operations and Supply Chain Management, First Edition. Valeria Belvedere and Alberto Grando.
© 2017 John Wiley & Sons Ltd. Published 2017 by John Wiley & Sons Ltd.

The new framework does not just add goals. It weaves the goals together, with human rights, the rule of law and women's empowerment as crucial parts of an integrated whole.

The global goals are universal.

You, the world's leaders, have committed to leave no one behind and to reach those farthest behind, first. We can build on the momentum this December in Paris with a robust agreement on climate change.

Remarkable changes are under way to reduce harmful greenhouse emissions. I have seen and visited vast solar power installations bringing a new energy future into being. There is wind in the sails of climate action.

Yet it is clear that the national targets submitted by the member states will not be enough. We face a choice: either raise ambition or risk raising temperatures above the degree Celsius threshold, which science tells us we must not cross.

Reaching our sustainable development goals means organizing ourselves better. Let there be no more walls or boxes; no more ministries or agencies working at cross purposes. Let us move from silos to synergy, supported by data, long term planning and a will to do things differently...

Source: Excerpt from speech by Ban Ki-moon at 70th UN General Assembly, 28 September, 2015. Available at http://gadebate.un.org/sites/default/files/gastate ments/70/70_SG_en.pdf.

As highlighted in the speech of Secretary Ban Ki-moon, sustainability is a global goal, encompassing several different areas: environment protection, climate change, social inequality, human rights, poverty and nutrition.

In the first part of this Chapter, the definitions of *sustainability* and *sustainable development* are introduced, and the major issues related to the imperative of nutrition are presented; in the second part of the Chapter, the impact of some *mega-trends* on these phenomena is underlined, and the main *pay-offs* and *reasons why* governments, institutions and companies are required to focus on sustainable objectives are pointed out. This Chapter aims at providing the general picture in which the main topics covered in this book – operations and supply chain management – have to be framed in the light of sustainability.

1.2 SUSTAINABILITY BEFORE SUSTAINABLE OPERATIONS AND SUPPLY CHAIN MANAGEMENT

To speak of sustainability, even from the specific perspective of Operations and Supply Chain Management, means confronting the question of how to pursue the objectives of the present – whether they are those of a company, an institution or a wider socio-economic system – while ensuring that adequate standards of development are also guaranteed in the future.

The subject of sustainability is therefore intrinsically connected to a vision of the future that postulates *intergenerational equity* and it is for this reason that we have decided to start our discussion with an analysis – albeit brief – of several scenarios that, most probably, will form the backdrop for the choices to be made by those that must make governance decisions, such as managers, entrepreneurs or heads of government. The socio-economic context in which future generations will live and companies and institutions will operate will largely be the result of the decisions made today and, in particular, of the actions to be taken due to these decisions. It is in the knowledge of this great responsibility, therefore, that it seems appropriate to rethink management choices, placing attention on a more extensive, complex, objective function than the one that traditionally characterises company operations, which is often summarised in the objective of value creation for shareholders. It involves, in fact, devising decision-making processes based on the values of responsibility, ethics and sustainability, within a time frame that is consistent with the ability of the system to generate and regenerate adequate resources for sustaining its development. The subject is complex and has both micro- and macroeconomic implications. It transcends the boundaries of a single discipline, encompassing aspects connected to the economy, management, economic policy, sociology, demographics and so on.

It therefore seems appropriate, right from the very beginning, to clearly define the specific perimeter in which the considerations contained in this work will be developed. This book focuses on some of the most important managerial processes – Operations and Supply Chain Management – and in this regard we have decided to examine the subject of corporate sustainability as systematically as possible. Indeed, it is not the intention of this study to thoroughly analyse the subject of corporate sustainability as a whole, which is why reference is made to many of the literature contributions (Benn et al., 2014; Tencati and Perini, 2011; Craig Smith and Lenssen, 2009), but rather to limit our analysis to the organisation and management of operations and supply chain processes, examined from a broad perspective (Cooper et al., 1997), and their interaction with the imperative of sustainability.

It may appear strange to start the discussion that will lead us to the subject area of this book, namely the topic of Sustainable Operations and Supply Chain Management, by looking at two factors considered to be available commodities today, at least in one part – the most fortunate part – of our planet: food and water.

The decision to dwell upon the growing scarcity of food and water, which are essential for survival, is based on a threefold consideration:

- First, because, however much it may appear obvious, these are two factors that are essential for the survival of the planet, the scarcity and unfair distribution of which already require an urgent response today in terms of global policies that guarantee the access and the availability of them to an increasing number of people.
- Second, because these two elements, food and water, are intrinsically dependent on one another: to produce food, a large quantity of water is consumed, and therefore raising the quality and quantity of food offered to those who need it, given current technology and lifestyles, will lead to an rapid shortage of water resources.

- Third, because the solutions that may be advised today to deal effectively with these problems concern the productivity of the agro-food system, the technology required for increasing the aforesaid productivity, the fight against waste and the responsible management of the connected supply chains – the main topics of this work.

We will attempt to develop these three points briefly next.

The global food system today is capable of producing 2800 calories per day per person compared to an average daily requirement of approximately 2550 calories. This means that today the planet would be capable of feeding its population of approximate 7 billion and, according to some studies, of sustaining 9 and even 11 billion people (Stuart, 2009; Hanley, 2014).

Nevertheless, about 2.5 billion people today live on less than $2 a day; the poorest families spend more than 70% of the their income on food (WB, 2010); 36 million people die every year due to malnutrition and undernourishment; about 870 million people are hit by malnutrition, 852 million of whom live in developing countries; and approximately 1.1 billion people are undernourished (FAO, 2012). At the same time, in a dramatic food paradox, more than 1.5 billion people are obese or overweight, a problem that is increasingly widespread, and almost 30 million people die each year from diseases linked to excess food (BCFN, 2012).

According to reliable projections (UNPD, 2015), demographic growth will drive the current 7.3 billion inhabitants on Earth to 8.5 billion by 2030 and more than 9.5 billion by 2050[1], meaning an increase of 30% in thirty-five years, who will have to be fed by extending agro-food production. Agriculture, however, is responsible today for 70–80% of the water consumption destined for food production and 33% of the global production of greenhouse gases – the main factors at the crux of climate change. Within the same time frame, it is estimated that arable land will be reduced by between 8% and 20% due to the effects of climate change, with the consequent modification of the geography of farming, which will lead to the conversion of tropical, subtropical and temperate forests into farmland. It is estimated that approximately 45% of these forests will be lost. More than 240 million people (most of them in rural areas) are projected to lack access to an improved water source by 2050, and almost 1.4 billion people will not have access to basic sanitation (OECD, 2012).

As already stated, there is a close interdependence between food production and water consumption. Currently 70% of freshwater withdrawals are destined for farm irrigation, whereas 22% are used by industry and the remaining 8% by domestic consumption (BCFN, 2012, p. 160)[2]. The consumption of freshwater is closely

---

[1] According to the most recent forecast, the world population will stabilise at around 11 billion people at the end of the century. The growth rate of the world population, which 10 years ago was 1.24% per year has dropped to 1.18% today; 83 countries, which represent 46% of the world population have a fertility rate lower than the rate of replacement, namely 2.1 children per woman, and in other countries, which represent a further 46% of the world population, births are slightly decreasing. Half of the predicted growth by 2050 will be in only nine countries, the majority of which are extremely poor (UNPD, 2015).

[2] These percentages refer to average consumption; the impact of agriculture is significantly higher in low/medium income countries or developing countries, where it may reach 95%, whereas in industrialised countries consumption linked to industry reaches 59% (BCFN, 2012).

connected to the food production chain and consumption behaviours in the most populated areas of the planet. For instance, it is enough to recall the impact of the above in terms of Water Footprint (also known as Virtual Water Content), which analyses different types of food, measuring the consumption of water expressed in litres for each kilogram or litre of food produced (cultivated or raised), handled, packaged, transported and made suitable (e.g. cooked) for consumption (BCFN, 2012). One kilogram of beef requires 15,500 litres of water, rice 3400, bread 1300, milk 1000, potatoes 900 and so on.

Table 1.1 below contains a summary of the environmental impact of several foods, expressed in terms of their carbon, water and ecological footprints.

It appears obvious that the demand for food implied in the social imperative to reduce the problem of malnutrition, or more simply induced by the evolution of the quality of consumption models, combined with the demographic developments described previously and in the absence of appropriate action, will risk producing a disastrous impact on the availability of resources such as water, which are also being diminished due to the effects of climate change and the gradual pollution of the groundwater caused by the growth in population.

Re-examining the data stated before, the expectation that several million consumers in other rapidly developing countries, in escaping situations of poverty, will gradually adopt 'western' eating patterns, translates into an easy prediction in terms of the Water Footprint, which may lead first of all to an increase in the price of this fundamental element – the blue gold – and then to much more dramatic scenarios. In the last twenty years the consumption of meat in China has doubled, and it is esti-mated to double again by 2030. Giving up one kilogram of rice and replacing it with one kilogram of beef translates into a consumption of resources expressed in a Virtual

TABLE 1.1 Carbon, water and ecological footprint of most common foodstuffs

Food	Carbon footprint (gCO_2 eq./kg or l)	Water footprint (Water kg or l)	Ecological footprint (m^2/kg or l)
Beef	26,000	15,500	109
Cheese	9500	5000	93
Butter	8600	5000	86
Eggs	4540	3300	16
Pork	4250	4800	28
Fish	3900	n.a.	71
Rice	3850	3400	12
Poultry	3600	3900	25
Oil	3200	5555	40
Pasta	3000	1775	15
Pulses	1600	3160	19
Milk	1300	1000	15
Bread	900	1300	7
Fruit	670	930	4
Vegetables	665	240	3
Potatoes	600	900	4

Source: Reproduced with permission of Barilla Center for Food & Nutrition.

Water Content that is 4.5 times higher, a Carbon Footprint that is 6.7 times higher and an Ecological Footprint that is a good nine times higher! By 2050, the need for water and its uneven distribution among countries will have dramatic effects on the 9 plus billion inhabitants of the planet, located in concentrated areas due to the growing phenomenon of urbanisation. In fact, some estimates predict that of the 9.3 billion inhabitants on earth, 67% will live in cities and the remaining 33% in rural areas (Van Audenhove et al., 2014).

Furthermore, it must be emphasised that, regardless of developments that will be introduced by technological innovation, current methods for managing production, distribution and food consumption processes hide enormous recovery margins and generate waste that, due to its extent, is extremely unacceptable, from an ethical point of view more so than an economic one. It is sufficient to quote the FAO: 'the global volume of food wastage is estimated to be approximately 1.6 billion tonnes of 'primary products equivalent' while the total wastage of edible part of food is 1.3 billion tonnes' (FAO, 2013, p. 6). This means that one third of global food production is lost, destroyed or wasted during conservation, transformation, distribution and consumption processes (FAO, 2011).

Once again, the unfair distribution of wealth and its connected models of production and consumption produce a clear difference between waste and scarcity. The waste produced along agro-business supply chains is known as *food loss* when dealing with the losses that occur upstream, and as *food waste* when dealing with waste that takes place during the industrial processing, distribution and final consumption processes. Food losses, or spoiling, take place at production, postharvest and processing stages in the food supply chain. Food losses occurring at the end of the food chain (retail and final consumption) are rather called 'food waste', which relates to retailers' and consumers' behaviour (Grolleaud, 2002; Parfitt et al., 2010[3]). In this case the causes and the distribution of losses and waste also differ depending on the countries: food losses mainly occur in developing countries due to limits in their cultivation, harvesting and preservation techniques and methods, or due to the lack of adequate transportation and storage infrastructures. Food waste, on the other hand, is more common in industrialised countries, notably during the final consumption phase (household consumption and catering), and in these countries there are significant wastes also during the production process (selection and packaging)

[3] A definition of food waste was given by the UN Food and Agriculture Organisation (FAO): 'Food losses refer to the decrease in edible food mass throughout the part of the supply chain that specifically leads to edible food for human consumption. Food losses take place at production, post-harvest and processing stages in the food supply chain' (Parfitt et al., 2010). Food losses occurring at the end of the food chain (retail and final consumption) are rather called 'food waste', which relates to retailers' and consumers' behaviour (Parfitt et al., 2010). 'Food' waste or loss is measured only for products that are directed to human consumption, excluding feed and parts of products that are not edible. As per the definition, food losses or waste are the masses of food lost or wasted in the part of food chains leading to 'edible products going to human consumption'.
Therefore, food that was originally meant for human consumption but which gets out of the human food chain is considered as food loss or waste, even if it is then directed to a non-food use (feed, bioenergy etc.). This approach distinguishes 'planned' non-food uses to 'unplanned' non-food uses, which are hereby accounted under losses (FAO, 2011, p. 2).

TABLE 1.2 Global food losses and waste along the supply chain

Supply chain stage	Million tonnes of food	%
Agricultural production	510	32
Post-harvesting and storage	355	22
Industrial processing	180	11
Distribution	200	13
Consumer	345	22
TOTAL	1590	100

Source: adapted from FAO, 2013, p. 13.

phase, due to the assertion of questionable sizing and aesthetic standards, and product quality or production surplus regulations. It has been estimated that Europe and the United States consume an amount of food that is equal to double the nutritional requirement of their population and, between food losses and food waste, approximately half of the food supplied is wasted along the cycle described previously (Stuart, 2009).

The quantity of food that is dumped in industrialised countries, estimated at 222 million tonnes, matches the food production available in sub-Saharan Africa, which amounts to 230 million tonnes (FAO, 2011).

Much of this waste is the result of incorrect purchase and management models related to the consumer in terms of excess purchasing, excess portions prepared, errors in food storage, and so forth; but a good part is also linked to errors in 'product planning stage', such as in the case of oversizing portions that produces waste, or the assertion, as already mentioned, of sizing and aesthetic standards that cause high levels of waste upstream, or supply chain management in terms of conservation technology and methods, packaging, transportation and distribution – the main subject of the following pages. As summarised in Table 1.2, in fact, of the 1.6 billion tonnes of primary products equivalent lost/wasted stated previously, more than 45% takes place during the stages linked to the Operations and Supply Chain Management, such as post-harvesting and storage, industrial processing and distribution.

Going back to the relationship between the consumption of water and food, it is sufficient to think, as effectively reported, that the quantity of water necessary to produce the quantity of food wasted every year on a global scale is estimated at 250,000 billion litres, equivalent to the current domestic water requirement of a city like New York for 120 years (Segré, 2015). In addition to this, the food produced but wasted requires 1.4 billion hectares of land per year, the equivalent of about 30% of the world agricultural land area and generates a carbon footprint of 3.3 billion tonnes of carbon dioxide. If food waste was a country it would be the third top emitter after the United States and China (Segré, 2015; FAO, 2013).

1.3 THE IMPACT OF CLIMATE CHANGE

The prospect of an increasing scarcity of resources, such as food, fuel, metals and farmland, and their unequal distribution throughout the world, will change the geopolitics of the planet and is already forcing many countries to take action, such as China, which is taking the lead in investing in the areas richest in resources, as well as many areas of Africa. For other needs the battle is well underway to gain the rights to exploit the resources preserved in the Arctic areas.

According to some interpretations, most of the recent wars, as those in Northern Africa and in the Middle East, occurred also because of the extreme poverty of the local communities, which has been worsened by a severe drought caused in turn by climate change, as in the case of Syria. A similar interpretation can be given to the root causes of the exponential growth of migration flows from these countries, which are resulting in a huge humanitarian emergency. The impact of climate change has been deeply analysed in the last ten years and several studies have predicted the effects on our lives (Lewis et al., 2001; Rockström et al., 2009; Monastersky, 2015). A recent study, developed thanks to the contribution of several research centres, institutes and universities from all over the world (Steffen et al., 2015), highlighted the impact of human development on the Earth System in terms of changes in biosphere integrity (ozone depletion, air pollution etc.), ocean acidification, biogeochemical flows (resources depletion, impact on biodiversity etc.), land-system change (land degradation, solid waste impact etc.) and freshwater use (water pollution and scarcity).

As is well-known, *climate change* is caused by the increase in the emissions of so-called greenhouse gases linked to the use of fossil fuels, which have led to progressive global warming. In 650,000 years there have been seven ice ages, and the level of carbon dioxide has never exceeded 300 parts per million; since 1950 this threshold has been exceeded, reaching 400 parts per million in just a few years from now. Global warming has increased significantly since the 1970s; this growth trend is dramatically demonstrated by the fact that the twenty hottest years ever recorded have occurred from 1981, ten of which in the last twelve years (NASA, 2015).

Unless changes are made through the radical alteration of the lifestyles of the world's population or through technological innovations capable of replacing the technologies that have the greatest impact or through policies aimed at limiting their use, it is estimated that emissions will double within fifty years, with irreversible consequences for the planet. Some scenarios (OECD, 2012) estimate an increase in gas emissions that could reach a concentration of 685 ppm – parts of CO_2- equivalent per million, which would cause an increase in the mean temperature of more than 2.5 °C at the middle of the century and between 3 and 6 °C by 2100, with possible catastrophic consequences for many areas of the planet. If it were possible to stabilise the concentration of gases below the threshold of 450 ppm, there would be a 50% chance of limiting the increase in the average temperatures to 2 °C, producing significant, but manageable, effects in terms of climate change.

The impact of these changes, the majority of which are already visible, will manifest themselves in terms of the progressive desertification of large areas of the planet, consequent deforestation, caused by the need to find new lands to cultivate, impact on biodiversity and the disappearance of many current species of flora and fauna.

Furthermore, the increase in the amount of polluting agents in the atmosphere, water and ground will have an increasing impact on the health of humans and animals. Warming seas will also intensify extreme meteorological phenomena, such as tornadoes and floods, the cost of which will be extremely high as measured in terms of human and animal lives, destruction of crops, impact on infrastructures and the flooding of extensive populated areas.

If most countries set themselves the objective of limiting the increase in average temperatures to 2 °C above the average temperatures registered in pre-industrial times (UNFCCC, 2010), current growth trends, although extenuated by the effects of the crisis, seem to exceed these values. The effects in terms of desertification, reduction of precipitation, increase in the number of hurricanes and other extreme meteorological phenomena would be felt more in the poorest areas of the world, which are located in the most exposed band of the planet, in medium and low latitudes. The melting of the glaciers and the consequent raising of sea levels, would consume thousands of kilometres of coastline, atolls would disappear, and approximately 150,000,000 people living in cities and coastal settlements would be affected. According to some studies (Church and White, 2006), the sea level has already risen by about 17 cm in the last century, with an increase in the last decade of double the amount recorded in the previous hundred years.

The progressive deforestation of vast green areas and the increasing pollution of the soil and water resources, together with expected demographic changes, risk speeding up the evolution of the trends and the phenomena stated earlier and generating further imbalances, which without widespread and decisive intervention, appear difficult to remedy.

The topics dealt with in this book, motivated by the knowledge that it is necessary to review operations and supply chain management processes in light of the imperative of sustainability, constitute only one component of an ever more urgent and general need, which must be embraced and converted into coherent action, not only at the level of national and supranational policy, but also in the daily actions of companies and their managers, and in the behaviour of consumers and all those that understand the importance of responsible behaviour.

1.4   MEGA-TRENDS AND SUSTAINABILITY

The scenarios and tendencies described previously may be accelerated or delayed and produce effects that are accentuated or mitigated by the parallel occurrence of other phenomena capable of significantly, if not radically, transforming the social, economic, political and cultural context in which people, companies and institutions will be forced to live and do business.

In particular, we are referring to trends and forces of change whose trajectory appears to be interconvertible – at least from the viewpoint of reliable forecasting – and capable of significantly modifying the framework of reference in which society develops. These trends, starting from the contribution of Naisbitt, who defined a 'megatrend as a general shift in thinking or approach affecting countries, industries and organisations' (Naisbitt, 1982, p. 3), have been given various names: Mega Trends (Naisbitt, 1982; Naisbitt and Aburdene, 1990; Singh, 2012), Global Forces (McKinsey G.I., 2010), Global Shift (Dicken, 2003; 2012), Global Trends (Malnight and Keys, 2013), to name but a few contributions.

Regardless of the differing definitions offered, a common trait emerges: Megatrends are global, sustained and macroeconomic forces of development and transformation (Singh, 2012). In the pages that introduce the main theme of our work, by drawing attention to the most relevant ones, we will highlight how the aforesaid mega-trends have a crucial impact on the topics described previously, as they are capable of aggravating or extenuating the alarming trends of unsustainability we have summarised.

1.4.1 Demographic Evolution

As already mentioned, the current world population is estimated at approximately 7 billion and is expected to grow to around 9.3 billion by 2050. According to recent estimations, the current population consumes approximately the equivalent of something between 1.5 and 1.8 planets of resources per year in terms of food, water, energy and other resources, and, given the current level of technological development and lifestyles, the destruction process of our natural resources will increase to two planets per year by 2030, growing to a little less than three planets by 2050. Likewise, the impact on the planet in terms of pollution, waste and other negative effects will rise. The world's population will grow (70% in less developed countries) at different rates depending on geographical area. In particular, it is estimated that China will remain almost stable, unless the effect of the recent abolishing the one child policy proves significant. Europe and Japan will see reduction or stability in their populations, and there will be a significant increase in Africa and India. The trends in terms of increases and decreases in population are linked, in addition to migratory phenomena, to the fertility rate of the different countries. Although different sources make forecasts that do not always coincide, the phenomenon of the progressive ageing of the population in several countries, linked to the increase in life expectancy, shows Incontrovertible trends. The number of people in the world aged over 60, is expected to rise from 510 million in 2011 to 1.6 billion by 2050 and to 2.4 billion by 2100 (Malnight and Keys, 2013). The over-65 population will double to 1 billion by 2030, once again with a marked geographical difference. In European countries the phenomenon will be accentuated, increasing the problems of growth in labour productivity and the sustainability of public spending linked to social welfare and health care. In general, in fact, older people save less, causing a decline in wealth accumulation and the consumption of more public spending. This fact, when faced with a progressive cut in public spending due to spending review policies, will offer many opportunities to private operators in many sectors linked to welfare that offer products and services dedicated to the ageing population. The working population, conventionally aged between fifteen and sixty-five years old, started to shrink in Europe and Japan in this decade, and it will shrink by 2020 in China too. By contrast, in some countries the number of young people will continue to grow. It is estimated in fact that, taking the Global Population into consideration, in 2015 there were 1.2 billion youth (aged between 15 and 24); by 2030 the number of youth is projected to grow by 7%, to about 1.3 billion. Nevertheless, even if Asia remains the most relevant region in terms of youth, the number of young people is projected to decline from 718 million in 2015 to 711 million in 2030 and 619 million in 2060. In contrast,

Africa shows a strong trend: 226 million youth in 2015 (19% of the global population) with a projected increase of 42% in 2030 (UNDESA, 2015). The impact of these trends on the capacity of the different countries to increase their growth rates is huge. It is enough to think that demographics alone explain 60% of GDP growth and 40% labour productivity growth (McKinsey G.I., 2010).

1.4.2 Urbanisation

The demographic growth described previously is associated with other phenomena, namely growing urbanisation and migratory flows from rural areas to the global metropolises. Whereas at the beginning of the last century, a little more than 20% of the world population lived in cities and 30% in the 1950s, today this proportion has risen to more than 54%, and it is estimated that it could reach a level close to 60% by 2030 and about 66% by 2050. Considering also that the total number of world inhabitants will grow by 30% between today and 2050, a total of approximately 6.5 billion people will be concentrated in vast urban areas (UNPD, 2014). Some studies estimate a further acceleration of these trends, estimating urbanisation levels at 60% of the world population by 2025 (Singh, 2012).

This migratory flow, comparable to the urbanisation of the nineteenth century, but on a much larger scale, is leading to the creation and development of urban mega-agglomerations, known as mega-cities, and more extensive areas with high population density, creating mega-regions and mega-corridors. Mega-cities, according to the definition of UN Habitat (2006), are urban agglomerations with more than 10 million inhabitants, such as Tokyo, Istanbul, Cairo, Mumbai, Delhi, Mexico City, London, Paris, Shanghai, Peking, São Paulo, Rio de Janeiro, Buenos Aires, Teheran, Calcutta, Jakarta, Manila, Moscow and Seoul. By 2025 there will be more than thirty-five mega-cities, the majority of which will be located in developing countries. It is also predicted that the first 600 world cities will generate 60% of the world GDP growth by 2025 and the first 100 approximately 35% of it. Of these 600, about 420 (about 70%) will be 'Emerging-market mega- and middleweight cities' that 'together are likely to contribute more than 45 percent of global growth from 2007 to 2025' (McKinsey G.I., 2011). Mega-cities like Bogota and Seoul account for more than 50% of the GDP of their countries, and Budapest and Brussels for 45% (Singh, 2012). Mega-regions with more than 50 million inhabitants are developing around these centres, consisting of a series of smaller cities and suburbs that are nonetheless strongly integrated with a mega-city, such as those around Pretoria, Lagos or Kinshasa, or greater Los Angeles and New York City. In particular, the number of mega-cities in old Europe will remain very small, whereas its geographical concentration has produced areas that are characterised by high population density and the significant ability to produce wealth that may be compared to mega-regions[4].

---

[4] This phenomenon has already been observed and analysed: for example, already at the beginning of the last century, Amsterdam–Rotterdam, Ruhr–Cologne, Brussels–Antwerp and Lille, with 59.2 million people and producing nearly $1.5 trillion in economic output or that of London–Leeds–Manchester–Liverpool–Birmingham combined, with about 50 million people and responsible for $1.2 trillion in economic output (Florida, 2008).

Mega-corridors are also being developed, or rather communication corridors between mega-cities, along which more than 25 million inhabitants settle, such as, for example, the Hong Kong–Shenzhen–Guangzhou corridors, which accounts for a population of 120 million inhabitants within an area of 120 km, or the industrial Delhi-Mumbai corridor, which is estimated to reach more than 200 million inhabitants by the year 2025 along its 1480 kilometres (Singh, 2012). These aggregates are the source of development of many nations, and will be even more so in the future, and at the same time they will be places of enormous and unacceptable inequality, with sections of the privileged population with immense wealth and much broader sections of the population seeking to survive, living within close proximity of one another. In many of these mega-cities, between 20 and 70% of the population will live in slums, favelas and bidonvilles.

The described changes appear to be huge, as illustrated in the following examples (Sander, 2012).

- São Paolo–Rio de Janeiro is a mega-region with 43 million inhabitants.
- New York has a GDP comparable to that of Spain and Canada.
- Ibadan–Lagos–Acra is an urban corridor extending for 600 km through Nigeria, Benin, Togo and Ghana, the economic engine of western Africa.
- Cape Town is a 100 km large city-region.
- Mumbai-Delhi is an industrial corridor, which may reach 1500 km as it develops.
- Bangkok is a city region, which in 2020 is expected to expand for 200 km from its current centre, going beyond the current population of 17 million.
- Hong Kong–Shenzhen–Guangzhou is a corridor hosting 120 million people.
- Tokyo alone represents almost 2% of the world GDP.
- From Beijing to Tokyo, via Pyongyang and Seoul, there is a 1150 km belt connecting at least 77 cities with a population of over 97 million people that actually merges four megalopolises of four different countries.
- Budapest represents almost half of Hungary's GDP.
- Brussels has a GDP percentage that is 4.4 times higher than the incidence of its population of Belgium.
- London has a GDP higher than that of Switzerland or Sweden.

1.4.3   Emerging New Consumers

The rise of developing countries (in Asia, Eastern Europe and Africa) is creating a new class of consumers, characterised by growing discretionary spending, but with different needs from consumers in the Western countries. This requires the ability to adapt the offer and adopt lower-cost business models. With reference to this phenomenon, several studies (McKinsey G.I., 2010) have already recently estimated the emergence of 300 million new middle-class/upper middle-class households, with a growth rate of 8% in ten years. In the upper-middle category, which accounts for 40 million households, approximately 40% are from eastern European countries and 20% from China. Within the range of a minimum annual income of $3200 (lower-middle-class), and a maximum of $4400 (upper-middle class), it is estimated that 864 million people, the equivalent of 62% of its population, will fall into this category in India alone by 2020, whereas China will see an increase in this band of the population from 65 million in 2005 to 949 million by 2020, Russia will witness an increase of the middle-class share of between 40 and 70% out of its population of 140 million by 2020 (Singh, 2012).

The increase in the number of these new consumers will have a significant influence on the offer models of all the companies involved in serving them (Court and Narasimhan; 2010). It is not a simple case of adapting or localising products and services, but often a case of completely rethinking them, both from the point of view of their functional features, as well as their positioning and pricing in order to respond to an enormous demand, quantitatively speaking, with price/performance features, however, that differ greatly from those experienced by consumers in western countries. In low-income markets it is therefore necessary to develop coherent product and distribution strategies that, for example, allow products also to be offered in rural areas with a modest population density and limited spending power. This, therefore, concerns making changes to product and distribution processes that may at times be radical, developing new business models, based on low prices, low margins and enormous volumes, aimed at the bottom of the pyramid (Prahalad and Hart, 2002; Prahalad and Hammond, 2002a; 2002). The development of these strategies makes it possible for economically sustainable results to be achieved only if a very high market penetration rate is reached. In many cases, distribution costs in rural areas are prohibitive and may counterbalance the margins generated by large economies of scale. In these situations, critical issues arise with regard to operating costs, distribution systems and the need to have local sales networks capable of developing the market through personal contact (Simanis, 2012). Therefore, it seems that there are various options in terms of supply and distribution strategies: in the cases where a company has a pre-existing logistics infrastructure that is designed to sustain other products aimed at richer market segments and where potential clients are aware of the purchase and usage models of the products and services offered, a distribution strategy based on low margins and high volumes may be sustainable. This possibility, together with the absence of costs for making customers aware of the product and teaching them how to use it, means that only the difference in costs linked to the distribution of the new products aimed at weaker segments of the market need to be covered. There are multiple examples of success stories, such as the Wheel detergents distributed in India by Unilever at a price that is 30% lower than the average price of its similar products or the case of Manila Water in the Philippines. In contrast, if the company has to develop its own distribution logistics in rural areas, in which the scale is based on the individual village and it is necessary to educate the customer on the purchase and consumption process, it is often necessary to significantly change the company's supply strategy. In this case a different option based on three elements is practicable, which are illustrated in detail by Simanis (2012), aimed at raising prices and margins and exploiting communication and training linked to the use of products. This option is based on:

1. *Localising and bundling base products*, or rather creating products that can reduce variable costs through the options of postponement and increasing prices and margins thanks to a richer value proposition. On the one hand, this means offering a basic product whose final processing prior to sale is done as close to the target market as possible, such as in the cases of packaging or bottling of detergents, the mixing of ingredients or the dilution of chemical elements for fertilisers, with the objective of exploiting low local labour costs. On the other hand, it involves proposing a sales bundle, offering more products, services and features in a single purchase, thus saving the consumer time and money, such as in the case of the sales bundles of several personal hygiene products or home-cleaning or multifunctional products. The idea of developing a family of products and reusing containers is the basis of the project developed in Ghana by S.C. Johnson with the support of the Bill & Melinda Gates Foundation, which is aimed at low-income consumers in two rural districts. On the one hand, the project focused on the concept of bundling, proposing several categories of products, such as insect control, home clearing and air care; on the other hand, it reduced distribution costs through the design of localised containers and filling systems.

2. *Offering an enabling service*, with the objective of sustaining pricing policies and higher margins and giving customers the knowledge and skills needed to maximise product features. Simanis (2012) quotes the case of Cemex, a Mexican company that supplies building materials to families, offering a service that costs $14 a week to help them to maximise the use of the products and to build their own homes at a lower cost.

3. *Cultivating customer peer groups*, in order to reduce communication and training costs related to the use of the products, and even their design. The use of customers, located locally, who inform, demonstrate and sell is a practice that was successful during the 1960s and 1970s in Europe and the United States. This policy is being successfully adapted and developed more and more often in emerging countries, allowing for low-cost widespread market penetration based on direct contact among users, such as, for example, the case of P&G sanitary products in Mexico (Hill, 2007) or the case of the distribution of pots and pans and kitchen utensils in India, or even the network of women that support the spread of Grameen micro-credit services in Bangladesh (Simanis, 2012). A different and more recent example is provided by the ChotuKool refrigerator, initially sold at less than $70 by the Indian group Godrej & Boyce in Maharastra, co-designed with the contribution of 600 women involved in different stages of its development, from concept development to the definition of its technical features and colour.

As clearly demonstrated in these brief notes, the development of these markets requires a complex rethinking of both the products and services on offer, as well as of underlying operations and supply chains.

1.4.4 Smart Technologies and the Digital Factory

It is estimated that by 2020 there will be more than 80 billion connected devices, 9 billion mobile phones, 5 billion Internet users and on average five connected devices for every individual, ten connected devices for every household and 500 devices with unique digital ID per square kilometre (Singh, 2012). The incredible development of the connectivity phenomenon between different applications and devices – the result of the diffusion of the Internet and new technology – will lead to the democratisation of information through collaborative platforms and knowledge-sharing, based on already widely distributed social media. The new archetypes of co-creation and knowledge-sharing will have an impact on all sectors, expanding the potential of increasingly sophisticated but less expensive hardware. The arrival and incredible development of the Internet has also led to the production and accumulation of enormous quantities of data. It is estimated that 2.5 quintillion bytes are created every day, 90% of the total bytes have been created in the last two years, and that in the next decade the amount of information managed by companies will increase by a good fifty times (Malnight and Keys, 2013). The demand to acquire new ways of extracting sophisticated information from this massive amount of data is leading to the development of new tools: analytics, capable of exploiting the information content of big data. At the same time, approaches concerning the co-creation of information among consumers and making this information available through the development of knowledge-sharing platforms in all fields will go through the roof.

The technological developments are also creating new waves of smart products[5]. Think, for example, that 'global smartphone penetration exploded from 5% of the global population in 2009, to 22% by the end of 2013. By 2017 more than a third of all people around the globe will be smartphone users' (Eagar et al., 2014, p. 15). Take also, for example, the new solutions such as innovations in smart home products, the evolution of the first home automation projects, called domotica, based on sensors capable of setting and adapting room temperature and lighting depending on the presence of people in the building and external environmental conditions, or guiding the use of electrical appliances remotely; as well as devices that suggest diets or nutritional adjustments and sporting activities depending on the evolution of vital and biological parameters, using smart tracker bracelets or smartwatches or even a fork that controls the speed and pace with which we eat that vibrates if food habits are incorrect, sending data to a smartphone app in order to suggest corrective action. Smart technologies are starting to form a part of the everyday life of a growing number of people in many fields of application, from remote medical diagnostics to home automation and smart buildings, from electrical network control systems or new generations of automobiles to machine-to-machine control devices.

---

[5] Smart products are products with an incorporated form of intelligence, made up of microprocessors, which allows them to connect to other devices, enabling two-way communication by transferring information in such a way as to allow them to modify their performance through corrective actions (Singh, 2012).

The success of this technology has created an exponential increase in the demand for connectivity and integration between the operators and the various parties, rendering the boundaries between competition and cooperation increasingly faint and stimulating the convergence of different industries.

With specific reference to the subject of this book, namely Operations and Supply Chain Management, the impact of ICT – Information and Communication Technologies on industrial processes has been translated into a series of revolutionary innovations that fall within what has been defined today as the 'Digital Factory' or 'Manufacturing 4.0' or 'Industry 4.0' (Lee et al., 2013; Brettel et al., 2014). Intelligence and connectivity, key features of the digital economy, are incorporated into equipments and machines defined as smart machines capable of interacting and cooperating with one another, producing and using a quantity of data and information flows that were unthinkable only a few years ago. According to a recent study (Manenti, 2014), new technologies supporting the digital factory are:

- *Systems capable of storing*, computing and networking unstructured and variable data, such as Cloud infrastructures, big data analytics, augmented reality software, a series of dedicated apps, for example 3D visualisation and simulation apps, which will enable business users to customise their business systems by downloading apps and integrating them in their IT platforms.
- *Systems capable of enabling connections between objects*, such as the Internet of things (or cyber-physical systems), or interconnecting devices equipped with intelligent systems, able to connect to the Internet and to communicate with one another. This is a business area that is showing enormous growth potential: the worldwide market for Internet of things is forecasted to grow from 1.9 trillion dollars in 2003 to 71 trillion by 2020 (Eagar et al., 2014).
- *Systems capable of using the received information and processing it* to produce goods, such as Advanced Robotics and additive manufacturing applications. The former are made up of machines capable of communicating and cooperating with other systems, and with one another, recognising parts, carrying out self-maintenance and changeovers and so on, making optimised decisions thanks to embedded sensors and intelligent systems on-board the machine. The latter, known as 3-D printers, are capable of producing complex pieces, with features that cannot be produced today, except for the assembly of components, such as, for example, pieces with internal cavities, thanks to stereolithography processes, laser sintering and coating processes applied to plastic materials and powdered metals.
- *Systems capable of guaranteeing the continuous traceability of data flows* and data collection in real time, such as RFID applications – Radio Frequency Identification Devices, mobile systems and the extensive use of well-known technologies, such as 2-D barcodes.

Another area that will certainly see very fast technological developments and applications that are useful to the farming, industry and service sectors is the use of drones, which can be used for monitoring, mapping and analysing land and other areas, checking areas that otherwise are not easily accessible and possibly transporting light loads.

Furthermore, the innovations linked to Autonomous Vehicles – also known as autonomous cars, self-driving cars or robotic cars – may affect sectors like freight transport logistics and personal transportation in the future. The application areas of such technology are potentially enormous and are conditioned more by legal aspects linked to the safety of land and air transport and the requirement to think of compatible infrastructures, than by the development of the underlying technology.

Moreover, from the perspective of consumer habits and purchasing patterns, models based on the so-called Sharing Economy are fast becoming more popular, such as the sharing of means of transport, holiday homes, or even actual production structures. In this regard, take, for example, the popularity of the phenomenon of 'makers', based on sharing equipment, machineries and tools to produce products, which are speeding up 'servitisation' processes (Beuren et al., 2013; Baglieri and Karmakar, 2014; Lay, 2015), in which users substitute the purchase of goods with the purchase of their utility function. These trends have significant repercussions in terms of environmental and social impact, as they increase the rate of saturation of the available production capacities or the utilisation rate of existing goods, limiting the creation of new ones and reinforcing sharing and solidarity phenomena.

1.5 MEGA-TRENDS, SUSTAINABILITY AND SUPPLY CHAIN MANAGEMENT

The mega-trends summarised here are only some of the most relevant examples of the many global forces that are remodelling the socio-economic profile of our planet. These trends combine with one another, producing different effects: in some cases, the overlapping of these tendencies may generate an increase in the phenomena that threaten sustainability; in others they produce compensatory and mitigation effects that may minimise adverse impacts. It is enough to think that, as reported by Bastein et al. (2013), it is estimated that the effects of urbanisation and changes in middle-class consumer habits, especially in developing countries, may lead to a tripling of consumption by 2050 (UNEP, 2011). Take, for example, that in the twentieth century, due to the impact of population growth, the extraction of construction materials increased by a factor of 34, minerals by a factor of 27, fossil fuels by a factor of 12 and biomass by a factor of 3.6 (UNEP, 2011). In contrast, it is to be highlighted that, as far as the quest for prosperity and the growth in population are concerned, these are inevitable trends that lead to an increase in consumption. However, technology and the growing attention paid to respecting natural resources have made great progress and will make even greater progress in future years. Just think, for example, that 'the world economy used approximately 30% fewer resources in 2005 to produce one unit of GDP than it did in 1980' (Bastein et al., 2013, p. 4).

Limiting our discussion to the implications linked to Operations and Supply Chain Management, the subject of this book, the possible scenarios generated by the statements previously have been taken into consideration.

The combined effects of demographic growth, especially in developing countries, and the phenomenon of population concentration in mega-cities, mega-regions and mega-corridors will give rise to a considerable increase in the demand for goods and services, starting from consumption goods, assessable in physical flows that have never been experienced before, with very important implications in terms of the supply chain, logistics and retailing. New procurement, transportation, storage and distribution models must be tested in order to be able to continuously and reliably feed the flow of goods from huge industrial areas to enormous consumption centres. Likewise, it will be necessary to design sustainable solutions for efficiently supplying populations that live in scattered rural areas.

The effects of climate change, the progressive desertification of arable land and the simultaneous increase in the world's population will strain the relationship between the demand and supply of food, water, fuel and other materials, where only technological innovation, the dissemination of new methods for producing agro-foods and greater attention to conscious consumption will be able to achieve sustainability. In this regard, investments in Research and Development and new technology aimed at increasing the productivity of agricultural cultivation and the reduction of waste in processing, preservation and distribution processes may be able to offset the deficit that is currently predicted.

The environmental impact caused by the growth in populations, their needs and their consumption, may be softened thanks to the development of clean technologies and the issuing of new environmental standards by supranational regulatory bodies. As far as the main subjects of this book are concerned, this will lead to the drafting of new methods for measuring the value created, or destroyed, by companies, sectors and nations, through the identification of metrics and key performance indicators (KPIs) capable of rating not only economic performance, but also the social and environmental impact of the managed processes.

New generations, called Z generations or digital natives, will partially make up for the loss in traditional occupations, thanks to the new opportunities offered by connectivity, which will enable alternative forms of employment and lifestyles to be developed, compensating for the difficulties of inter-urban mobility in mega-cities. The pressure of the regulators and the increased sensitivity of the new generations towards the subjects of sustainability will lead to an increase in low-impact urban mobility initiatives, such as the use of fleets of mini electric cars, car-sharing platforms, the tendency to purchase and consume green products and greater attention to more environmentally and social-conscious behaviour. This will lead to an increase in waste separation systems and implicit requirements during product design and two-way (forward and back) logistics flows (see Chapter 7).

The development of new technologies and the progression of connectivity trends will greatly increase the effectiveness and potential of instruments that have already been used today with success. In order to limit ourselves once again to the field of investigation of this book, take, for example, the potential of RFID – Radio Frequency Identification technology and satellite geolocation systems already in use today to optimise the routing, tracking and tracing of transport and logistics flows, and their possible integration with information, which is becoming increasingly sophisticated, accessible with ease and cost-effective. Or even the impact of 3-D printing, nowadays widely used for prototyping and also the production of parts in many sectors, such as aeronautics, which shows huge potential also from the perspective of economic and environmental sustainability; the use of additive manufacturing logics that makes it possible for waste and production leftovers to be minimised as only the material necessary for the manufacture of the product is used; the possibility of building spare parts on demand, for example, which reduces investments in stock and related risks of obsolescence and overproduction; the use of printed material in the proximity of users, which may contain the transportation costs of goods, reducing the connected environmental impact; and the production of complex, lighter parts and cables that will simplify several industrial processes, containing maintenance and production costs.

Another area in which new technology will produce considerable increases in productivity that can contribute to reducing environmental impact is defined as Precision Farming (Stafford, 2000; Auernhammer, 2001; Phillips et al., 2014). Take, for example, the studies underway using machine-to-machine protocols for interfacing drones that use specific sensors to assess the areas on agricultural land that require more water or fertiliser. This information can be transmitted to tractors and farming machinery that can plough, water and fertilise the same field using satellite navigators and digital maps, optimising the use of scarce resources such as water, as well as minimising the use of fertilisers and consequently producing a higher level of efficiency and lower environmental impact. The use of drones with cameras or infrared optical tools also makes it possible today to map forest areas and to detect fires or areas susceptible to landslides or, with the use of computer tools, the levels of atmospheric pollution and air quality.

The growing complexity linked to globalisation, together with a greater understanding of the finiteness of the resources guaranteed by our planet, may lead to increasing conflict or, hopefully, forms of international cooperation between different public and private stakeholders, as is already happening in many cases between consumer associations, producers and distributors, regulatory bodies and so on, such as, for example, the multiple local production and consumption initiatives, those linked to the recovery and redistribution of unsold products or, again, those linked to the minimisation of the environmental impact of waste and packaging. In this regard, efforts focusing on the design of reverse logistics systems, the recovery and use of products and their components to the end of their life cycle and design for environment logics, that is, products designed to have minimum environmental impact, will be intensified.

1.6   SUSTAINABLE DEVELOPMENT AND CORPORATE SOCIAL RESPONSIBILITY

The picture described here highlights how the topic of sustainability will be of increasing importance on all levels: in the choice of government policies and national and supranational regulatory bodies, in the managerial decisions of public and private companies, in the actions of many not-for-profit organisations, in purchase and consumption patterns and in people's lifestyles.

The development of awareness in this important field has led, mainly, to the different origin of the concepts of Sustainable Development, which for the most part refer to environmental impact and attention to the ecosystem, and Corporate Social Responsibility, which concerns guidelines on social matters for business managers. The two tendencies, however, have found elements of convergence and integration over time, in the sense that CSR is becoming an important tool that public actors and companies can use to pursue sustainable development objectives.

The most widespread definition of Sustainable Development is, in fact, the one that refers to the possibility of promoting development by looking not only at current needs, but also future ones. More precisely, Sustainable Development is defined as the:

'*development that meets the needs of the present without compromising the ability of future generations to meet their own needs*' (Brundtland, 1987, p. 54).

According to the Commission work, this definition *contains within it two key concepts*:

- *the concept of needs, in particular the essential needs of the world's poor, to which overriding priority should be given; and*
- *the idea of limitations imposed by the state of technology and social organization on the environment's ability to meet present and future needs* (Brundtland, 1987, p. 54).

With reference to the 'needs' component, apart from increasing awareness of the topic of waste, consumer choices and methods for the use of goods, specifically in relation to food (food and water), which companies can certainly contribute to in terms of awareness and communication, little can presumably be done from a corporate perspective. With regard, on the other hand, to the subject of limitations, namely the development of technology, processes, products and practices that enable current limitations to be overcome, the responsibility of companies and institutions seems paramount. Nevertheless, it is important to emphasise how empirical evidence has shown that the greatest environmental impact, and also social impact, occurs upstream, along the stages of the supply chain and during consumption, depending on the more or less conscious behaviour of the consumer/user. This evidence, within the context of this work, clarifies why, in addition to internal or 'end-of-pipe' checks carried out by the focal company dominating a supply chain, performing checks inside the entire supply chain becomes important, which, in general, occurs less and less frequently as one moves slowly upstream towards the extraction or cultivation of raw materials (Tencati and Pogutz, 2015).

In this regard, the role that the company ought to promote responsibly is that of developing business strategies, technology innovations and practices that enable business and sustainability objectives to be pursued together from a dual social and environmental perspective, in the interest of all stakeholders, in a broad sense and in the long term.

The increasing attention of society to the subjects of sustainability and sustainable development has led to progressive attention, also on the part of companies, to the integration of CSR – Corporate Social Responsibility – objectives and practices in the formulation of their development strategies and their pursuit of objectives. The literature has coined several definitions of CSR, and there are numerous studies that have analysed the origins and evolution of the concept of sustainability over time and its implications on a corporate and public policy level (Perrini et al., 2006). From among the many, keeping the aims of this book in mind, we will only dwell upon on a few, focusing on their basic elements, to be considered as an overall framework, within which the subjects of Sustainable Operations and Supply Chain Management can be developed.

- *CSR is a concept whereby companies integrate social and environmental concerns in their business operations and in their interaction with their stakeholders on voluntary basis* (EC, 2001, p. 6).
- *CSR is the continuing commitment by business to behave ethically and contribute to economic development while improving the quality of life of the workforce and their families as well as of the local community and society at large* (WBCSD, 1999, p. 3).

Whereas initial definitions, such as the one developed by the World Business Council for Sustainable Development (1999) or the one drawn up by the European Commission following the Lisbon Summit of 2000, focused on clarifying the concept of CSR, over time attempts have been made to place greater emphasis on its strategic implications and clear methods for the implementation of CSR practices. From the point of view of the policy maker, this translates into the possibility of pursuing three priorities, namely the promotion of best CSR practices, giving credibility to CSR claims and the development of coherent public policies (Perrini et al., 2006). From a corporate point of view, on the other hand, this translates into the imperative to integrate socially responsible objectives and conduct into the formulation and implementation of business strategies and consequent business choices.

More recently the European Commission (2011) produced a new definition of CSR, as *the responsibility of enterprises for their impacts on society*. In the same document the Commission specifies:

Respect for applicable legislation, and for collective agreements between social partners, is a prerequisite for meeting that responsibility. To fully meet their corporate social responsibility, enterprises should have in place a process to integrate social, environmental, ethical, human rights and consumer concerns into their business operations and core strategy in close collaboration with their stakeholders, with the aim of:

- *maximising the creation of shared value for their owners/shareholders and for their other stakeholders and society at large.*
- *identifying, preventing and mitigating their possible adverse impacts'* (EC, 2011).

It is within the framework of this definition that the interaction between business, environmental and social objectives is discussed next, with specific reference to the role played by Operations and Supply Chain Management.

1.7   THE DEVELOPMENT OF SUSTAINABLE OBJECTIVES
FROM THE TRIPLE BOTTOM LINE PERSPECTIVE

Sustainability objectives therefore refer to three performance levels, defined as the Triple Bottom Line (Elkington, 1994; 1997; Kleindorfer et al, 2005; Pagell and Wu, 2009; Pagell, Wu, Wasserman, 2010; Gimenez et al., 2012), or the 3P, illustrated in Figure 1.1, which each company must try to jointly maximise:

- *Profit:* expression of the performances that lead to economic and financial sustainability and its development prospects in the medium to long-term.
- *Planet:* refers to the performances that guarantee environmental sustainability, in terms of environmental protection and the overall impact of the business on the environment.
- *People:* connected to the performances that measure the social impact of the business, in terms of social equity and cohesion, economic prosperity and the protection and promotion of fundamental rights.

Unfortunately a deep-rooted vision in several business contexts may be in contrast with these objectives, a vision that presumes that the maximisation of profit may justify paying less attention to the subjects of environmental and social sustainability, as well as to conduct that does not respect these imperatives. The trade-off between

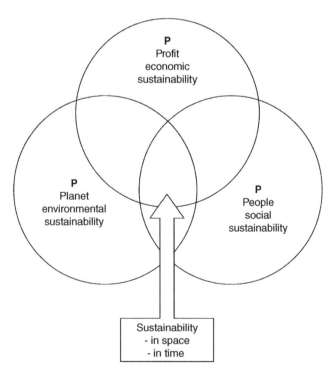

FIGURE 1.1   3Ps and Triple Bottom Line.

these objectives must, however, be rejected, first of all for ethical grounds and, second, by extending the scope of the analysis of the results attainable by each company, with reference to both the time frame of the aforesaid results subsequent to managerial or public policy decisions and the type of stakeholders that the achieved results are measured against.

If economic and financial sustainability is the main objective of value creation and it is connected to the interest of shareholders, the support of the other two sets of performances, linked to environmental and social sustainability, extend the ultimate purpose of the company to all stakeholders, be they current or future, with the objective of guaranteeing an overall quality of life on the planet and fairness in standards of living in terms of time and space:

- *In space*, in terms of the better distribution of the value created between more fortunate populations, located in the areas that, although representing a minority (20%) of the world population, absorb far greater wealth (80%) and the remaining part that find it hard in many cases to reach the threshold of survival.
- *In time*, with reference to the need to guarantee intergenerational equity, offering future generations the same opportunities that are offered to those of today's generations and progressively encouraging balance in all forms of growth and development.

In this regard, economic and financial sustainability must not only refer to the economic entity capable of producing it, that is, the company, but to society as a whole, which, by hosting and interacting with it, contributes to its creation and must therefore benefit from it. The concept of the Triple Bottom Line therefore refers to broad objectives, which must be summarised nevertheless using performance, metrics and specific indicators, as will be described in Chapter 8. From this point of view, the interdependence of the economic and financial, environmental and social profiles of sustainable development recurs in many models and guidelines developed to support companies and institutions in the implementation of best sustainability practices.

1.8   SUSTAINABILITY: THE REASONS WHY

The main advantages of an approach oriented towards sustainability are ascribable to Sanders (2012):

- *Financial pay-offs*, connected to the possibility on the one hand of reducing business costs, administrative costs and invested capital and, on the other hand, increasing returns and market appreciation.
- *Consumer-related pay-offs*, linked to the ability to increase customer satisfaction, market share and the reputation of the company, as well as developing product innovation and new business development.
- *Operational pay-offs*, connected to process innovation, aimed at increasing productivity and the yield of the used resources, reducing process times and minimising waste.

- *Organisational pay-offs*, deriving from increased employee satisfaction, better relationships with stakeholders, the reduction of risk and interventions of regulatory bodies, and an increase in organisational learning.

The possibility of obtaining these benefits depends on the ability to jointly and deliberately pursue economic, environmental and social sustainability objectives, as mentioned in reference to the Triple Bottom Line. The drivers that may lead a company to increase its compliance with the principles of sustainability differ from one another, even if overlaps among them can be found. In particular, a distinction can be made between the various reasons, examples of which are given next in reference to the area being examined in this book (Fiksel, 2012; Sanders, 2012):

- *Legal reasons:* in many national and supranational contexts, laws and regulations that impose consistent behaviour and that sanction elusive or illegal behaviour are drafted. For example, with regard to environmental impact, there are regulations that impose the use of systems to reduce polluting emissions, such as filters, catalysers and other equipment or those that prohibit the use of materials that are toxic and dangerous for health and the environment, such as asbestos, Freon gas and plastic packaging waste. Similarly, with regard to social impact, there are laws that are aimed at resisting forms of social dumping and child labour, those that impose the installation of protective systems for accident prevention in the workplace or alarm and isolation systems in the event of toxic gas leaks or leaks of radioactive substances. These regulations are mainly aimed at preventing the risk of occurrences that may cause damage to people or the environment or that may create situations of social injustice during the design of a production and logistics system (industrial assets used, such as buildings, systems, machinery, storage and transportation systems) and the processes and practices that may be adopted within them (safety procedures, accident prevention regulations, laws that protect workers etc.). Alongside these are the laws and regulations aimed at guaranteeing the monitoring of system performance (measurement of polluting emissions, characteristics of waste water etc.), the use of appropriate input (materials, energy, labour etc.), the maintenance and adaptation to new system standards, as well as the communication of these regulations and training of workers. Over time, the regulatory bodies have progressively acknowledged the urgency of responsible behaviour and have expanded the regulatory framework regulations and inspections in this field.
- *Compliance reasons with regard to specific certifications and accreditations:* A second reason originates from the will of the company of its own accord to respect the regulations issued by certification or accreditation bodies, such as ISO standards. In this case the choice to adapt behaviour and internal processes to the regulations of the aforesaid systems may be due to competitive opportunities, such as the need to possess certain certificates in order to be admitted to the supplier portfolio of certain clients, or to participate in tenders or, even, to obtain licences in order to set up business in certain areas or countries. In other

cases, it concerns adapting to industry practices or using the visibility linked to certifications and accreditations for internal and external communication purposes, the revision of internal processes aimed at improving quality or recovering efficiency, or for the actual practical implementation of boosting values and ethical motivations. In these cases, the compliance choices are used to pursue objectives that can be classified in one of the three categories stated next:

o *Reasons connected to relationships:* with particular reference to the community of stakeholders. The need to maintain high levels of reputation in the markets, to encourage dialogue with local governments or the workers' or consumers' representatives, especially in the case of companies exposed to greater environmental and social risk, may force the top management of the company to set up sustainability projects. From this point of view, many companies develop codes of conduct and systems for measuring and reporting their sustainability performance, inspired by the principles of transparency and accountability. This the case, for example, of the Sustainability Reporting Guidelines released by the GRI – Global Responsible Initiative, or, in the field of education the PRME – Principles of Responsible Management Education.

o *Reasons linked to profitability opportunities:* In many cases setting up sustainability projects is accompanied by clear objectives to increase economic and financial performance, through actions that may reduce costs or increase returns, such as, for example, investments in clean technology that reduces energy consumption or replaces conventional energy sources with renewable sources or has low environmental impact, or design for logistics and design for packaging choices, aimed at minimising or rationalising packaging in order to increase the value density of transported goods and consequently reducing transport flows.

o *Ethical or values-based reasons:* these concern initiatives that start 'from the bottom up', that is, from the community of employees or the sensitivity of top management. They often involve projects that are created from the will of enlightened entrepreneurs and managers, aware that success also comes from the opportunities offered by the community and who want to give something back. The cases of companies that invest in company welfare through the setting up of day-care facilities for the children of their employees, the distribution of incentives and bonuses (e.g. practices of matching funds) linked to sustainability projects, the financing of works and promotion of donations for the local community, the creation of foundations for social or cultural purposes or environmental recovery, the involvement of employees in philanthropic projects, or the provision of their know-how in kind for not-for-profit organisation initiatives, are become increasingly frequent.

It goes without saying that the reasons stated here, far from being secluded, often mix, overlap and reinforce one another, resulting in sustainability projects and models each with their own unique character and effectiveness.

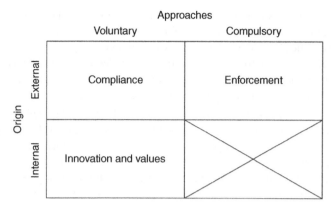

FIGURE 1.2   Origins and approaches in the development of sustainability projects. *Source:* Sanders 2012. Reproduced with permission of John Wiley & Sons.

In summary, the adoption of sustainability models in corporate environments may therefore be due to voluntary compliance or compulsory obligations and may have internal or external origins, as illustrated in Figure 1.2.

- The first case – *Enforcement* – refers to an external and binding obligations linked to laws and regulatory requirements on environmental and social responsibility imposed by regulatory bodies or national or supranational governments, such as, for example, the EU 2001 Polluter Pays Principle asserting that who pollutes pay (OECD, 2002), the Extended Producer Responsibility, affirming that the producer is responsible for the product throughout its entire life cycle (OECD, 2001), the WEEE directive – Waste Electrical and Electronic Equipment (Goodship and Stevels, 2012), which requires each nation to set collection, recycling and recovery targets for electronic products or the RoHS, Restriction on Hazardous Substances, to phase out the use of lead, mercury, cadmium, hexavalent chromium and other toxic materials, as well as the related variations to these regulations in the different countries of the European Union. With reference to social sustainability, the labour standards and the legislative body promoted by ILO – International Labour Organisation – on the prevention of child labour and all forms of discrimination is a prominent example.
- The second case – *Compliance* – originates from the voluntary choice of a company to comply with practices and models generally linked to sector certifications or accreditations with bodies that propose environmental and social responsibility systems, such as, for example, voluntary compliance with the family of ISO 14000 standards and the EMAS certification – Eco-Management and Audit Scheme regarding the requirements for appropriate environmental management, or the SA 8000 certification concerning the voluntary universal standard for companies interested in auditing and certifying social performance, or even the GHG – Greenhouse Gas Reporting Program created by the U.S.

EPA – Environmental Protection Agency – and so on. As already mentioned, more and more frequently companies are undertaking to develop codes of conduct inspired by the guidelines of third parties, such as, for example, the GRI – Global Reporting Initiative – which has developed guidelines relative to labour rights and decent work practices, human rights, society and product responsibilities, or the standards promoted by the United Nations and the CEDAW – Convention on the Elimination of all Forms of Discrimination Against Women.

- The third case – *Innovation and Values* – is based on a voluntary choice of the company and is inspired by internal reasons linked to improvement objectives in terms of internal efficiency or external visibility and presence on the market, or again, as has already been stated, by choices based on basic ethical values. This is the case in companies that set up process innovations aimed at reducing polluting emissions or energy consumption, or product innovations to reduce the use of toxic materials, or management innovations, such as, for example, vendor selection methods that take the environmental and social practices of its suppliers into account, or projects linked to company welfare or philanthropic investments.

2

SUSTAINABLE OPERATIONS AND SUPPLY CHAIN MANAGEMENT AS COMPETITIVE FACTORS

2.1 INTRODUCTION

Barilla is an international Group that operates in the food sector. It is a world leader in the markets of pasta and ready-to-use sauces in continental Europe, bakery products in Italy and crispbread in Scandinavia. Respect for principles and values that are consolidated but that can be renewed over time, HR management as a key asset, and production systems that are cutting-edge in terms of output and sustainability have made Barilla one of the world's most highly respected food producers, a byword for Italian knowhow. In 2014, with more than 8130 employees worldwide and investments amounting to 155 million euros, the Group has reached a turnover of 3254 million euros, selling 1821 thousand tonnes of product. Barilla has a global presence attested by 26 headquarters and 30 production sites. Approximately 50% of its sales are in Italy; almost 30% in Europe; 17% in the Americas and approximately 5% in Asia, Africa and Australia.

Barilla Group has an ambitious aspiration: to double its business while continuously reducing its footprint on the planet and promoting wholesome and joyful food habits. To this end, it has chosen five strategies to ensure success:

1. Be the number one choice of brand and product: Nurture people's taste, mind and heart; Build iconic brands that create meaning and sense of belonging; Commit to product quality, sustainability and safety from field to

*consumption; Innovate towards further accessibility, convenience, afford-
ability, local adaptation and better nutrition.*

2. *Win in the marketplace: Persistently foster expansion in the emerging markets
through a winning and adaptive model; Achieve a ruthless in-market execu-
tion, putting customers, shoppers and consumers first; Build win-win partnerships with our current and future customers to better serve our shoppers;
Simplify the business for the customer and the choice for the shopper.*

3. *Drive continuous improvement: Relentlessly enhance our competitiveness,
with increasing levels of efficiency, simplification and agility; Be recognized
as preferred supplier by our customers.*

4. *Only one way of doing business 'Good for You, Good for the Planet':
Care for the present and future wellbeing of people, the Planet and
the company in everything Barilla does, from field to consumption;
Encourage open, transparent and caring partnerships with the communities in which Barilla operates.*

5. *Proudly be the Barilla people: Be the ambassadors of Barilla's identity,
values and food culture; Be a great company to work for, promoting diversity and a balanced sustainable lifestyle; Foster empowerment, commitment, results-oriented leadership and accountability.*

*What the world calls 'sustainability' is for Barilla a unique way of doing business:
'Good for You, Good for the Planet'.*
Several of the 2020 goals defined by the Barilla Group are:

'Good for You'

- *100% of Barilla's product volume aligned to the most up-to-date standards
for quality and food safety proven by external certification bodies (currently
98.5% of Barilla's product volume).*
- *Raise the global volume of products in line with Barilla's Nutritional
Guidelines from 70% to 90% (currently 85.5% product volume sold).*
- *Offer people scientifically relevant information on food and nutrition
through brand activities (currently 80% of websites contain nutritional
facts and 53% of websites presenting Barilla products provide suggestions
for a healthy lifestyle.*

'Good for the Planet'

- *100% of Barilla products in the lower section of the environmental pyramid
(currently 93% of Barilla products).*
- *Reduce CO_2 emissions and water consumption in the production process
by 30% per ton of finished product compared to 2010 values (currently
reduction of CO_2 emissions and water consumption by 20% per ton).*
- *100% of strategic raw materials purchased responsibly (currently 6% of
strategic raw materials).*

'Good for the Communities'

- *By 2020 Barilla will promote the inclusion of people through programs for access to food, educational projects and the promotion of diversity.*
- *Increase the number of farms involved in projects that improve the competitiveness of local agriculture (currently about 1000 farms).*
- *Promote the social inclusion of people in need through food donations, social projects and support in the event of emergencies (Currently more than 2000 tons of products have been donated in the world).*

Source: Barilla Group, 2015, www.buonopertebuonoperilpianeta.com, accessed 10 August 2015.

The case in the introduction illustrates how the Barilla Group, in the creation of its vision and development strategy, integrates ambitious business goals and sustainability goals, reflected in the values of the company and its characteristics. The motto 'Good for You, Good for the Planet', which has been accompanied in recent years with 'Good for the Communities', aims to convey both within and outside the company that its growth and profitability goals are strictly interdependent on the goals of attention to the individual and the planet, in line with the orientations cited in the Triple Bottom Line. In a manufacturing company like Barilla, these objectives are found in all company processes and, in particular, in operations and supply chain management. It is evident how the values linked to sustainability translate into goals and performance targets that take on the same importance as those of profit and business, and how the choices linked to company processes are always made taking the environment, people and the community of stakeholders into consideration.

This Chapter, therefore, will start with the analysis of relevant scientific literature, first of all it will illustrate the traits qualifying and differentiating the areas investigated here – Operations, Logistics and Supply Chain, their management profile and the elements that characterise their role in the pursuit of sustainability goals. Then, it describes the crucial subject of the *strategic alignment* of corporate and functional strategies, the decision-making process arising from strategic choices, the concepts of order qualifiers and order winners and the role of management in controlling operations and supply performance in the *creation of competitive advantage*. In the second part of the Chapter, we will go into more detail on several relevant aspects of Sustainable Operations and Supply Chain Management, proposing a framework of analysis that enables the impact of economic, environmental and social sustainability profiles of the decision-making process made along the phases of an ideal product life cycle and the role of the players inside and outside the supply chain involved in these phases. The Chapter concludes by illustrating how each of the different components of the proposed framework are expressed and analysed in detail in the following Chapters of this book.

2.2 OPERATIONS, LOGISTICS AND SUPPLY CHAIN MANAGEMENT IN MANUFACTURING AND SERVICE INDUSTRIES

As introduced in the previous Chapter, the pursuit of sustainability goals means that decisions must be made on both a macro level, in terms of policies and regulations, as well as on a corporate level, from the perspective of strategy and management choices. In this book, we have decided to take a corporate view in order to offer useful reflections aimed at the promotion of responsible choices, by designing and managing systems capable of jointly pursuing the economic, environmental and social sustainability goals.

Special attention in particular is paid here to the areas most closely connected to operations management, namely the company processes that govern the design, production and distribution of goods and services. From this perspective, the activities carried out within each individual company become relevant, as well as those connected to interaction with any other companies involved, through different levels of cooperation, collaboration and partnership (Secchi, 2012) with the aim of satisfying the final customer. This goal is pursued by different functions and processes linked to the management of the physical flow: by Operations in the management of intra-company processes and by Logistics or the Supply Chain in inter-company relations.

Even if the topics of operations, logistics and supply chain have become increasingly relevant in the current economic environment, it is widely believed both in practice and in literature that there are multiple interpretations and definitions of these concepts (Monczka et al., 1998; Cox et al., 2001; Mentzer et al., 2001, Kathawala and Abdou, 2003; Quayle, 2003; Simchi-Levi et al., 2003; Mentzer, 2004; Chopra and Meindl, 2007; Sanders, 2012). Although it is not the aim of this work to go into the details of this debate, it is necessary to explain the standpoints from which the subjects dealt with in the following Chapters have been arranged and analysed. To this end, it is appropriate to make some preliminary remarks on how the different definitions found in literature do not always coincide. Without being exhaustive, first of all we will examine some of the most relevant definitions of *Operations, Logistics and Supply Chain*, and then we will take a closer look at the main implications of these definitions in terms of management, including those linked to the subject of sustainability, which will be dealt with next. Figure 2.1 shows the proposed path of analysis presented in the following pages.

Operations is the business function responsible for producing a company's goods and services in an efficient and cost-effective way. It is the function responsible for transforming a company's inputs, obtained by sourcing function, into finished goods and services, which marketing sells to final customers (Sanders, 2012, p. 123).

This function oversees a complex system of means, labour, machineries, resources and knowledge defined as the Operations System, which exchanges information physical and financial flows, interacting with other business units.

Operations Management, according to several well-known definitions, 'is the activity of managing the resources which are devoted to the production and delivery

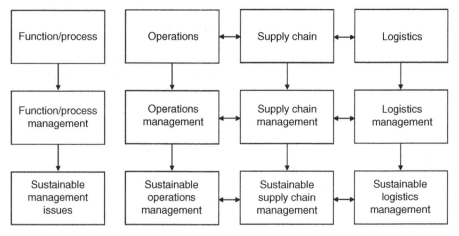

FIGURE 2.1 The proposed path of analysis.

of products and services' (Slack et al., 2007, p. 4) or 'the management of the processes that produce or deliver goods and services' (Greasley, 2006, p. 5), or, even,

> *is responsible for planning, organizing, and managing all the resources needed to produce a company's goods and services. This includes people, equipment, technology, materials and information* (Sanders, 2012, p. 123).

In other words, the main task of Operations Management lies in the organisation and management of processes that guarantee the transformation of input – resources made up of materials and information, as well as, in the case of services, the customers themselves (input *to be* transformed), and machines, personnel and methods (input *for* transformation) – into output consisting of goods, services and operating conditions. Transforming input into output does not simply mean transforming leather into shoes, cotton into shirts, metal into pans or, in the case of services, a patient into a healthy person or, even, a hungry customer into a satisfied one; it also means doing this by offering the market goods and services using processes that enable them to be purchased and consumed efficiently and effectively. Such conditions refer to time, cost, quality and other performances that accompany the manufacturing of a good or the provision of a service that are an integral part of the value transferred to the customer. Furthermore, positive or negative outcomes generated by a production system, often overlooked or defined as an 'externality', are associated with the product or service offered: for example, employment, creation of wealth, reuse of recyclable materials and reduction of environmental impact among the positive ones; unemployment, pollution and destruction of resources and practices that are disrespectful to the rights of workers among the negative ones. This book, although focusing on Operations and Supply Chain Management choices, will also look at the need to integrate these fundamental aspects into the set of corporate goals.

The more a company has to increase the level of collaboration with other players located upstream and downstream in managing its business, the greater is the need to extend responsibility and coordination along the supply chain and its main actors, which contribute to the value creation for the final customer. These actors can be suppliers, subcontractors or other manufacturing, commercial and services-providing companies, which operate by exchanging physical, information and financial flows, interwoven with the different players belonging to several supply chains.

As mentioned, not all companies need to design units to oversee these inter-organisational processes, even if the growing technological complexity, as well as the increasing variety and variability of the products, the vertical disintegration of processes and the globalisation of markets today lead the majority of companies to review and extend their collaborative networks. In some cases, in fact, where the level of integration with upstream suppliers and the downstream companies is limited and relatively straightforward, it is often sufficient to set up the supervision of an *Operations Management Function*, focused on the coordination of internal processes, and of some logistics responsibilities interacting upstream and downstream. On the other hand, if the level of integration between the players placed upstream and downstream is high and is characterised by close coordination or collaboration, frequently a *Supply Chain Management Function* is set up to oversee inter-company processes. Therefore, in some cases, characterised by a low level of integration with upstream and downstream partners, the goal of sustainability, like other specific company goals, is mainly an internal concern and can have a significant impact on the choices to be made by Operations. This can be the case of a steelworks that needs to guarantee the safety of workers and to keep harmful emissions within legal limits – it can manage these problems by focusing mainly on its internal operations. In other companies, where the level of integration with external players is more complex, Operations become an element constituting the most extensive Supply Chain, which must be managed with a view to coordination and unity, also in the light of the imperative of sustainability. This is the case, for example, in companies that operate in manufacturing sectors, such as in the clothing, footwear or mechanical industries, in which outsourcing choices expose the companies to the risks of social dumping by suppliers and subcontractors and of environmentally unfriendly practices to be dealt with responsibly by the focal company.

As already mentioned, companies that extend the scope of management influence to other upstream and/or downstream players along the supply chain, through the orchestration of inter-company processes and with the goal of creating value for the final customer, generally define the responsibilities for the coordination of the entire network of players underlying the supply chain concept. By analysing some of the many definitions given in literature, it is possible to understand the scope of the concept of supply chain and, consequently, the extension of the responsibilities assigned to Supply Chain Management. In fact, *Supply Chain* means 'the network of organizations that are involved, through upstream and downstream linkages, in the different processes and activities that produce value in the form of products and services in the hands of the ultimate consumer' (Christopher, 1998, p. 15). Consequently,

Supply Chain Management is the integration of key business processes from end user through original suppliers that provides products, services, and information that add

value for customers and other stakeholders (Cooper et al., 1997, p. 2; Lambert et al. 2006, p. 2[1]).

It is also defined as

The management of a network of relationships within a firm and between interdependent organizations and business units consisting of material suppliers, purchasing, produc- tion facilities, logistics, marketing, and related systems that facilitate the forward and reverse flow of materials, services, finances and information from the original producer to final customer with the benefits of adding value, maximizing profitability through efficiencies, and achieving customer satisfaction (Stock and Boyer 2009, p. 706).

Having clarified the difference between Operations and Supply Chain Management, it is now necessary to define *Logistics* and *Logistics Management*, which are often used as synonyms of Supply Chain and Supply Chain Management. In business practices, in fact, there is not always a clear distinction between the Supply Chain Management and Logistics Management functions. Since different interpretations are given also in literature (Naslund and Williamson, 2010), in the following we have adopted the view of those who have emphasised the differences between logistics and the supply chain, among whom Sanders (2012), who states:

- *Supply chain is the network of all entities involved in producing and delivering a finished product to the final customer. This includes sourcing raw materials and parts, manufacturing, producing and assembling the products, storing goods in the warehouses, order entry and tracking, distribution and delivery to the final customer* (p. 3); and that
- *Logistics is the business function responsible for transporting and delivering products to the right place at the right time throughout the supply chain. In essence it is about movement and storage of product inventories throughout the chain* (p. 179).

Because there are various opinions on the differences or overlaps between the concepts of Logistics and the Supply Chain, a debate on the differences or overlaps between the concepts of Logistics Management and Supply Chain Management has emerged from an organisational and management perspective. Over time, however, the prevailing opinion has agreed that logistics is a relevant component of the broader concept of the supply chain. In particular, *Logistics Management* refers to activities carried out in a single company, from our perspective the focal organisation, and the management of its inbound and outbound flows of goods, services and related information. These flows are managed so as to create value for the dominant player, or rather, as expressed by Mentzer (2004, p. 4) are 'focused on what we call the focal organization...'. In contrast, *Supply Chain Management* pursues goals from the perspective of all the players involved in the supply chain, or rather,

---

[1]This definition is taken from the one developed by the study coordinated by Lambert (1994), at The International Center for Competitive Excellence, University of North Florida, which then transferred to Ohio State University with the new name The Global Supply Chain Forum.

'Supply chain management is the systematic, strategic coordination of the traditional business functions and the tactics across these business functions within a particular company and across businesses within the supply chain, for the purposes of improving the long-term performance of the individual companies and the supply chain as a whole' (Mentzer et al., 2001, p. 22).

Another element that distinguishes the two concepts is the heterogeneity of the business processes embedded in the concept of supply chain management, including those most specifically assigned to logistics functions. In this regard, in our opinion, the analysis proposed by Cooper et al. (1997) is still convincing; in their review of specialist literature they observed that 'it is unclear what specific characteristics differentiate the two disciplines' and again 'for many the contemporary understanding of SCM is not appreciably different from the understanding of integrated logistics management, however broadly logistics is defined' (p. 4). Starting with the consideration of the weakening of the functional differences, to the advantage of organisations that are becoming more and more oriented towards processes, and the increasing importance of all the business processes that go beyond intra- and inter-company confines, Cooper et al. stated: 'The new vision of Supply Chain Management ideally embraces all business processes cutting across all organizations within the supply chain, from initial point of supply to the ultimate point of consumption' (p. 5). In the proposed framework of Supply Chain Management, several logistics activities, such as order fulfilment, manufacturing flow management and procurement, are either business processes or components of the more extensive concept of Supply Chain Management, which also includes other relevant business processes, such as customer relationship management, customer service management and product development and commercialisation.

In order to explain the differences between the two definitions and the scope of each one of them, a useful contribution was recently offered by the CSCMP – Council of Supply Chain Management Professionals, according to which:

- *Logistics Management is that part of supply chain management that plans, implements and controls the efficient, effective forward and reverse flow and storage of goods, services and related information between the point of origin and the point of consumption in order to meet the customers' requirements* (CSCMP, 2012).
- *Supply Chain Management encompasses the planning and management of all activities involved in sourcing and procurement, conversion, and all logistics management activities. Importantly, it also includes coordination and collaboration with channel partners, which can be suppliers, intermediaries, third-party service providers, and customers. In essence, supply chain management integrates supply and demand management within and across companies* (CSCMP, 2012).

In brief, and this is the view taken later in this book, it can be said that Logistics Management is to be understood as a subset of Supply Chain Management, in three different respects:

1. The *horizontal extension* of the sub-processes controlled by the function, which, in the case of Logistics Management, include mainly the effective

and efficient management of physical flows and the related information flows between the individual players, both upstream and downstream, that interact with the focal company. In the case of Supply Chain Management, on the other hand, this is extended beyond, connecting all the possible players involved along the supply chain and improving their long-term performances.

2. The *uniqueness or the variety of players* in the interest of whom goals are pursued, be they cost or profit goals or even others. In the first case the choices to optimise the objective function refer to the focal company, whereas in the case of Supply Chain Management the pursuit of goals refers to all the players involved in the supply chain.

3. The *structure and complexity* of the business processes underlying the area of responsibility, which in the case of Logistics Management refers mainly to forward and reverse flows in terms of transportation, storage and the other activities closely linked to these, such as handling or some logistics postponement operations, and so on. In contrast, in the case of Supply Chain Management, other key processes, such as new product development or customer relationship management, are also included.

Therefore, with reference to both Operations, Logistics and Supply Chain processes, and to reverse flows, which are just as important from a sustainability perspective (namely Reverse Logistics and the Closed-Loop Supply Chain – see Chapter 7), we will adopt the distinction explained earlier, which defines Operations Management as activities referring to intra-company flows, and Supply Chain Management as those referring to inter-company exchanges, within which the subject of Logistics Management is found, as a specific subset, mainly dealing with transportation and storage activities. With reference, in particular, to the management of physical flows and the connected information flows, the relation between the three concepts – Operations, Logistics and Supply Chain Management – is exemplified in Figure 2.2.

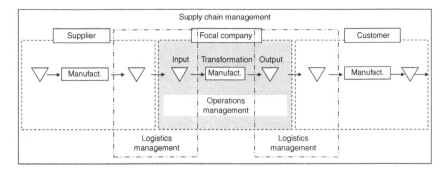

FIGURE 2.2 FGC Operations, Logistics and Supply Chain Management and the development of the management of physical flows.

2.3 OPERATIONS, SUPPLY CHAIN MANAGEMENT AND COMPETITIVE ADVANTAGE

2.3.1 Strategic Alignment

Operations and Supply Chain Management decisions must be aligned with strategic business choices, which represent 'the direction and scope of an organization over the long term: ideally, which matches its resources to its changing environment, and, in particular, its markets, customers or clients so as to meet stakeholder expectation' (Johnson et al., 2008 p. 3). The process of strategy formulation generally goes in a top-down direction and is carried out along three levels – corporate, business and function – where goals become more and more specific (Greasley, 2006, p. 27):

1. On the first level, *corporate*, the long-term goals and guidelines for the entire organisation, frequently summarised in the *company vision*, are developed.
2. On the second level, *business*, the different plans for each Strategic Business Unit are developed in order to define the elements underlying the creation of competitive advantage, for the products and services offered to specific markets, or for each business area defined on a corporate level.
3. On the third level, *function*, the long-term plans to be assigned to the functions – operations, marketing, finance and so on – or to any other selected organisational unit, are developed, so that these can support the creation of competitive advantage, defined on a business level.

The hierarchical process described here, although mainly based on a top-down approach, imposes a two-way interaction, where choices to be made on a functional level can contribute to the definition of goals on a business level and so on, going in a bottom-up direction. Indeed, the decisions taken at the functional level can have significant implications, as highlighted by the theories of the *emergent strategies* (Mintzberg and Waters, 1985), according to which a strategy can also emerge from everyday operating experience, rather than from a long-term hierarchical planning approach.

The Operations and Supply Chain Strategy is therefore found on the third level of the process described earlier, like all other functional strategies, such as marketing and finance, and so on, and can be implemented according to two different perspectives (Greasley, 2006, p. 39):

1. The first, defined *market-based strategy* (Hines, 2004), according to which corporate choices are derived from positioning goals in target markets and is followed by appropriate approaches of organisation, management and control of operating processes. Take, for example, the case of some fast-food chains that try to achieve a high market share through a business model characterised by an acceptable level of food quality, low costs, quick service, and a clean environment and so on. These restaurants pursue performance goals related to quality, speed of service and cost-effectiveness, based on the design and management of highly standardised processes, the use of properly trained staff,

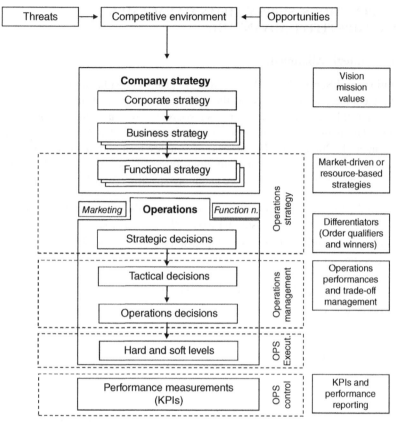

FIGURE 2.3   Strategic Alignment Process, Operations Strategy and Operations Management. *Source:* Grando et al., 2010, adapted from Greasley, 2006.

ad hoc technologies and ergonomic infrastructures, and the careful selection of suppliers, selected on the basis of their capabilities and performance.

2. The second, defined *resource-based strategy* (Grant, 1991), according to which business choices must be taken leveraging the internal competences, on the basis of which a set of operating capabilities (operations and supply chain management capabilities) necessary for pursuing competitive success in the target markets can be set up. This is the case, for example, of the 3M Corporation, which, thanks to its competence in the field of adhesive materials technology, continues to develop successful products, or the recent cases of several web application design companies that, thanks to the competences of their researchers and designers and the availability of laboratories and technology, develop capabilities to create and customise wide ranges of products and services.

The two approaches may find appropriate integration methods, as illustrated in Figure 2.3. Over time, there may be cases in which one approach prevails over the other; in other cases there can be little movement or, on the contrary, a high acceleration due to the dynamic nature of markets and the necessity to develop new competences.

In order for a company to compete effectively in its competitive arena, it must identify differentiators, or rather, attributes linked to its core competences, capable of providing a long-lasting competitive advantage and enabling successful product offerings (Grant, 2013). In this regard, it is necessary to look at the competitive factors in Figure 2.3 and the performance goals to be reached, which may be divided into two categories, defined as *order qualifiers* and *order winners* (Hill, 2005). Order qualifiers are made up of all the performance profiles characteristic of a product or service that are required in order for the product/service to even be considered by a customer; these are minimum levels of performance and define the short list of competitors playing in the same competitive arena. Order winners are the specific elements and performances that make a company win the order, outperforming the other shortlisted companies. Guaranteeing performance that qualifies the company to be in a certain market segment does not necessarily lead to competitive success, but simply enables the company to participate in the competition in the first place. A minimum threshold, such as, for example, a level of reliability or quality considered acceptable, must be reached within these performance profiles (order qualifiers), and consequently within the underlying priorities of operations and supply chain management, under penalty of exclusion from the competition. Once this threshold has been reached, improvements to the performance profiles, however, guarantee only a limited increase in sales. On the contrary and only after having offered adequate qualifying levels of performance (order qualifiers), competitive advantage lies in the ability to offer distinctiveness in the performance profiles that customers consider to be winners (order winners). All the automobile manufacturers that compete within a specific segment offer products and related services, guaranteeing performance in terms of quality, cost, delivery and after-sales services that is often comparable, but in the end customers choose the set of performances that best satisfies their needs, and the order is collected by just one of the competitors.

2.3.2   Operations, Supply Chain Management and Decision Making

In order to achieve adequate performance levels, and thus create value, it is necessary to design the Operations and Supply Chain system managing a number of 'levers', which may be grouped into Hardware Levers and Software Levers.

These design levers cannot be used without identifying the primary goals of the Operations and Supply Chain Management system, which in turn are derived, as already stated, by the Vision, Mission and Strategy of the company. The latter permeate the entire activity of the company and, in indicating the areas where the management team ought to concentrate its improvement efforts, define strategic goals and, then, functional sub-goals. As illustrated in Figure 2.3, and within the perimeter of the processes discussed in this book, there may be a large number of sub-goals, which are often antithetical. Take, for example, a logistics system that attempts to jointly pursue limited investments in stocks and a high service level, or a production process that requires maximum saturation and production flexibility. The traditional approach towards Operations and Supply Chain Management choices is therefore based on the concept of focalisation (Skinner, 1974): in the presence of diverging goals (trade-offs), it is necessary to focus on priorities and to consider the others to be secondary, just like dependent variables. Competing on cost, for example, may involve good, but not excellent, quality and service; a high service level can be achieved thanks to high investment in stock.

Once the set of goals assigned to the Operations and Supply Chain Management System has been defined, it is necessary to shape the organisation that has to pursue these goals, which must be capable of providing an adequate response to the identified needs, through the use and consistent integration of all its components, or Design Levers. The Design Levers available to managers can be grouped according to the degree of irreversibility of the choices that characterise them (Grando, 1995).

Hardware Levers – also called Configuration Levers – can therefore be defined as the choices concerning infrastructure, the type of systems and technology adopted, the installed production capacity, the degree of vertical integration and the possible off-shoring or outsourcing of production processes. The decisions concerning these issues are taken for medium- to long-term periods and shape the permanent features of the production system. *Software Levers* – or Management Levers – on the other hand, are those regarding the planning and control systems of the core operations and supply chain management processes, such as materials management, transportation and shipments, quality control, maintenance activities, the management of production-related employees and so forth. These decisions can be changed more frequently and affect the production system over the short/medium term.

Software Levers are generally embedded in a defined hardware system, bringing it to life and guaranteeing its optimal performance. This means that decisions concerning Hardware and Software Levers must be consistent and share the same visions and goals. Frequent negative behaviour arises from inconsistencies between the choices concerning the production system and its management processes. This is the case in situations where the Hardware Levers have been managed so as to achieve specific competitive goals, which over time have changed due to market pressures. In these cases, in order to cope with such variability in the competitive arena, the company may need to manage its Software Levers accordingly, in an attempt to adapt its production system to the new challenges. However, these incremental adjustments can result in an inconsistency between the structural and managerial aspects of the production system. Take, for example, the case of a company that, having chosen to outsource its production to a low-labour-cost country (hardware choice), finds out that it is difficult to establish an appropriate local supply base and that, consequently, it is not possible to keep using Just-in-Time principles in procurement processes (software choice).

2.3.3   Operations and Supply Chain Performance Management and Control

The performance goals pursued by the Operations and Supply Chain Management units are, as illustrated in Figure 2.3, the basis for the creation of competitive advantage, as they support the positioning of a company in its market. These units, as

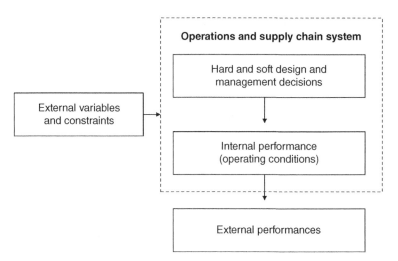

FIGURE 2.4 Performance and operating conditions. *Source:* Bartezzaghi and Turco 1989. Reproduced with permission of Emerald Group Publishing Ltd.

already stated, must organise resources and processes in order to guarantee levels of corporate performance that meet the needs of its target customers.

The need for the performance goals to have a unique and systematic framework has inspired countless studies on the subject, which will be discussed later, in Chapter 8. In terms of implications for management, it is necessary first and foremost to make a distinction between the performances outside the production system (external performances or performances *stricto sensu*), that is, the performances that can be measured directly by the customer or by the top management of the company (at business unit or corporate level), and the performances within the production system (internal performances, also called operating conditions or configuration parameters), namely those features that characterise the productive factors and the activities of the Operations and Supply Chain processes (Bartezzaghi and Turco, 1989).

The latter lead to the determination of the former, as they are the features that make the system work, as illustrated in Figure 2.4.

External performance typically derives from the goals assigned to the Operations and Supply Chain units and expresses the degree with which these goals are achieved: it concerns, for example, measures, such as the level of service provided in terms of delivery dependability or speed, the product quality, the factors productivity and the level of emissions, and so on. *Internal performance*, on the other hand, is derived from the design choices of the system and the set of constraints it is subjected to and refers to elements such as process lead times (Gallmann and Belvedere, 2011), plant utilisation and efficiency (Grando and Turco, 2005; Cigolini and Grando, 2009), scrap rates (Crosby, 1979; 1984a; 1984b; Flynn et al., 1994), and health and safety at the shop-floor level (Silvestri et al., 2012; Alston and Millikin, 2015) and so on. Operations and Supply Chain managers, in fact, have to undertake actions to modify operating conditions in order to improve external performance. In this regard, in highly competitive situations, since the customer is able to make a selection by comparing the performance offered by several competitors, according to the order qualifiers and the order winners described above, measuring and managing the final performances offered to the market (i.e. quality, time, flexibility and cost etc.) become crucial.

It is to be noted that the performance attributes indicated above are closely interdependent, and have an influence on one another. Take, for example, the case of a production system that generates defective output due to insufficient levels of reliability in its manufacturing process. If the defect is detected and corrected prior to the delivery of the products to customer (in-house defect), the need to carry out recovery and correction activities will lead to higher costs; even if the customer will receive a good quality product, a higher price will be charged (or a lower margin earned by the manufacturer). On the other hand, in the case where the defective product enters the market (in-field defect), the possibility of limiting the negative impact of such an event is linked to the opportunity of offering appropriate in-field services (such as repairs under warranty), which will affect company margins.

Similarly, the use of non-conformant materials or an excessive emphasis on productivity and production rates can cause an increase in accidents involving workers or lead to the manufacturing of products that are harmful to consumer health. The performance delivered by an Operations system is therefore characterised by close interdependence and mutual conditioning: in fact, several internal performance levels – the result of choices made during the design and management of the Operations System – contribute to the achievement of certain external performance levels. The increasing need expressed by many companies to have efficient and comprehensive systems to control the performance of their processes, both internally and externally, has led to the design of 'dashboards' or 'tableaux de bord' suitable for measuring the manufacturing and logistic performance of the company, for identifying improvement areas and supporting the management decision-making process through the analysis of a few relevant indicators (Belvedere, 2015).

The discovery of any variations between expected performance and actual performance is the start of the process that leads to the design and implementation of corrective action to improve the system. This process can be observed at different levels of the decision-making hierarchy of the company.

To properly design an effective performance measurement system, a dual approach is required: feed-back control and feed-forward control (Da Villa, 2000). *Feed-back control*, or *reactive control*, means a simple ex post assessment, aimed at assessing the gap that may be observed between estimated, target or standard values and actual values. In addition, a performance measurement system must also enable a *feed-forward process*, strongly inspired by interpretative or diagnostic objectives, aimed at explaining the deviations of past phenomena and therefore at providing instructions to improve the Operations system.

The measurement of appropriate KPI – Key Performance Indicators – is therefore a fundamental pre-requisite for the correct management of the levers that can be managed in order to achieve goals.

2.4 PERFORMANCE AND TRADE-OFF MANAGEMENT

Operations and Supply Chain Management therefore consists of the set of decision-making processes that enable a manufacturing or services company to create a competitive advantage by offering products, services and performance whose value, in the perspective of the customer, is perceived to be at least equal to that of competitors (order qualifier) and, if possible, higher (order winner).

The main task of Operations and Supply Chain Management is to deliver performances that comply with internal and external requirements; these performances are conventionally summarised in four categories (Slack et al., 2007):

1. *Cost*, linked to overall efficiency and productivity of the factors employed. In this regard, the total productivity, an expression of the relationship between output evaluated at standard manufacturing cost and the value of the set of production factors, can be broken down into several partial productivities, with reference to the individual factors employed, mainly: capital, labour, materials and energy (Grando and Turco, 2005; Cigolini and Grando, 2009).

2. *Quality*, mainly assessed from two different perspectives, represented by design quality and conformance quality. Design quality is generally measured with specific indicators, depending on the features of the product or service and the technology incorporated therein, such as, for example, the toughness and resilience of a metal, the elasticity of a fibre, the power of an electric motor or the viscosity of a lubricant set in the design stage. Conformance quality, on the other hand, is defined as the correspondence of the product or service to design specifications. In the analysis of a production and logistics system, the measurement of conformance quality, which is assessed at different times and points of the manufacturing process, becomes particularly relevant: internally or in-house, that is, prior to the delivery to the customer, and externally, or in-field, that is, when the product is available at the site of the customer. In the former case, the most common indicators aim to measure the impact of scraps and defective volumes compared to the total volumes produced, as well as the costs incurred to repair non-conformant items. In the latter case, the most recurrent KPIs refer to the number of hours or assistance provided under warranty, compared to the number of units sold, the frequency of complaints and so on (Feigembaum, 1991).

3. *Flexibility*, observable from many perspectives, all linked to the ability to deal with the variety and variability of requests and their impact on the production system. Therefore, the general concept of flexibility is often broken down into several elementary types of flexibility, such as, for example, mix flexibility (ability to vary the range of products manufactured in a cost-effective manner in a given amount of time), product flexibility (ability to engineer and launch new products in a limited period of time, referred to as 'time to market'), plan flexibility (ability to accept order variations, also with short notice periods) and volume flexibility (or elasticity, which is the ability to change production volumes cost-effectively and in a limited period of time) (Gerwin, 1987; Beamon, 1999; Slack, 2005).

4. *Time*, in terms of the speed of introduction of new products and delivery speed and dependability. The former aims at promptly meeting new customer's needs with adequate products, while the latter refer to the ability to deliver items in a timely manner and to comply with the promised delivery dates (Beamon, 1998; Reichhart and Holweg, 2007).

The pursuit of these performances is functional to the achievement of a sustainable competitive advantage, either through choices to differentiate and enhance the goods and services offered, or through the reduction of costs and consequently price-based competition. More recently, due to the pressures from consumers, the diffusion of Corporate Social Responsibility (CSR) principles among companies, as well as more stringent limitations imposed by the regulator or different forms of certification, social and environmental sustainability goals, which have already been described, are to be added to the main goal of economic sustainability. All companies, in the continuous process of value creation for their stakeholders, must integrate the goals linked to environmental and social sustainability into the set of goals pursued. As stated by Sanders and Wood, in fact,

> *in pursuit of social and environmental improvements, OM [Operations Management] strategy still should be based on a company's unique core competencies, resources, technologies and supply network. Sustainable OM strategy includes value creation for social and environmental stakeholders as a competitive priority. Together these elements create the building blocks of a firm's unique strategic sustainability architecture or sustainable operating system* (Sanders and Wood, 2015, p. 264).

In many companies, therefore, the types of performance identified here have also been expressed in light of environmental and social sustainability goals, without necessarily being detrimental to the goal of economic sustainability. Take, for example, the decision to select suppliers that hold an Environmental Certification ISO 14001 or EMAS Registration, or the reduction of costs by choosing to use materials originating from recycling processes and not only virgin raw materials, or the development of energy recovery systems, the decisions to develop products and industrial processes aimed at reducing the consumption of scarce resources, like water, the creation of working environments that are respectful of the needs of workers, investments in gyms and areas for employees to socialise, or day-care facilities for their children, and other policies that are becoming increasingly widespread in companies that take care of the welfare of their employees.

2.5   SUSTAINABLE OPERATIONS AND SUPPLY CHAIN MANAGEMENT: A REFERENCE FRAMEWORK

The need to combine the subjects of Operations and Supply Chain Management (which includes Logistics Management, as mentioned) with new sustainability and sustainable development demands has gradually encouraged the development of definitions and models that aim to integrate sustainability goals within the framework of the processes governed by these functions.

With regard to the definitions of Sustainable Operations and Supply Chain Management, the following are considered to be among the most recent contributions of literature: Kleindorfer et al. (2005); Linton et al. (2007); Carter and Rogers (2008); Pagell and Wu (2009); Cetinkaya et al. (2011); Stroufe and Melnyk (2013); Sanders and Wood (2015):

- *Sustainable OM [is] the set of skills and concepts that allow a company to structure and manage its business processes to obtain competitive returns on its capital assets without sacrificing the legitimate needs of internal and external stakeholders and with due regard for the impact of its operations on people and environment* (Kleindorfer et al., 2005, p. 489).

- *Sustainable Operations Management is the management of the transformational process to reduce resource consumption, pollution and waste while benefiting employees, customers and communities in order to reduce short-term risks and shore-up long-term cash flows* (Sanders and Wood, 2015, p. 261).

- *Sustainable Supply Chain is the strategic, transparent integration and achievement of an organization's social, environmental and economic goals in the systemic coordination of key interorganizational business processes for improving the long-term economic performance of the individual company and its supply chains* (Carter and Rogers, 2008, p. 368).

- *Sustainable Supply Chain Management practices include stakeholder engagement, product/process design, life cycle assessment (LCA), materials selection and sourcing, manufacturing processes, waste transportation of final products and services to consumers as well as end-of-life management of products, and closed-loop systems* (Stroufe and Melnyk, 2013, p. 7).

In accordance with these statements regarding the difference between Operations Management and Supply Chain Management, where the former focuses on intra-company processes and the latter embraces the widest spectrum of inter-company processes, also in terms of sustainability, we will maintain the same distinction. As suggested in the framework for a sustainable supply chain proposed by Mollenkopf (2006), *Internal Operations* is a component of a broader system made up also of 'upstream suppliers, downstream customers and product development and stewardship'.

With reference to the subject under analysis and its management choices – Sustainable Operations and Supply Chain Management – several building blocks can be found in the definitions previously, which can be used to develop the topics dealt with later in this book:

- The *strategic intention to clearly integrate* the profiles summarised previously with *the 3Ps* – Profit, Planet, People – of economic, environmental and social sustainability, included in a wider objective of competitiveness, into the set of pursued goals.

- The *pressure to achieve sustainable goals* that create long-term value for the individual company and for the other players in the supply chain that it belongs to, through collaboration and value-sharing practices.

FIGURE 2.5   Sustainable Supply Chain Management. *Source:* Carter 2008. Reproduced with permission of Emerald Group Publishing Ltd.

- The *involvement and accountability* not only of shareholders, but *of all stakeholders*, along the entire life cycle of the product or service offered.
- The *extension of the framework* to all relevant inter- and intra-company business processes, in accordance with the meaning of Operations and Supply Chain illustrated earlier.

The need to design and manage Sustainable Supply Chains has therefore led some authors to look more closely at the areas that companies have to manage in relation to sustainability goals. As illustrated in the framework set out in Figure 2.5, the design of Sustainable Supply Chains must be based on a more articulated and stronger company orientation to be transferred into strategic and management choices (Carter and Rogers, 2008).

Carter and Rogers (2008), on the one hand, highlight many elements that must to be taken into consideration by any organisation that is about to embed sustainability into its corporate goals, in terms of strategy, organisational culture, risk management and transparency requirements. On the other hand, they emphasise how 'the social and environmental dimensions of SCCM (Sustainable Supply Chain Management) ... must be undertaken with a clear and explicit recognition of the economics goals of the firm' (p. 369). This is the reason why they place a question mark over the term 'good', where the intersection is limited to environmental and social performance, without considering these objectives within the broadest strategic and financial goals of a company.

Consistently, since they have witnessed a broad debate regarding the possibility of applying win-win goals among the components of the Triple Bottom Line, they emphasise that 'There are a variety of environmental and social issues that a firm can undertake which can both improve as well as harm the economic bottom line', and conclude by speculating: 'The proportion of environmental and social initiatives which result in enhanced economic performance is relatively large' and 'the highest level of economic performance will occur at the intersection of environmental, social and economic performance' (p. 370).

Although there is a debate on the existence of trade-offs between sustainability and economic competitiveness, a growing number of authors have produced evidence that goes beyond this position, putting forward analyses that are built on broader horizons and wider ranges of assessment (McWilliams and Siegel, 2000; Porter and Kramer, 2002, 2006, 2011; Salzmann et al., 2005). For example, at the beginning of the 1990s, Porter (1991, p. 96) stated 'the conflict between environmental protection and economic competitiveness is a false dichotomy based on a narrow view of the sources of prosperity and a static view of competition'. In order to understand how to reconcile the possible trade-offs among sustainability elements, and to express these concepts within the scope of operations and the supply chain, it is necessary to identify the stages in which management decisions have to be taken to jointly achieve not only economic, but also environmental and social sustainability

It is, therefore, useful to propose a reference framework, which makes it possible to show the possible integration of the triple goal of sustainability with the stages that make up the *life cycle* associated with a product, from a cradle-to-cradle perspective (Braungart et al., 2007; Linton et al., 2007). This framework is also suitable for explaining the structure of this book and introducing its Chapters.

In this regard, we build on the proposal contained in the seminal work of Corbett (2009), which puts forward an effective approach for outlining the areas of possible interaction between the business processes developed during the lifetime of a product and their implications in terms of sustainability. For our purposes, the original model has been modified and integrated with the goal of emphasising the link between the stages of the life cycle of the product and the players along an ideal supply chain involved in their management. As illustrated in Figure 2.6, and as already stated in the previous paragraphs, the goals assigned to the departments and managers of the different phases of a product life cycle must necessarily derive from broader strategic goals, typically linked to positioning choices of the focal company that governs the supply chain, and shared, although through mediation processes, with other players. The consistency between higher-ranking corporate goals and sub-goals pursued on a functional level or in a subset of the supply chain must emerge in the medium to long term, guaranteeing, as mentioned earlier, strategic alignment (also defined strategic fit) and a focus on defined priorities.

The central part of the diagram compares, on the one hand, the three components of sustainability, previously summarised in the *Triple Bottom Line* concept (Elkington, 1998), and, on the other hand, the typical phases along which the LCA – *Life Cycle Analysis* – of a product is developed, according to the cradle-to-cradle approach, assuming a circular life cycle of the product (see Chapter 3).

This perspective is based on the development of products and processes designed so as to generate (or save) value in several life cycles through the reuse of their parts (or at least some of them) at the end of their lifetime.

In order to integrate the proposal of Corbett (2009) based on Life Cycle Analysis with the need to give evidence to all the main players in the supply chain and

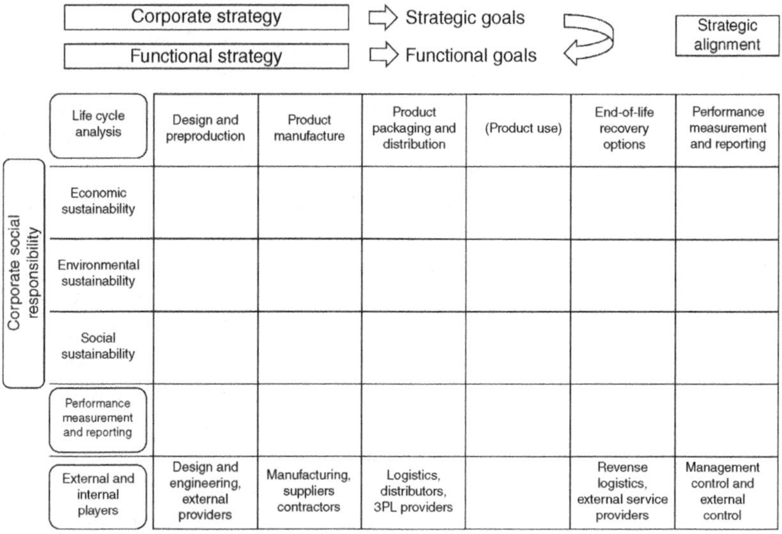

Corporate strategy	⇨ Strategic goals	⇨	Strategic alignment
Functional strategy	⇨ Functional goals		

	Life cycle analysis	Design and preproduction	Product manufacture	Product packaging and distribution	(Product use)	End-of-life recovery options	Performance measurement and reporting
Economic sustainability							
Environmental sustainability							
Social sustainability							
Performance measurement and reporting							
External and internal players	Design and engineering, external providers	Manufacturing, suppliers contractors	Logistics, distributors, 3PL providers			Reverse logistics, external service providers	Management control and external control

(left vertical labels: Corporate social responsibility)

FIGURE 2.6 A reference framework for the development of Sustainable Operations and Supply Chain Management. *Source*: Corbett 2009, http://www.jiem.org/index.php/jiem/article/viewArticle/15. Used under CC BY 3.0 http://creativecommons.org/licenses/by/3.0/

accountable for its management, the figure also illustrates the sequence of internal and external players and departments involved in each stage of the product life cycle. In this regard, the main phases can be summarised as follows:

- *Design and pre-production*, which, based on principles of Design for Environment (see Chapter 3), are crucial in determining the possibility of recovering value along the life cycle of a product and, in particular, at the end of its lifetime.
- *Production* of the product, which, in terms of the organisation of the players involved along the supply chain, can be divided into two stages, involving the supply system (see Chapter 4), which is increasingly relevant in an environment dominated by outsourcing choices, and the production activity carried out by the focal company (see Chapter 5).
- *Packaging and distribution* of the product (see Chapter 6), crucial in terms of sustainability due to the impact of primary and secondary transportation, and the possibility of minimising and reusing packaging; also in this case, the focal company can use third-party logistics providers for the activities necessary to reach the final customer, especially for consumer goods in business-to-consumer (B2C) systems.
- *Use* of the product by customers, who play an increasingly relevant role in directing corporate choices through their preference for products that respect environmental and social sustainability principles, and in the development and diffusion of a culture of accountability that is implemented through specific actions, such as the tendency to save energy, to focus on the reduction of waste

and to separate recyclable waste and so on. This stage, however, is beyond the scope of this book.

- *End-of-life management* of a product, through Reverse Logistics and the adoption of different recovery options (see Chapter 7), which, if planned and managed properly, can offer the possibility of extracting residual value, through processes that range from high-impact choices, such as reuse, remanufacture and recycle processes, to low-potential processes like the choice to dispose the exhausted products or send them to incineration plants.

The proposed model is completed with the analysis of *performance measurement* and reporting systems. In all systems that are geared towards on-going improvement it is, in fact, necessary to monitor the performance of the processes under analysis, designing KPIs suitable for measuring targets and achievements (see Chapter 8). In this regard, as previously mentioned, it is worth highlighting how these measures should have a double purpose: on the one hand, in accordance with feed-back control logics, to highlight any variance between target values and actual ones; and on the other hand, following the principles of feed-forward control, to be a diagnostic tool, able not only to express the size of the gap, but also, if possible, to highlight the main causes behind it and, thus, to lead to the implementation of appropriate improvement measures. Take, for example, a company that has consumed more energy than its target values or has used lower volumes of recycled materials than expected. The usefulness of a deviation analysis as an end in itself appears to be limited to an ex post assessment of the increased cost, or lower saving, obtained through a comparison with the expected values. A reporting system that enables an in-depth analysis of these deviations, such as, for example, a deployment of the energy losses or of the materials wasted in the various phases of the production process, will make it possible to reconsider previous choices and to implement appropriate corrective actions.

As highlighted by the references to the following Chapters, the previously proposed framework is central to our entire work, and therefore will be taken up and detailed later, in terms of the organisation of relevant business processes and players involved along the supply chain.

As suggested by Corbett (2009), the general table in Figure 2.6 offers various layers of analysis of both the dimensions observed. On the one hand, in fact, it is possible to deploy the general goals of sustainability, summarised in the Triple Bottom Line, into more detailed ones, until the single measures to be set as targets in the control and reporting system are reached. On the other hand, the life cycle phases, overseen by various links in the Supply Chain, underlie the business processes that can be broken down until their specific activities, roles and responsibilities can be identified. It is evident, in organisational terms, that the development of KPIs aimed at measuring the performance of the players involved in these processes can be implemented with different levels of detail and reliability, for both internal organisation units (business divisions and departments involved) and external ones (suppliers, subcontractors, distributors and service providers).

At the bottom of the framework represented in Figure 2.7 there is an example of the sustainability goals that become increasingly detailed until the point of their

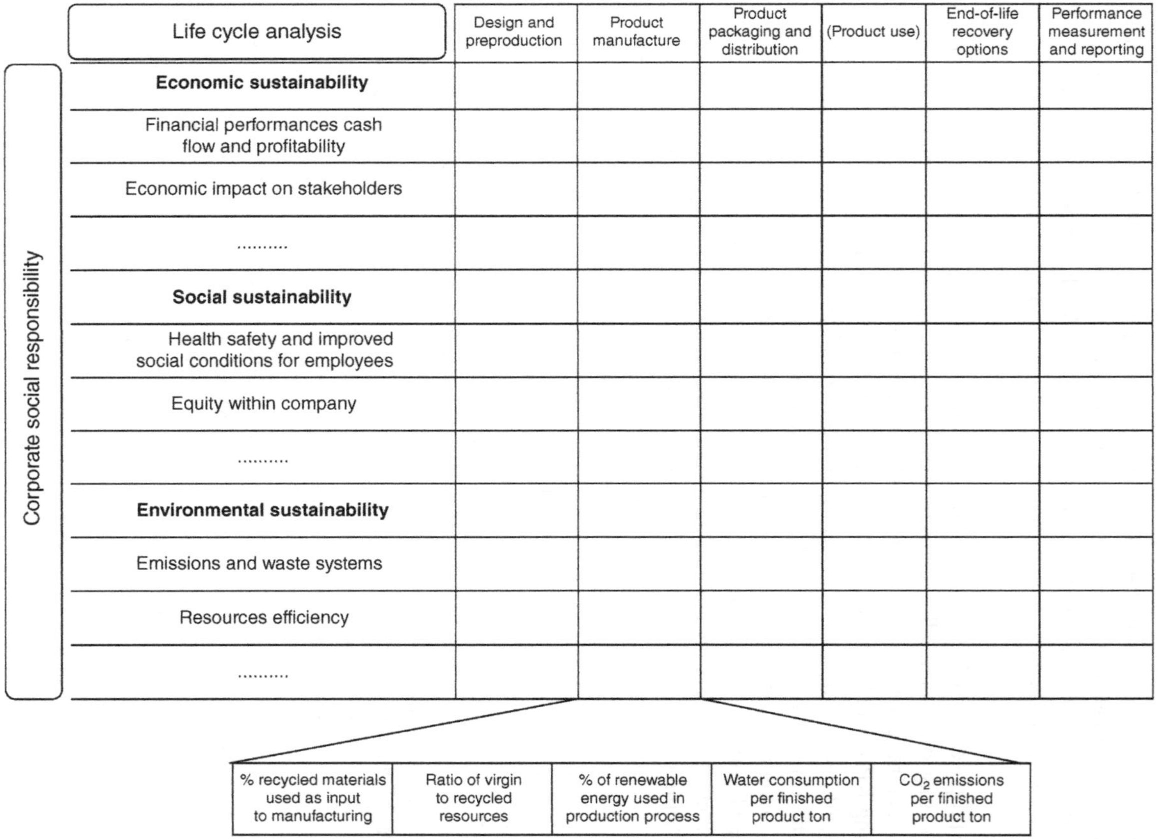

Life cycle analysis	Design and preproduction	Product manufacture	Product packaging and distribution	(Product use)	End-of-life recovery options	Performance measurement and reporting
Economic sustainability						
Financial performances cash flow and profitability						
Economic impact on stakeholders						
....						
Social sustainability						
Health safety and improved social conditions for employees						
Equity within company						
....						
Environmental sustainability						
Emissions and waste systems						
Resources efficiency						
....						

Corporate social responsibility

% recycled materials used as input to manufacturing	Ratio of virgin to recycled resources	% of renewable energy used in production process	Water consumption per finished product ton	CO_2 emissions per finished product ton

FIGURE 2.7 An example of the layering and segmentation of Supply Chain processes. *Source:* Corbett 2009, http://www.jiem.org/index.php/jiem/article/viewArticle/15. Used under CC BY 3.0 http://creativecommons.org/licenses/by/3.0/

deployment into environmental sustainability KPIs peculiar to a specific stage of the entire life cycle, namely product manufacture.

In the introductory Chapter of this book, reference was made to the mega-trends that are shaping the socio-economic environment in which companies operate. These forces will also have an impact on supply chain flows, changing their characteristics and generating needs to which companies must provide adequate responses. Take, for example, new urbanism phenomena, which, on the one hand, will create the need to guarantee the uninterrupted flow of products in densely populated areas and, on the other hand, the need to devise distribution models for populations in rural areas with a low population density; or even the impact of new technologies, such as the revolutionary applications of 3-D printing and additive manufacturing that may, in a growing number of sectors, do away with or reduce storage requirements and guarantee outsourced build-to-order operations, impacting on stock and transportation costs. Or even the undisputed dynamics of demographic trends, which will cause significant changes to the range of products and services on offer in countries where the subject of aging is emerging dramatically and those where the driving force of younger generations will become more intense.

It is therefore evident that operations and supply chain management will have to change and will also become more and more important in the future. For example, according to a recent survey, the production of internationally traded goods accounts for approximately 30% of global CO_2, while agriculture is responsible for the consumption of about 70% of worldwide freshwater resources (UNEP, 2010). The globalisation of trade increases the need for companies to pay attention also to the environmental and social impact of their choices, especially for those that act as the focal companies of their supply chains. Recalling one of the scenarios illustrated in the first Chapter, regarding the increasing scarcity of water on earth, it is worth drawing attention to several actions undertaken by leading global industrial groups, which have been described in a recent report (Gasson, 2014): Coca Cola has spent almost 2 billion dollars since 2003 in order to reduce water consumption in its 863 production plants, and more than 1 billion dollars for the development of water treatment systems and recycling processes. Nestlé, another food and beverage giant, spent 31 million euros on the introduction of new water treatment technology in 2013. In its Spanish factory, it managed to reduce the consumption of water per tonne of product by 60% with an investment of 1 million euros. Google is experimenting with the use of sea water to cool its digital archive in Finland and is testing the use of rainwater for another factory in South Carolina, whereas it is using water from the sewerage network in a US factory in Georgia. In 2014, Barilla, the Italian leader in the production of pasta, reduced the consumption of water for each tonne of finished product by 20% compared to 2010, in addition to cutting CO_2 emissions by 20%, and has set forth the goal of reducing both by 30% by 2020 (Barilla, 2015).

3

SUSTAINABILITY AND NEW PRODUCT DESIGN

3.1 INTRODUCTION

Ricoh, with a turnover of almost 2232 billion yen developed in approximately 200 countries and regions worldwide, approximately 110,000 employees, 229 consolidated companies (as of March 31, 2015), produces a wide range of products for different segments:

- *Office Imaging: MFPs (multifunctional printers), copiers, laser printers, digital duplicators, facsimile, scanners, related parts and supplies, services, support and software.*
- *Production Printing: cut sheet printer, continuous feed printer, related parts and supplies, services, support and software.*
- *Network System Solutions: personal computers, servers, network equipment, related services, support and software.*
- *Industrial Products: thermal media, optical equipment, semiconductor devices and electronic components, and -digital cameras.*

The Ricoh Group develops products that – throughout their life cycles – will keep their environmental impact below the limit at which the global environment becomes unsustainable. First, Eco Balance data on the environmental impact caused by overall business activities are identified, and, based on the results, targets for products covered by the action plans are set (Plan). LCA-based designs are then drawn up, and production process technologies are developed to achieve

Sustainable Operations and Supply Chain Management, First Edition. Valeria Belvedere and Alberto Grando.
© 2017 John Wiley & Sons Ltd. Published 2017 by John Wiley & Sons Ltd.

the targets (Do). Results from these designs and process technologies are again reviewed alongside the Eco Balance data (Check) before being reflected in the next targets (Act). In addition to technological development directly related to products, we also work on technological development that will help reduce the environmental impact of society as a whole. We are promoting various activities – such as the development of new/alternative materials, creation of a paperless environment through information technologies, and introduction of reuse/rewritable technologies to replace paper – to further evolve Ricoh's core technologies into environmental technologies that can be applied in a wider variety of areas.

In addition to energy saving, global warming prevention, resource preservation, recycling and pollution avoidance, Ricoh design proposes methods of easing human participation in ecological activity, and thereby contributes to the realization of a society that is sustainable.

According to the Ricoh Group CEO

The Ricoh Group is in a position to make tremendous contributions to protecting the global environment by implementing measures against climate change and improving resource productivity through its business activities. In order to enhance our sustainable environmental management, which means making the growth of our business compatible with environmental conservation, we are actively developing environmentally oriented businesses. As part of this effort, we will launch the new RICOH Eco Business Development Center in Gotemba City, Shizuoka, in 2015, thereby further accelerating the development of our environmental technologies and businesses. At the development center, we will conduct trial studies of environmental technologies, develop reuse and recycling technologies, and implement and optimize these technologies to create new businesses that extend beyond the boundaries of our conventional business domains. By developing businesses in the energy and other sectors to help our customers implement their own environmental measures, we will contribute to the creation of a sustainable society.

Our efforts at sustainable environmental management are supported by four pillars. Three of them – conserving energy and preventing global warming; conserving natural resources and encouraging recycling; and preventing pollution – support reduced environmental impact from our own business pursuits, and the fourth – protecting biodiversity – is vital for the planet to raise its capacity for self-recovery. These pillars are built upon a basis for sustainable environmental management, forming an infrastructure for effective and efficient activities across the board.

Source: Ricoh Group Sustainability Report, 2014, www.ricoh.com; consulted on 24 August, 2015.

Ricoh is one of the many multinational groups that has set sustainability goals that it pursues through continuing innovation in technology, products with, operations and supply chain management processes. In order to effectively pursue these goals it is fundamental right from the beginning, during the concept design phase, to create products and technology taking sustainability into consideration. The ability to develop the Research & Development processes of new products and to innovate underlying technology with a view to the Triple Bottom Line therefore plays a central role. In this Chapter, we will first of all illustrate the evolutionary path followed by many companies that have tackled the subject of sustainability, starting with a reactive orientation to the search for external bodies (compliance or enforcement), then to the triggering of more proactive processes; the latter are linked to the knowledge of the environmental impact of a product along its life cycle and the possibility of implementing innovative processes based on *DFE – Design for Environment*. Therefore, in the first part of the Chapter the concepts of LCA – *Life Cycle Assessment* – and Cradle-to-Cradle will be introduced and analysed, in contrast to the outdated *Cradle-to-Grave* design approaches. Subsequently, a distinction will be made between logics oriented at eco-efficiency and those oriented at eco-effectiveness. In the second part of the Chapter, we will go into more detail on the design philosophies defined as Design for X, with particular attention to DFE – Design for Environment – and its founding principles.

3.2 THE ENVIRONMENTAL ORIENTATION PATH

As illustrated in the previous Chapter, in the search for higher levels of performance companies are constantly trying to align higher corporate goals, which are linked to competitive long-term challanges, with the sub-goals assigned to the specific departments involved in company management. In this regard, new product development departments, such as Research & Development and Engineering in particular, play a vital role.

For the reasons illustrated in Chapter 2, from among the many goals pursued by companies, in recent years respect for the environment has emerged with increasing intensity, which is translated in the Environmental Management Orientation, defined as 'the set of objectives, plans and mechanisms that determine the responsiveness of operations to environmental issues' (Klassen and Johnson, 2004, p. 230; see also Klassen, 2001; Klassen and Whybark, 1999; Klassen and McLaughlin, 1996). In the framework proposed by Klassen and Johnson (2004), this orientation can have different stages of maturity, starting from a basic reactive orientation to a more complex and sophisticated pro-active orientation, meaning the evolutionary process, which can be summarised in the following steps:

- *Actions motivated by reactive choices made in response* to pressure from regulators, the market or value-based choices, which in turn mean compliance choices, such as certifications or the participation in voluntary improvement programmes related to environmental impact.
- *Actions involving end-of-pipe pollution control*, aimed at capturing pollutants and wastes, or limiting their impact, through the improvement of production processes and investments in technology. These actions generally affect production processes within and along the supply chain, especially upstream,

through the introduction of further phases in the operations and end-of-cycle stages, without significantly modifying the products and the supply chain itself.

* *Actions connected to the design and management of reverse flows*, developed downstream, to capture end-of-life products' value, by leveraging any possible recovery options, such as remanufacturing, part harvesting, recycling and so on (see Chapter 7).

* *Actions more oriented at pro-active choices* (Leong et al., 1990), such as those linked to pollution prevention and the analysis of environmental impact along the product life cycle, through the development of techniques such as the LFA – Life Cycle Assessment – and product design choices oriented at respecting the environment, like DFE – Design for Environment. These actions, in contrast with pollution control, mostly involve product design, internal manufacturing processes, and those managed along the supply chain.

The impact of these actions is witnessed in the areas dominated by Operations and Supply Chain Management, progressively involving all the players located up and downstream of the focal company, requiring a coherent Supply Chain Orientation (Shin et al., 2000), which is characterised by a wide range of competences, such as purely transactional skills, the ability to structure partnerships with suppliers and customers, or to coordinate the entire supply chain network. If, for example, certification or pollution control interventions may demand a supply chain orientation that is limited to the management of internal operations or relations with suppliers, using transactional processes that may at times be irregular and oriented at the short term, the most evolved pollution prevention, reverse flow management and *Design For Environment* choices require a supply chain orientation capable of closely coordinating the behaviour of upstream and downstream players through the definition of long-term partnerships and network orientation, whose supply chain management assumes a fundamental role in the creation of competitive advantage. The relation between Environmental Orientation and Supply Chain Orientation is shown in Figure 3.1.

As illustrated earlier, the most evolved interventions in terms of company environmental orientation, which play a fundamental role in supply chain management from the perspective of the creation of competitive advantage, refer to the approaches linked to product design in compliance with the principles of respect for the environment along its entire life cycle. These design and management approaches are summarised by DFE – Design For Environment.

DFE, as a fundamental lever, can be placed within the broadest set of actions and approaches that attempt to provide an answer to the dilemma linked to the trade-off between population growth and its aspirations to prosper and the requirement to reduce the pressure on the environment and to preserve the planet's resources. The need to provide clear answers to this dilemma, defined as 'absolute coupling' at both macro-level (in the drafting of consistent policies) and at micro-level (influencing the conduct of companies and supply chains) has led to the development of the approach known as the *Circular Economy* (Ellen MacArthur Foundation, 2012; 2013), understood in this Chapter as the arrival point of the evolution summarised before.

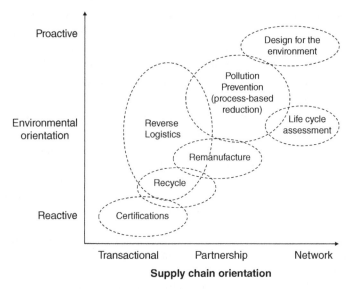

FIGURE 3.1   Aligning Environmental and Supply Chain Orientation. *Source:* Klassen 2004. Reproduced with permission of Oxford University Press.

This approach sets forth the need to base the development of an economy and its industrial system on the reuse of products and raw materials, and, as far as possible, the need to replenish natural resources. As will be described in detail next, the principles underlying the Circular Economy are based on (Ellen MacArthur Foundation, 2012; 2013):

- *A circular vision of the life cycle* of manufactured goods, which must be created and designed for multiple life cycles, according to cradle-to-cradle logics.
- *The need to implement up-cycling logics*, namely the creation – and not the reduction (down-cycling) – of value, through processes aimed at reusing products and materials that create new products and materials of a higher quality and with improved features.
- *The need to think* of the relationship with natural resources *in terms of resource effectiveness and not resource efficiency*, taking into consideration the requirement to re-insert natural resources so far as possible into the biological cycle that transforms waste into food.
- *The incentive to use renewable resources* and to take strict action against all forms of the depletion of natural resources, the use of hazardous materials and greenhouse emissions and so on.

In fact the Circular Economy is essentially based on the possibility of intentionally contemplating an industrial and economic system in which all waste streams and emissions can be a source of value creation, limiting environmental impact and moving towards the search for decoupling forms that allow for sustainable development and the restorative capacity of natural resources.

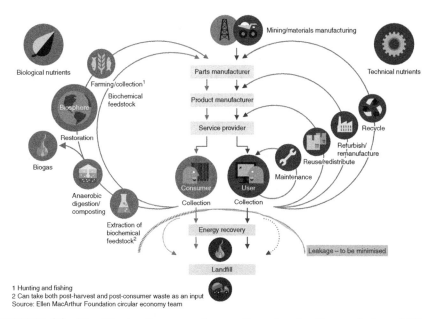

1 Hunting and fishing
2 Can take both post-harvest and post-consumer waste as an input
Source: Ellen MacArthur Foundation circular economy team

FIGURE 3.2 The Circular Economy. *Source:* Reproduced with permission of Ellen MacArthur Foundation.

As shown in Figure 3.2, the traditional development of an industrial cycle, shown in the centre of the diagram, proceeds according to a linear logic that starts with the extraction of raw materials and moves towards production, consumption and the destruction of value though waste disposal. On the contrary, sustainable development must be based on circular cycles, shown along the sides, which differ due to the nature – that is, the '*biological and technical nutrients*', respectively – of the reusable materials and products concerned: the former are non-toxic and can be composted, hence guaranteeing the restorative capacity of natural resources, and the latter must be designed to have multiple life cycles from a perspective of cradle-to-cradle, achieved through their reuse with the aim of minimising the impact on environmental resources.

In particular:

- As far as *Biological Nutrients* are concerned, the cycles shown in the diagram demonstrate how biomasses and biotic waste streams ought to return to the soil as nutrients, once their capacity to create value has been exhausted. Prior to this, however, the value of these nutrients may be increased through cycles based on the *Cascade of Processes* in which valuable feedstocks can be extracted and put back into circulation through composting or biorefining processes, aimed at extracting high quality materials such as biofuel and bio-gases from the biomasses, which are useful for the production of energy, such as methane, or even fertiliser for farming.

BOX 3.1   THE POWER OF CIRCULAR ECONOMY

The power of the inner circle refers to minimising comparative material usage vis-à-vis the linear production system. The tighter the circle, that is, the less a product has to be changed in reuse, refurbishment and remanufacturing, and the faster it returns to use, the higher the potential savings on the shares of material, labour, energy and capital embedded in the product and on the associated rucksack of externalities (such as greenhouse gas (GHG) emissions, water, toxicity).

The power of circling longer refers to maximising the number of consecutive cycles (be it reuse, remanufacturing, or recycling) and/or the time in each cycle.

The power of cascaded use refers to diversifying reuse across the value chain, as when cotton clothing is reused first as second-hand apparel, then crosses to the furniture industry as fibre-fill in upholstery, and the fibre-fill is later reused in stone wool insulation for construction – in each case substituting for an inflow of virgin materials into the economy – before the cotton fibres are safely returned to the biosphere.

The power of pure circles, finally, lies in the fact that uncontaminated material-streams increase collection and redistribution efficiency while maintaining quality, particularly of technical materials, which, in turn, extends product longevity and thus increases material productivity.

Source: Reproduced with permission of Ellen MacArthur Foundation.

- As far as *Technical Nutrients* are concerned, on the other hand, the feedback loops shown in the diagram are based on the possible lengthening of the life cycle of products through design choices and the improvement of maintenance and repair methods or through recovery options that range from the reuse and reselling of products on secondary markets to the refurbishing and remanufacturing of parts and components that can re-enter industrial processes and the recycling of reusable raw materials. These subjects will be discussed in more depth in Chapter 7.

The study promoted by the Ellen MacArthur Foundation (2012) offers much insight, as well as operating instructions that are useful from both a macro and a micro perspectives. With reference to Figure 3.2, it appears evident that the different feedback loops shown in the diagram offer possibilities of creating value that are qualified by varying intensity. Box 3.1 – The Power of Circular Economy – summarises the main ways of creating the value implied by circular economy logics.

3.3   LIFE CYCLE AND CRADLE-TO-CRADLE APPROACHES

In order to fully understand the value of sustainability-oriented design and management choices, it is necessary to introduce several concepts at the root of the most popular approaches followed today in new product development.

The sustainability profile of a product and the processes that accompany it from its development to its exit from the market may in fact be evaluated by projecting its estimated impact along its entire life cycle: from the extraction of raw materials to its production, the manufacturing processes used to make the product, its distribution methods and usage by consumers, up to its end-of-life phase and destruction and disposal. In fact, during its lifetime, a product generates impacts that may range from energy, water and land consumption, to the destruction of raw materials and the emission of polluting gases, as well as impacts in terms of toxicity or global warming and so on.

For this purpose, one of the most widely used tools is the LCA – Life Cycle Assessment or Analysis (Klassen and McLaughlin, 1996): this is a useful approach for monitoring the impact of sustainability along the entire life cycle of a product or a system, from its creation until its end. In product design, the LCA 'evaluates the types and quantities of product inputs such as energy, raw materials, and water, and of product outputs, such as atmospheric emissions, solid and water borne wastes, and end-product' (EPA, 1992, Ch. 7)[1].

Nevertheless, a vision that is more attentive careful? to the subject of sustainability must take the options for the reuse of a product or a system for multiple cycles, also after its technological end or economic obsolescence, into consideration, according to the mentioned logic of 'Circular economy' (World Business Forum, 2014; Ellen MacArthur Foundation, 2012; 2013). This vision proposes replacing the classic 'take, make and dispose' approach, by designing and managing products with a view to their future full or partial reuse, with the primary aim of extracting residual value and limiting or eliminating the waste of resources. In order to get an idea of the scale of the opportunities for companies and the community, it is sufficient to think that in the 'fast-moving consumer-goods industry, about 80% of the 3.2 trillion dollars' worth of materials it uses each year is not recovered' (Nguyen et al., 2014, p. 51).

This concept is summarised perfectly in the Cradle-to-Cradle approach, which, in contrast to the traditional Cradle-to-Grave vision, is based on the observation of biological systems and cycles in nature, in which 'waste is food' or what is considered to be waste by several living organisms becomes food for others (McDonough and Braunghart, 2002; Stahel, 2010).

More specifically, it is possible to distinguish between (Souza, 2012, p. 45):

- *Cradle-to-Gate*, if the effects caused along the life cycle from the extraction of raw materials to the production, packaging and distribution phases are evaluated. In this case, impact is evaluated up to the release of the product by a company to its transfer to other actors downstream or its introduction to the market.

---

[1]The aim of the LCA is to analyse and measure the environmental impact, and at times the social impact, of a product or a process along its entire life cycle, from extraction of the raw materials to its end-of-life and disposal. Generally elements such as energy consumption, the depletion of minerals and fossil fuels, toxicity, global warming etc. are evaluated and measured using measurements in equivalent units, such as the Carbon Footprint or Water Footprint, etc. Guidelines for conducting a LCA can be found in various ISO standards, in particular in ISO 14040, 14041, 14042 and 14043.

- *Cradle-to-Grave*, when the phases linked to the usage cycles of the product in question by consumers in the primary and secondary markets are added to the previous phases, until its end-of-life and disposal.
- *Cradle-to-Cradle*, in the cases where, as mentioned before at the end of its life cycle, either a part of or the entire product can become a useful component in new life cycles of the goods it generates.

In considering the Product Life Cycle (and the connected Process Life Cycle), it is necessary to distinguish between two different perspectives that, although closely inter-related, differ from the point of view of time scale, responsibility and sustainability (Fiksel, 2012, p. 79–80):

1. The first perspective is the *Physical Life Cycle (PLC)*, which interprets the life cycle of the product through a series of phases and physical transformation processes of materials and energy, such as the extraction and manufacturing of materials, their transformation and assembly, their distribution, their use on the market and the recovery and recycling of the product materials. In the case of the PLC, time scale is linked to the duration of the useful life of a product, which may range from a few days for a consumer good to years for a durable good. The responsibility of the PLC and its connected impact on the market is divided among the various actors involved in the different phases of the purchase, production and distribution processes. Take, for example, the design, production, delivery, use and dismantling of a complex good such as industrial machinery: the responsibility for the proper management of its physical life cycle depends on how it is designed and built, but also on the methods of its use and maintenance, the possibility of ensuring a second life through the transfer of useful components to the secondary market or their reuse and the recycling of recoverable materials at the end of the cycle. The ability to optimise sustainability along the PLC is therefore also distributed among the different parties involved in the production and distribution processes, due to their ability to acquire materials and energy in an effective and efficient manner and to create different recovery and recycling options at the end of the useful life cycle.

2. The second perspective refers to the *Business Life Cycle (BLC)*, which involves a sequence of different management activities and process phases, sequenced according to the stage and gate approach (Cooper, 1975), such as the creation of the product concept and its development, launch, production, maintenance, re-evaluation and renewal into next-generation products. In this case, the time scale depends on technological developments and the obsolescence ratified by the markets. The responsibility of the BLC and the connected business impact, to be understood in terms of the profits and losses generated, as well as its sustainability, are substantially referable to the individual company producing the good, and its capacity to innovate by developing product extensions or revisions that are capable of satisfying the demands of the markets. For example, this is the case for mobile telephones that, over time, mainly through incremental innovations and accessibility to apps that can be also downloaded online, have extended the functions of the mobile phone, rendering an object that was originally created

to communicate by voice into a device that can manage email, take photographs, search for information, geo-localise positions and routes on a map and so on.

Product designers and developers, traditionally, have mainly acted from the BLC perspective, making design and management choices that are in keeping with the goals to reduce time to market, using concurrent engineering and product-extension approaches, through simultaneous engineering and product revitalisation with product upgrading and so on. More and more frequently, however, considerations related to the PLC emerge during new product development, in particular with regard to the need to evaluate *ex ante* the environmental implications of the choices made on the materials used, packaging, assembly systems, storage and transportation and the implications of these decisions in terms of recovery options at the end of the life cycle.

Therefore, next we will refer to both perspectives, in consideration of the fact that the design choices implemented during the Business Life Cycle may significantly condition the margins of discretion available to the parties responsible for the management of the Physical Life Cycle of the product, from a Cradle-to-Cradle perspective. This means, for example, that the designer who is attentive to sustainability trends must select the materials used or the industrial treatments to transform them or even energy solutions that can be adopted. These choices have to be based not only on the objectives to quickly launch the product on the market or to develop platforms created to release several generations of products, which are typical objectives linked to BLC, but also on PLC objectives, focusing on minimising the riskiness of the materials themselves, maximising the use of renewable energy sources, or their greater ease of reuse versus their disposal at the end of their life cycle.

3.4 ECO-EFFICIENCY AND ECO-EFFECTIVENESS

By analysing these phenomena from an evolutional perspective, the ability to interpret the life cycle as a Cradle-to-Cradle logic, going beyond the Cradle-to-Grave logic, can be observed in the simultaneous growth of the practices of systems oriented at *eco-efficiency* (Fiksel, 1996) compared to the more evolved systems oriented at *eco-effectiveness* (Souza, 2012).

The concept of eco-efficiency, some times called zero emission, connected to the Cradle-to-Grave vision, was defined by the World Business Council for Sustainable Development:

> *Eco-efficiency is achieved by the delivery of competitively-priced goods and services that satisfy human needs and bring quality of life, while progressively reducing ecological impacts and resource intensity throughout the life cycle to a level at least in line with the earth's estimated carrying capacity.* (Schmidheiny and WBCSD, 1992)

Seven key principles must be taken into consideration during product development in order to reach eco-efficiency goals (WBCSD, 1992):

1. Reduce the material intensity of goods and services, pursuing dematerialisation processes.
2. Reduce the energy intensity of goods and services.

3. Reduce toxic dispersion.
4. Enhance materials recyclability.
5. Maximise sustainable use of renewable resources.
6. Extend product durability.
7. Increase the service intensity of goods and services.

In this approach, adopted by numerous companies in order to evaluate the environmental consequences of their actions, a vision in which the design of products and processes ought to be aimed at reducing environmental impact along their life cycle prevails. During Research, Development and Engineering stages, emphasis is placed on energy consumption, the reduction of toxic materials, cautiousness in the use of scarce raw materials or the minimisation of waste production in industrial processes or at the end of the life cycle of the product. Take, for example, the design of refrigerators that have replaced products that contained gases that were harmful to the environment; or the imposing of laws that do not allow the use of asbestos in buildings; or the choice to refrain from using glues, dyes or surface treatments that may risk the health of humans and the environment.

The development of *eco-efficiency* practices originates from previous efforts to control and treat pollution or from interventions, often imposed by environmental regulations, aimed at controlling and reducing the amount of emissions and affluents released into the atmosphere through the adoption of end-of-pipe technologies, developed to reduce or remove the polluting agents emitted during the production process. Examples are filtration and depuration systems for waste water or treatments to purify the air using systems to reduce hazardous dust or even sound insulation systems to curb noise pollution. A much more proactive approach was developed over time to this purely reactive and ex-post control approach, based on an 'anticipate and prevent' logic, aimed at developing integrated environmental strategies and cleaner production programmes (UNEP, 2004). The key feature of this development consists of a shift upstream, during the product development and industrialisation phases, of the attention to be paid to the reduction of practices that have an impact on the environment, through pollution prevention rather than end-of-pipe pollution control. The increasing awareness that it is possible to reach both profit targets and goals to reduce environmental impact has therefore led to the affirmation of eco-efficiency principles, based on tools that measure the environmental impact of products and services, such as the Life Cycle Assessment and cradle-to-grave logics.

Over time, a more evolved concept has replaced the traditional concept that views the production of a good as a linear process, ranging from its creation to its disposal along a single life cycle. The more evolved concept interprets this process as circular or closed-loop, in which, as already mentioned, the product is 'reincarnated' into new products at the end of its life cycle, repeating subsequent life cycles in the cradle-to-cradle logic. This may occur through the use of recovery options (see Chapter 7), such as the reuse, remanufacturing or recycling of products, materials and components, in such a way as to minimise the extraction and consumption of virgin raw materials.

The goal, therefore, is not to minimise the flow of cradle-to-grave materials and their dematerialisation, but rather to exploit them in subsequent life cycles. This is the case, for example, in products made entirely from natural raw materials, such as fabrics and carpets made from natural, biodegradable fibres that may be reused as compost or as inputs in new productions; or the case of manufactured products, such as bags and backpacks made by reusing lorry tarpaulins or advertising canvases, recovered after use; or the use of scrapped-wood chips from timber mills to create cross-laminated timber panels used in construction.

The arrival point of this evolutionary trajectory lies in design choices based on *eco-effectiveness*, which go beyond the quest to eliminate all forms of environmental impact and, by completely prohibiting the use of toxic materials or materials that have an impact on the environment, aims to develop products and processes that maintain, or better, increase the quality and productivity of the resources used along life cycles repeated in the cradle-to-cradle logic. 'The concept of eco-effectiveness proposes the transformation of products and their associated material flows such that they form a supportive relationship with ecological systems and future economic growth' (Braungart et al., 2007, p. 1338).

Whereas eco-efficiency approaches claim that 'less is better', or that a reduced use of toxic or scarce materials is beneficial to the environment by limiting their impact, eco-effectiveness systems are based on the affirmation that 'bigger is better', where bigger means the possibility of developing products and businesses that enable the resources of the planet to be regenerated, through, for example, regional development initiatives, such as those linked to interventions aimed at replanting, repopulating, feeding and so forth, with the objective of producing a positive foot-print (McDonough and Braungart, 2002, pp. 77 and 78). From an industrial point of view, take, for example, the possibility of using plastic materials largely used in packaging and products such as polyethylene, polypropylene, polystyrene or others that, due to their high carbon content, may provide a source for carbon-based value-added products, such as light hydrocarbons, carbon black/activated carbon, carbon fibres, carbon nanotubes and graphene, which can be used in new generations of products, like sports gear based on composites, electrodes, electronics, photovoltaic devices and so on (Zhuo and Levendis, 2014). Another example is Dunlop Wellington boots, which are made from polyurethane, PVC and rubber, and completely recycled through the re-grinding and re-manufacturing processes of old boots collected from customers (Ulrich and Eppinger, 2012).

Going back to the concept of the Circular Economy, eco-efficiency is connected to a *linear vision* of industrial processes, based on a cradle-to-grave approach, whereas eco-effectiveness is based on a *circular vision* of the multiple life cycles typical of the cradle-to-cradle vision.

This distinction is at the root of the concepts of down-cycling and up-cycling (Pauli, 1998; McDonough and Braungart, 2002; Souza, 2012). *Down-cycling* is defined as the case where a material loses value during the recycling processes, because several or all of its properties change, meaning that it can therefore only be used in alternative or secondary productions, as is the case of recycled paper used to make newspapers or several plastics that can be used for low-performance products. On the other hand, *up-cycling* is the ability to recycle materials and components for use in the same original products, or better, in higher-value productions, as is the case mentioned earlier of sports gear made of carbon that comes from the up-cycling of polymers.

3.5 THE DESIGN FOR APPROACHES

As already mentioned, the choice to act in accordance with the principles of sustainability and to measure business activities from the Triple Bottom Line perspective (Elkington, 1998) affects all business processes and decisions. This way of thinking must, therefore, be implemented right from the concept-design phase of a new product or process, permeating the logics that each business uses to manage its innovation processes. The importance of careful product design is in fact often underestimated by companies that develop a general outline of products and prototypes, and then proceed with the modifications and the completion of the bill of materials at a later time, often once production has already started. In various studies it has been estimated that more than 70% of the life cycle costs of a product are conditioned during the design phase (Gatenby and Foo, 1990; NRC, 1991) and that a modification made during the design phase costs one-tenth of the cost of the same modification during the prototype phase and one-hundredth of the cost of the same modification to be made to the launched product (Stroufe and Melnyk, 2013). Therefore, the attributes that also render a product consistent with sustainability requirements must immediately form a part of the skills and knowledge of the designers, as well as the design specifications of the product and its packaging, in addition to the process to manufacture it.

In the majority of sectors, these activities are generally delegated to the Research, Development and Engineering departments, since, in other environments characterised by a high level of creativity, they are the responsibility of the design or styling or 'collection development' department. Regardless of the heterogeneity of the industrial sectors in which innovation takes place and the organisational units responsible for its development, what stands out is the vision that underlies product innovation. In the production of consumer goods or durable consumer goods in particular, innovation processes are generally aimed at creating a product suitable to be used in a single life cycle, at the end of which it is disposed of and replaced by a more recent and high-performing version of the product. According to this consolidated approach, the attention of the designer is therefore focused on optimising the quality/cost ratio of the product, based on its expected positioning and the target market segment to which it is proposed, focusing on raising the numerator of this ratio in terms of aesthetics, features and intrinsic performance or reducing its denominator, especially in terms of variable costs. This objective, as expressed also in the paradigm of the Triple Bottom Line, remains valid, because each profit or not-for-profit business providing goods or services must generate margins that are to be reinvested according to its institutional goals and must compete in an environment of scarce resources.

Nevertheless, in the new product development process environmental and social sustainability objectives must also be placed side by side with economic sustainability objectives. This can be achieved by considerably modifying the logics underlying the new product design processes and the production and distribution processes associated with the product, guiding the logics towards a different and more complex vision: the

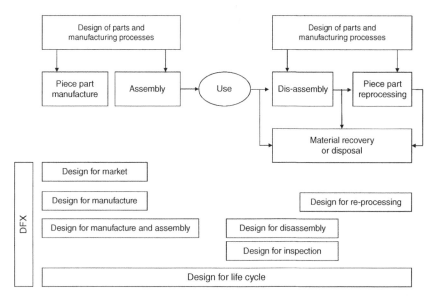

FIGURE 3.3 The Design for X approaches. *Source:* Reproduced with permission of The British Standards Institution[2].

product must generate uses in more timeframes and along more life cycles, in order that it may be reused – partially, in full or through possible transformation processes – with a view to optimising its environmental and social impact.

The adoption of this vision was codified in a series of practices, guidelines and principles that are included in the approach defined as Design For Environment – DFE. As will be explained in more detail next, the main objective of DFE is to combine economic sustainability with environmental sustainability in the broad sense; it also comprises several components of social sustainability.

DFE is one of the approaches that can be counted among the design logics that belong to the *Design For X* (or Design for eXcellence) family. In fact, Design For X (Chiu and Okudan Kremer, 2011) means the multiple approaches and techniques, developed over the years by design and development bodies, all aimed at using ad hoc design solutions to anticipate the subsequent management of problems linked to business processes that involve a new product along its production, distribution, use and disposal phases. Several examples of this are the techniques of Design for Manufacturing, aimed at facilitating automated manufacturing processes; Design for Assembly, in which product components are designed taking the efficiency of the subsequent assembly methods into account; Design for Quality, aimed at improving product quality and facilitating its control; Design for Logistics, aimed at improving efficiency in transportation, storage and the use of packaging materials; and Design for Recycling, aimed at encouraging recovery processes at the end of life cycles and so forth, as exemplified in Figure 3.3.

---

[2]To provide guidelines to design with consideration for the whole product life cycle, British Standards Institution (BSI) published BS 8887-1 series (2006) Design for Manufacture, Assembly, Disassembly and End of Life processing (MADE). The series of original regulations (2006) as a result were subsequently updated.

By analysing these methods in many cases solutions can be created, as a sub-objective of the primary objective for which the methods were devised, that can indirectly generate beneficial effects in terms of environmental impact. Take, for example, the following cases, in which a Design for X techniques may be advantageous from an environmental perspective:

- In Design for Quality, the replacement of materials with high environmental impact with others that are more respectful to the environment or the reduction of waste through the redesign of component structures or better nesting systems.
- In Design for Assembly/Disassembly, the design of assembly cycles that may facilitate the disassembling of similar parts, thus making them easier to separate, recycle or reuse.
- In Design for Logistics, the reduction of packaging or the design of reusable packaging, aimed at a lower environmental impact, or the miniaturisation of products so as to increase the transported value density and to reduce the amount of transport and connected impacts of CO_2.
- In Design for Maintenance, the simplification of construction and assembly criteria, aimed at encouraging easy and fast maintenance, may support the subsequent disassembling aimed at product remanufacturing or dismantling practices.

3.5.1   Design for Environment

Although, as highlighted, several of these approaches may demonstrate positive effects in terms of environmental impact, they were designed with the primary objective of improving business competitiveness, through the reduction of costs or the improvement of quality and other performance features of the product. Thanks to the growing emphasis placed on sustainability, only recently has a series of studies aimed at paying more attention to the subject of environmental and social impact emerged, which deliberately focus on the design of sustainable products from these perspectives (Spangenberg et al., 2010). These methods have been given different names (Bevilacqua et al., 2012), such as Green Product Development, Green Design, Sustainable Product Design, Ecodesign, Life Cycle Design, Sustainable Design, Design for Eco-efficiency, Design for Disassembly, Design for Reuse & Recycle and so on. Next, for the sake of simplicity, we shall refer to these approaches with the term DFE – Design For Environment.

In order to have a better understanding of what is meant by DFE, it is worth analysing several definitions taken from the most recent literature:

Design For Environment means designing products that minimise environmental impact throughout their life cycle, including raw material extraction, transportation, manufacturing, packaging and distribution, use by consumer, and end-of-life.
(Souza, 2012, p. 65)

Design For Environment is the systematic consideration of design performance with respect to environmental, health, safety and sustainability objectives over the full product and process design. (Fiksel, 2012, p. 6)

Design for Environment is a way to include environmental considerations in the product development process… . DFE provides organizations with a practical method to minimize these (environmental) impacts in an effort to create a more sustainable society. (Ulrich and Eppinger, 2012, p. 231)

Several important aspects emerge from these definitions, which can be summarised as follows:

- First of all, there is the repetition of the need to appreciate the *impact of design throughout the entire life cycle of the product*, from the extraction of raw materials to its end of life choices, from the perspective defined earlier as Physical and Business Life Cycle thinking.
- Second, emphasis is placed on the *systematic character of the proposed approach*, which must become an integral part of design routines and the objectives of all organisations, as well as the knowledge, methodological approaches and mindset of managers and designers.
- Third, focus is placed on the fact that *sustainability requirements* and the attention placed on them during the design phase *must not concern simply the product and its materials and components*, but also the processes for the acquisition of the latter, the manufacturing of the product, its distribution and the recovery of its residual value at the end of its life cycle, according to the managerial approach defined Closed-loop Supply Chain (see Chapter 7).

Business management must therefore devise specific programs, strategies and practices, aimed at directing new product and process design efforts towards the pursuit of environmental sustainability objectives. In this regard, different Design for Environment strategies can be drawn up, which can be associated with the different stages of the product's life cycle, as exemplified next (National Center for Design – RMIT, 1997):

Raw material extraction and processing
- Design for resource conservation.
- Design for low-impact materials.
- Design for biodiversity conservation.

Manufacturing, packaging and distribution
- Design for cleaner production.
- Design for low-impact packaging.
- Design for efficient distribution.
- Design for maintenance.

Product use
- Design for energy efficiency.
- Design for water conservation.

- Design for minimal consumption.
- Design for low-impact use.
- Design for service and repair.
- Design for durability.

End of life

- Design for environment.
- Design for reuse.
- Design for remanufacturing.
- Design for disassembly.
- Design for recycling.

As already stated, the traditional approach, which interprets the creation of a product designed to perform for a single life cycle – cradle to grave – according to a linear view, foresees the development of a one-way flow from the extraction of the raw materials until the final disposal of the product. The analysis of impact in terms of sustainability of such a process can be conducted in the first place using tools such as the Life Cycle Assessment Matrix (Crowther, 1999), in which impact is assessed in terms of energy use, resource depletion, waste and pollution, social issues and so on, during the different life cycles of a product, as illustrated in Figure 3.4, which uses the case of a cement producer as an example.

This example suggests that the aforesaid table can be adapted to different sectors and more details can be provided in terms of the analytics of the phases along the vertical axis and the type of impact along the horizontal axis, as well as in terms of quantitative measurements for the assessment of impact (CO_2, cubic metres of waste, kilowatts absorbed etc.) and it can be used to compare the environmental impact of different projects.

Impact in terms of sustainability can be significantly modified if, as mentioned several times, the principles and approaches of the DFE are introduced, shifting the focus of product design and manufacturing from the cradle-to-grave logic to that of cradle-to-cradle (from eco-efficiency to eco-effectiveness), or imagining – according to a circular view – the possibility of reusing all or part of the manufactured product and the identification of possible return flows and recovery options for product life cycles repeated over time.

Careful planning may in fact create recovery options, such as:

- The relocation and reuse of the product, if it is designed with criteria of versatility of use and if a secondary market exists.
- The reuse of components, if the design has adopted a modular structure and standardisation criteria.
- The recycling and, if it is possible, up-cycling, of materials, if materials that can be easily disassembled and separated are used.

Stages	IMPACTS					
	Energy use	Resource depletion	Waste and pollution	Species and habitat loss	Human health	Social issues
Extracting resources: - Limestone quarry	*	*****	**	*****	**	
Processing Materials: - Stone crushing - Staker and reclaimer	***		*		*	
Processing materials: - Feeder - Raw mill - Separator	***				*	
Klinker production: - Precalciner - Rotary kiln - Cooler	*****		*			
Cement production: - Cementer mill - Air classifier - Cement silos	***		*		*	
Packaging and transportation: - Trucks - Train - Bulk	**		***	*	**	***
Quarry rehabilitation	**	Positive impact				

*= Low impact
***** = High impact

FIGURE 3.4   Life Cycle Assessment matrix in a cement producer.

In order to be able to introduce a different sensitivity to the subjects of sustainability to businesses and design bodies and to encourage the systematic and structured adoption of the logics of Design For Environment, over time a series of guidelines and measures have been designed and improved that can be summarised under different headings, such as, among the most common, those that underpin the methods known as Design for Disassembly, Design for Remanufacturing and Design for Recycling (Pahl and Beitz, 1996; Deasi and Mital, 2003; Vezzoli and Manzini, 2008; Hatcher et al., 2011).

3.5.2   DFE Principles

The possibility of developing projects according to DFE logics can be taken and integrated into the cultures of product design and development bodies by basing design choices on a series of principles.

Among the different classifications and incentives drawn up by scientific literature and management practices, see, for example, the ten Golden Rules (Telenko et al., 2008) or similar guidelines (Luttropp and Lagerstedt, 2006). Next, we will dwell upon the classification which, in our opinion, is the most complete and well known, paying close attention in particular to the first four principles (Fiksel, 2012):

1. *Embed Life Cycle Thinking into the product development process*

   The design of a product or process must be inspired and guided by Life Cycle Thinking, or by an awareness, supported with stringent methodologies and practices, that forces designers to consider the impact and consequences of their choices along the entire life cycle of a product and its Physical Life Cycle in particular. The attention generally paid to product performance, its features or cost must be combined with environmental sustainability and social impact considerations. Once again, at each stage of the various processes, from sourcing (materials, components, energy etc.), the making process (manufacturing, assembling, packaging etc.), the delivering (transporting, stocking, repackaging etc.) and the support along the life cycle (maintaining, repairing, upgrading etc.) to the final recovery options (reusing, remanufacturing, recycling etc.), Triple Bottom Line goals must be taken into consideration. The creation of value for the shareholder must go hand in hand with the creation of value for the stakeholder, with the constant quest to exploit recovery opportunities and to seek revalorisation in each phase of the process, as well as in technological and management choices. For example, through the use of technologies that minimise industrial waste or processes that enable it to be reused or re-introduced into the economic cycle, logistic choices can be made that minimise the frequency of transportation and production processes that enable the reuse of waste to produce energy, such as thermo-valorisation.

2. *Evaluate the resource efficiency and effectiveness of the overall system*

   Since the actors at the various stages of the value chain form a part of a broad economic system, they ought to assess the impact of their own design choices on the overall system and not limit themselves to the supplier-client links to which they belong. Environmental and social impact analysis goes well beyond the boundaries of the economic transactions of the focal company with its direct external partners and is extended to the upstream and downstream processes of the entire chain, involving all the subjects along the way. The upstream processes refer to the methods for extracting materials and the production of components, as well as the use of energy to produce the product, whereas downstream refers to the storage, packaging, distribution, possible maintenance and repair methods until its final disposal. Multiple environmental and social effects are generated along all the phases of these processes, which must be evaluated by focusing on maximising the efficiency and effectiveness of the entire system. In this respect, the attention of the designer must be focused on actions that favour eco-effectiveness solutions, in addition to eco-efficiency solutions, as described previously. The choice of materials that can be used in recycling processes is a step in this direction, such as the case of packaging that, once recovered and processed, can become input for further processes or products.

By extending design logics to management choices that lead to the production of a product, the concept explained here still stands. Take, for example, the impact, in terms of social sustainability, of the increasingly common practices of global sourcing or off-shoring in countries that do not have strict controls in terms of protection of workers and employment regulations. There is a growing number of cases in which companies, including those with a high reputation, entrust production phases to subcontractors that do business through the unacceptable behaviour of social dumping, based on the exploitation of child labour or the subjection of their employees to inhumane working conditions or even the use of toxic materials or the implementation of uncontrolled and highly polluting processes.

3. *Select appropriate metrics to represent product life cycle performance*

As will be explained in more detail in Chapter 8, the need to create performance measurement systems that are consistent with sustainability goals and reliable reporting systems has become widespread on a single process, company or even economic systems level. Take, for example, the guidelines and business metrics developed by international institutions as GRI – Global Reporting Initiative, or UN Global Compact (GRI, 2015; UN GC, 2013).

Limiting our analysis to the context of the company, the possibility of planning performance measurement systems, aimed at monitoring the environmental and social impact of the choices made, translates into different solutions depending on:

- The objectives with which key performance indicators (KPIs) and reporting systems are designed; in this regard – as already mentioned (see Chapter 2) – a distinction is made between the look-back systems, namely the systems aimed at the ex post control of variance compared to the target or planned values, and look-forward systems, namely those predominantly aimed at attempts to interpret and diagnose the monitored processes, with the goal of finding useful pointers for the implementation of continuous improvement projects.
- The different degree of effectiveness in accordance with the appropriate performance measurements, produced in different ways from contexts in which sustainability trends are enforced by regulations and legal controls, choices to comply with voluntary certifications or more simply by ethical approaches, be they justified by communication objectives or by elements that identify the company values.
- The degree of integration with other performance measurements, such as, for example, economic and financial, market, operations or company

environment measurements. This case involves more extensive integrated reporting systems, as is the case in the well-known and widespread approaches developed with reference to Balanced Scorecards (Kaplan and Norton, 1996, 2001) or other systems designed with the intention of creating management dashboards (reporting systems containing the relevant key performance indicators to lead a company) aimed at continuous improvement (Lynch and Cross, 1991).

The measurements are generally industry-specific, even if some, such as the level of use of toxic materials or energy consumption, are frequently and widely used together with other company performance indicators. In this regard, please refer to Box 3.2.

4. *Maintain and apply a portfolio of systematic design strategies*

All companies ought to bear their own design experience and the design experience of others in mind when adopting design practices that are consistent with sustainability objectives. In order to do this, it is necessary to draw up and codify guidelines and to promote them through training and education initiatives, paying careful attention that they are applied systematically and correctly by designers. In various sectors, *ad hoc* design guidelines have been developed. One of these sectors is construction, in which regulations and green labels for the use of design and construction practices that are environmentally friendly have been implemented for years, such as, for example, LEED – Leadership in Energy and Environmental Design Certification (USGBC, 2015); a further example is the use of different Energy Labels, such as those used to define the different Energy Efficiency Classes of domestic appliances.

BOX 3.2   EXAMPLES OF PERFORMANCE INDICATORS LINKED TO SUSTAINABILITY

Metrics used for Product Recovery Options (reuse, remanufacturing and recycling), Time required for product recovery

- *Percentage recyclable/reusable materials available at the end of product life.*
- *Percentage product volume or weight recovered and reused.*
- *Purity of recycled materials recovered.*
- *Percentage recycled materials used as input to manufacturing.*
- *Percentage product disposed.*
- *Fraction of packaging or containers recycled.*
- *Core (return product) return rate.*
- *Ratio of virgin to recycled resources.*
- *Ratio of materials recycled to materials potentially recyclable.*
- *Percentage product (or weight or volume) disposed in landfills.*

The development of a new product generally is divided into the following phases, according to the approach known as stage-gate: planning, concept development; system-level design, detail design, testing and refinement, production ramp-up (Ulrich and Eppinger, 2012):

- *Planning:* starting with corporate strategy, with an evaluation of the technological development of market objectives; this phase defines the main objectives and components of a project, such as the target market, expected volumes, possible risks, and constraints and so on.
- *Concept development:* in consideration of the selected target market, in this phase alternative project concepts are created and evaluated, restricting the field to those to be subjected to further development and testing phases.
- *System-level design:* in this phase the architecture of the product and its decomposition into subsystems and components are defined, as well as the main methods to be used during its production and assembly processes.
- *Detail design:* in this phase specific design techniques, structures and manufacturing tolerances are identified, and dimensional drawings, production instructions and specifications for the provision of the components and materials are developed, as well as all the necessary information to define the estimate of cost of the product and its performances.
- *Testing and refinement:* once the specifications have been defined, prototypes, samples and pre-series are made, aimed at evaluating the different characteristics and performances of the product, such as, for example, the coupling of modules and components, several features and performances, several market tests, the study of the methods of manufacturing and assembly on the part of the engineering department and so on.
- *Production ramp-up:* in this last phase the prototypes and the pilot processes are abandoned in order to manufacture products in increasing volumes with the technology and production processes studied in order to achieve full production. At the same time, the reliability of the processes is evaluated, together with the quality of the product, the reactions of the client or selected market segments.

Design guidelines, and therefore also those related to sustainability, must be observed right from the concept design phase, in which the product concept is devised since, as already stated, it is in this phase and the subsequent system design phase that the majority of the choices and costs that will emerge along the entire life cycle of a product are determined. Two types of guidelines can be set (Fiksel, 2012, p. 118):

- *Prescriptive guidelines,* in which binding rules are established, or prohibitions on the use of materials, such as, for example, asbestos due to its carcinogen impact or the CFC – Chlorofluorocarbon gases for their ozone-depletion effects.

- *Suggestive guidelines,* which are not binding and originate from the experience that each company and sector accumulates.

From a managerial point of view it is more interesting to dwell briefly upon the second set of guidelines, as the first set are imposed by laws and regulations. The design strategies that are widely applied in many manufacturing businesses are described in brief next. These guidelines can be grouped into four sections (Fiksel, 2012, p. 119):

- *Design for dematerialisation,* which aims to reduce the quantity of materials and energy used.
- *Design for detoxification,* which aims to minimise and, if possible, put an end to the use of materials that are toxic and hazardous for the environment and humans.
- *Design for revalorisation,* which aims to make the most out of the recovery options in place for each residual material and for the energy produced at each stage of the life cycle of a product, focusing on minimising the production of waste and the use of virgin raw materials.
- *Design for capital protection and renewal,* which refers to the objective of ensuring the safety, productivity and continuity of economic, human and natural resources used.

All actions based on these guidelines must refer explicitly to the product design and the related processes for the acquisition of materials, manufacturing production, distribution, use and disposal of the product along its entire life cycle. In Table 3.1 these main strategies are examined one after the other under specific guidelines and then in more detailed and precise best practices.

These strategies demonstrate different impacts and take on a different value compared to the general objective of sustainability.

- *Dematerialisation processes* are, in fact, the best solution for releasing economic growth from the consumption of the resources of the planet; an example of this is the production of packaging that is becoming thinner and thinner in such a way as to use as little material as possible, as is the case in PET – Polyethylene bottles, or the replacement of components originating from raw materials with remanufactured or recycled materials, as in the production of recycled plastic parts or, even, the adoption of more efficient processes in terms of the use of energy or water resources, as is the case in modern dyeing processes in which wastewater is purified and reused.
- *Detoxification strategies* are aimed at reducing the environmental impact of hazardous materials and emissions. This is the case of chemical products that are reformulated to reduce the content of solvents or that are treated with special technology to reduce levels of toxicity. In several cases, the use of certain hazardous chemical products, such as those used as flame retardants for many

TABLE 3.1 Design for environment strategies, guidelines and best practices

Strategies	Guidelines	Best practices
1. Design for dematerialisation	1.1. Design for energy and material conservation	• Life cycle resource intensity reduction • Recycled or renewable material specification • Remanufactured or refurbished components • Product functionality extension • Product life extension
	1.2. Design for source reduction	• Product size and mass reduction • Process scale reduction • Auxiliary material and packaging reduction
	1.3. Design for servisation	• Resource management service from suppliers • Leased product services to customers • Substitution of services for products
2. Design for detoxification	2.1. Design for realisation reduction	• Toxic and hazardous substance removal • Process emission and waste reduction • Life cycle waste stream reduction
	2.2. Design for hazard reduction	• Product reformulation • Toxic and hazardous material use reduction • Water-based technologies
	2.3. Design benign waste disposition	• Responsible treatment and disposal • Waste sequestration • ecosystem adsorption • Biodegradation
3. Design for revalorisation	3.1. Design for product recovery	• Secondary utilisation • Reusable components and packaging • Component or product refurbishment • Remanufacturing
	3.2. Design for product disassembly	• Product simplicity • Disassembly sequencing • Component accessibility • Component and material separability
	3.3. Design for recyclability	• End-of-life material recovery • Closed-loop material recycling • Waste composition and homogeneity • By-product synergy and industrial ecology
4. Design for capital protection and renewal	4.1. Design for human capital	• Workplace health, safety and ergonomics • Product safety, integrity and efficiency • Public health, safety and security
	4.2. Design for natural capital	• Climate change mitigation • Water resource protection • Ecosystem integrity and biodiversity protection • Land conservation and restoration
	4.3. Design for economic capital	• Process reliability, safety and security • Business continuity and supply chain resilience • Asset utilisation and resource productivity • Reputation and brand protection

Source: Fiksel 2012. Reproduced with permission of McGraw-Hill.

products (like, for example, electrical cables and for telecommunications) are restricted by specific regulations and at the end of their life cycle the products must be recovered and treated by the companies that manufactured them. While these strategies reduce the environmental impact of dangerous emissions, they do not necessarily minimise the consumption of scarce resources; take, for example, the development of new products such as water-based paint, which is slowly replacing the use of polluting solvents, but on the other hand uses up water resources.

- *Revalorisation choices*, similar to those of dematerialisation, which encourage development by limiting the consumption of resources, where the objective is to reuse the residual value of materials and the energy generated during the various stages of the product life cycle; this is the case in the reconditioning of used products, such as toners, or the reuse of materials, such as PET – polyethylene in plastic bottles to produce fleece garments, aluminium tins for multiple uses or the co-generation of energy or thermo-valorisation processes. For example, Ricoh designed its new line of photo-copiers and office printers – Green Line – with the aim of maximising the reusability of products and components and minimising the use of raw materials. Reusing recovered, inspected and reused materials, originating from leasing agreements through local facilities, Ricoh estimates that it will be able to reduce the cost of materials and components used by 30% (Nguyen et al., 2014, p. 53).

- *Capital protection and renewal practices*, in their different forms – human, natural, economic and social – must be understood in a broad sense, as they concern the possibility of maintaining, and if possible developing, all forms of capital. Taking only human capital into consideration, represented, for example, by the employees of a company, the practices involve the design of factories, offices and spaces that guarantee dignity, opportunities to socialise and professional development or the more and more frequent cases of company welfare projects that offer support to employees and their families through education structures, day care facilities and so on.

5. *Use analysis methods to evaluate design performance and trade-offs*

Taking the environmental impact of a design solution into account must lead the designer to develop and apply methods for assessing the possible options and their implications in strict and objective sustainability terms, on a par with the assessment of other design choices. Similar to the activities generally carried out during the design and development phase, in which the performance of a product is estimated and assessed in terms of its features, or the performance of a geometric component in terms of its acceptable tolerance during assembly or a material or fabric in terms of its resistance to scratches or traction, or even the viscosity of a lubricant or the power of electric motor, the assessment of design for environment choices must be made using methods and techniques that are capable of quantifying, or at least rating in comparative terms, whether these choices fit with design objectives.

There are a large number of techniques and approaches for conducting analysis that enable the expected performance, the connected risks, the costs and the impact in financial terms of the different options to be measured during the design phase. Depending on the specific design objective, according to Fiksel (2012, p. 166), the assessment process must follow three phases:

- *Screening*, using methods that make it possible to restrict design options to the respecting of the defined goals.
- *Performance assessment*, using methods that enable the expected performance of the different design choices to be measured and evaluated in compliance with the defined goals.
- *Trade-off analysis*, adopting methods that enable the comparison of different design choices, based on cost and associated sustainability performances.

As already stated, there are many methodologies used in the different phases, such as checklists, like the one developed for NECTA Vending Solutions, the European leader of drinks and food vending machines (Vezzoli and Sciama, 2006), or scorecards, like the one developed by Wal-Mart to evaluate packaging alternatives (Souza, 2012, p. 70), or footprint indices, like the one used by Barilla to measure impact in terms of water consumption and CO_2 emissions (Barilla, 2015).

6. *Provide software capabilities to facilitate the application of DFE practices*
   The development of complex projects that ought to keep countless variables under control, on the one hand, and the need to accumulate specific know-how in appropriate repositories and knowledge-sharing systems, on the other hand, have led to software applications that can be used during the design, testing and simulation phases, such as the CAD/CAE – Computer Aided Engineering and Computer Aided Design systems, as well as the technical, economic and financial assessment phases.

   Furthermore, nowadays the diffusion and pervasiveness of ICT systems – Information and Communication Technology – offer innumerable software and application tools to measure the impact of design choices and the use of materials or processes in terms of Carbon Footprint or other similar metrics. The growth in prototype technology and modelling based on 3-D printing applications and additive manufacturing has also opened new frontiers in the design of complex parts, minimising the use of materials. The possibility of extracting value from end-of-use products is also connected to the ability to trace the use of the product itself, the maintenance carried out and the replacement of parts and components during its life cycle and so on. Take, for example, technology such as RFID systems. Radio Frequency Identification Devices make it possible for the history of a product to be memorised in special databases and for useful information on the intensity and duration of its use to be provided. Another example is the systems that are capable today of providing diagnostics in real time on the functions of complex components, such as engines or electronic components. Using Analytics, nowadays we have the extraordinary possibility of using accessible technology and approaches to extract and archive data that can be used to make future improvements during the design and engineering phases, to model and simulate the behaviour of products, components and materials and to evaluate with an increasing degree of reliability their useful life and ability in terms of performance, impact in terms of cost and risk and, last but not least, the most relevant profiles in terms of sustainability.

7. *Seek inspiration from nature for the design of products and systems*

This last principle appears to be rather general and aims to encourage discussion on the amazing abilities of nature and the possibility of drawing inspiration from its observation. Take, for example, the structure of a beehive, made up of perfectly combined hexagons and often used in honeycomb structures, which has the characteristic of minimising the use of material by guaranteeing adequate levels of resistance, or the perfect shape of a water droplet that takes its form as a result of the resistance of the liquid to air, which has inspired aerodynamic solutions. Many innovations have drawn inspiration from nature, such as Velcro, which was created by observing the adhesive capacity of insects' feet.

From the perspective of environmental sustainability, the greatest lesson shared by nature is, as already stated, that 'waste is food' for subsequent biological cycles, and it is precisely this that designers must draw their inspiration from, for example, in their choice of materials and in the identification of possible future uses of a product in terms of recovery options. From this perspective, as mentioned before, emphasis is placed on how a distinction can be made between two fundamental types of materials that can be used in the design and creation of a product: *biological nutrients*, which are biodegradable and can return to the biosphere, and *technical nutrients*, which are not biodegradable, but can be reused in the production of the same products they came from (up-cycling). These materials can also be defined as Biological Materials and Technical Materials and follow, as explained, different recovery and revaluation cycles. According to the approach proposed by the Circular Economy (Ellen MacArthur Foundation, 2012; World Business Forum, 2014), in fact, components and materials must be separated into consumables and durable components. As far as the former are concerned, the objective to be pursued during the design phase is to use pure or non-toxic materials, in such a way that they can be easily reintroduced into the biosphere, restoring the natural cycle and regenerating them; with regard to the latter, on the other hand, the main objective is to design their use in such a way that they are easily disassembled and reused or upgraded into other products, hypothesising the highest number of life cycles possible.

According to the Circular Economy approach, represented in Figure 3.5, along a product life cycle, energy and other resources are consumed, emissions and waste are generated and an environmental impact is always produced.

To guarantee a sustainable closed-loop system, three challenges of product design arise (Ulrich and Eppinger, 2012, pp. 232–233):

- Eliminate use of nonrenewable natural resources.
- Eliminate disposal of synthetic and inorganic materials that do not decay quickly.
- Eliminate creation of toxic wastes that are not part of natural life cycles.

In the first group, we have natural fibres, such as cotton, wool and leather treated by vegetable tanning, and in the second group we have some plastics and metals. The underlying principle is based on the awareness of the finiteness of available resources and the need to design products that to some extent are 'rented' to the community, to then be withdrawn and reused as much as possible.

These two materials must be kept separate, in order to avoid the creation of *'monstrous hybrids'* (Souza, 2012, p. 77). These hybrids are created in particular when the two types of materials are used together, thus creating a material that is difficult to separate and that therefore ends up in down-cycling processes, wasting resources and causing risks to the environment. Examples of this are leathers that are tanned with the use of chrome, or some fabrics dyed with toxic dyes or products made of wood treated with chemical impregnating agents or even product packaging made of cellulose fibres and synthetic films. However, the attention that must be paid to these aspects during design must obviously not reduce the ability to offer the market high-quality products that meet consumers' expectations. A valid example of how this can be done is provided by the choices introduced by Nike when it designed and produced a series of eco-friendly shoes. One shoe, in fact, contains many materials that are

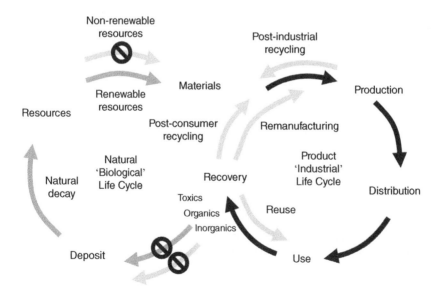

FIGURE 3.5   Natural Life Cycle and Product Life Cycle. *Source:* Ulrich 2012. Reproduced with permission of McGraw-Hill.

not environmentally friendly, such as synthetic materials, glues and biological nutrients treated with chemical components or dyes that must often be disposed of or recycled in productions with a lower value at the end of the product life cycle. Using biological nutrients, such as untreated leathers, and stitching rather than the traditional toxic adhesive and biodegradable, interchangeable soles, Nike launched products on the market that were fashionable and environmentally friendly at the same time.

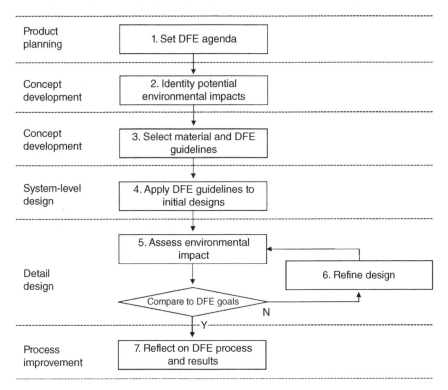

FIGURE 3.6 The Design for Environment implementation process. *Source:* Ulrich 2012. Reproduced with permission of McGraw-Hill.

Companies focused on developing sustainable products can take a great advantage from the adoption of DFE techniques and guidelines. In order to properly and effectively implement DFE in their activities, as suggested by Ulrich and Eppinger (2012), designers and product development teams should follow some steps synthesised in the path reported in Figure 3.6.

4

SUSTAINABILITY AND PROCUREMENT

4.1   INTRODUCTION

illycaffè is an Italian company established in 1933 by Francesco Illy that specialises in the production and distribution of coffee.

Its coffee is currently served in more than 10,000 public retailers and in over 200 'Espressamente Illy' retail points at a world-wide level. With a turnover of € 390,8 million and 1,084 employees in 2014, illycaffè is a major player in this industry and is renowned, in particular, for the high-quality of its blends. The Vision statement of the company claims,

> *Our objective is to become a reference point at worldwide level in the culture and excellency of coffee: an innovative enterprise offering the best products together with the best location for their taste, achieving always higher level of standards, aiming to be leader in the highest level of quality in the sector.*

This search for excellence, as far as the quality of the product is concerned, is coupled with the commitment toward sound values, explicitly declared in the official documents of the company that, focusing on the distinctive features of illycaffè's ethics, claim: 'We create and share with stakeholders a long term vision with high added value, through our commitment to excellence, to transparency, to sustainability and to the personal growth and improvement.' These values have driven the procurement policy carried out by illycaffè, which has heavily invested in its suppliers, in order to achieve the highest possible quality level of raw materials, especially green coffee. In fact, illycaffè does not buy it on the market,

Sustainable Operations and Supply Chain Management, First Edition. Valeria Belvedere and Alberto Grando.
© 2017 John Wiley & Sons Ltd. Published 2017 by John Wiley & Sons Ltd.

but directly from farmers, mainly located in Brazil and other Central America countries, paying them a significantly higher price to reward the better quality standards of their products. Because the company is aware that most farmers need to be supported in order to achieve higher and higher performance levels, several initiatives have been undertaken over time to achieve this goal. The first relevant project, launched when the company arrived in Brazil, was the creation of the 'illycaffè Brazil Quality Espresso Coffee Award' in 1991, aimed at finding the best growers by means of a competition. In 1999, the 'Clube illy do Cafè' was established, with the aim of strengthening the relationships between the company and its suppliers. Most of all, in 1999 illycaffè created the University of Coffee, which has now twenty-three premises around the world that deliver training programs to promote the dissemination of knowledge on the culture of quality along the coffee supply chain, from the production of raw materials to the distribution of the finished product. All of these initiatives have strongly supported the suppliers not only in improving the quality levels of their harvests, but also in enhancing their managerial competences, with wide-reaching effects in several performance areas, including also environmental and social ones. In the company's view, only a long-term relationship with the suppliers can determine mutual benefits and the achievement of the essential features of a sustainable supply chain, which according to illycaffè's culture concern the following aspects:

- *Safety of products, services and processes, to pursue through compliance with the most severe regulations.*
- *Excellence of quality and welfare, to be offered to all stakeholders of the company.*
- *Integrity and value sharing, which involve that suppliers must adopt and respect the requirements mentioned in the ethical code of the company.*

Given the relevance of supply management for the quality of the product and for the sustainability of the business, in 2011 illycaffè certified its supply chain management system according to the standard 'Responsible Supply Chain Process', developed by DNV GL, an independent certification agency. According to these guidelines, the company must strive to achieve socially and environmentally sound processes along the entire supply chain, ensuring that suppliers too are compliant with a wide set of requirements that build on the most relevant international standards in the field of sustainability (ILO Convention 182, 29 and 105, 100 and 111, 87 and 98; OECD Guidelines for multinational enterprises; UN Convention against trans-national organised crime, protocol on trafficking and smuggling; Stockholm Convention on Persistent Organic Pollutants and Rotterdam Convention on Prior Informed Consent). To achieve this challenging goal, illycaffè has establish a process of vendor selection and control based on the analysis of several parameters, which also cover social and environmental sustainability and are based on mandatory regulations, as well as on requirements considered highly enabling.

This process involves the systematic analysis of performance indicators, classified in terms of relevance, and periodical inspections, aimed at identifying the main improvement areas and planning appropriate actions. Since the start of this program in 2010, the company has visited 1,500 suppliers' premises, 184 of which in 2014, for a total workload of 1,050 days devoted by illycaffè's technicians to this activity. Furthermore, since 2010 more the 5,500 participants have attended the training courses delivered by the company to disseminate best practices among suppliers and to address the main areas of improvements highlighted through the audits.

Sources: illycaffè Sustainable Value report 2014, available at http://valuereport. illy.com/assets/download/isvr_IT_2014.pdf, viewed 1 March, 2016; Perrini and Russo, 2008.

The illycaffè case study witnesses the relevance of the procurement process for the sustainability of business activities. In fact, it shows that, on the one hand, the performance level of the finished product can be strongly affected by the features of the inputs (i.e. raw materials, components, sub-assemblies) delivered by suppliers, especially if the purchasing company has a low level of vertical integration. This holds also for the environmental and social outcomes of the product along its life cycle, as its overall safety or its carbon footprint, which heavily rely on operating conditions and practices adopted by the suppliers. On the other hand, illycaffè demonstrates that vendors also have to be viewed as stakeholders of the company, who must be supported in order to promote their improvement in several performance areas, including sustainability.

In this Chapter, we will discuss how companies should manage their procurement process so as to pursue and achieve its sustainability in this twofold perspective.

4.2   THE ROLE OF PROCUREMENT IN DELIVERING SUSTAINABLE SOLUTIONS

In 2014, the Center of Advanced Purchasing Studies Research (CAPS, 2014) reported that the average total spend for bought-out materials and services, expressed as a percentage of company's sales, is close to 52% in industrial manufacturing companies, and similar values can also be observed in service companies. This is clear evidence of the important role played by a company's procurement department. As a matter of fact, this data shows that procurement is the major cost driver for most organisations and that, consequently, any cost-cutting strategy that a firm would be willing to pursue must first of all focus on the expenses incurred to buy materials and services. While CAPS research points out the relevance of procurement as a cost driver, there is clear empirical evidence that it is also an important determinant of the overall economic performance of the company, since the adoption of best practices specific to this function can result not only in lower costs, but also in superior product performance, higher customer satisfaction and ultimately an increase in the company's turnover (Narasimhan and Schoenherr, 2012; González-Benito and González-Benito, 2005; Carr and Pearson, 2002). Among these practices, those concerning ethical and sustainable procurement have gained momentum (Krause et al., 2009). In fact, especially due to lower labour costs that are characteristic of some areas, outsourcing and off-shoring solutions have recently become popular among both manufacturing and service companies, thus leading organisations to operate in countries that are unfamiliar to them. In such cases subcontractors and suppliers could use their production resources according to standards that do not always comply with what can be considered fair and safe working conditions or environmentally sustainable practices. In this regard, the way in which companies can address the challenge of ethical and sustainable procurement is twofold (Gimenez and Tachizawa, 2012). On the one hand, suppliers and sub-contractors that can guarantee that adequate levels of environmental and social performance should be preferred. This is achieved through the adoption of vendor-assessment tools that embed these principles. On the other hand, companies could adopt a more challenging approach based on a broader definition of the boundaries of their responsibility, extending them beyond the reach of the corporation's ownership and direct control. According to this view, companies should promote the diffusion of social and environmental practices among their supply chain partners, in particular if the latter are small-sized enterprises, structurally unable to invest in wide-reaching projects, and/or when they are located in developing countries, where such practices are seldom imposed by local legislation. In particular, while until recently the ethical dimension of procurement was primarily based on the 'green' performance of the suppliers, the current predominant approach regards sustainability in the sourcing processes as the ability to achieve both high social and environmental standards along the supply chain, even going beyond the requirements of national legislations (Miemczyk et al., 2012). This evolution is witnessed by the various definitions of 'sustainable procurement', some of which are stated next:

'Green supply refers to the way in which innovations in supply chain management and industrial purchasing may be considered in the context of the environment' (Green et al., 1996, p. 188).

'Environmental purchasing is defined as the purchasing function's involvement in supply chain management activities in order to facilitate recycling, reuse, and resource reduction' (Carter and Carter, 1998, p. 660).

'Supply management activities that attempt to improve the environmental performance of purchased inputs, or of the suppliers that provide them' (Walker et al., 2008, p. 75).

'Managing the optimal flow of high-quality, value-for-money materials, components or services from a suitable set of innovative suppliers in a fair, consistent, and reasonable manner that meets or exceeds societal norms, even though not legally required' (Eltantawy et al., 2009, p. 101).

'Sustainable procurement (SP) is procurement that is consistent with the principles of sustainable development, such as ensuring a strong, healthy and just society, living within environmental limits, and promoting good governance' (Walker and Brammer, 2009, p. 128).

'Sustainable procurement can be defined as buying goods and services in environmentally, socially and economically conscious ways' (Walker et al., 2012, p. 3558).

Also in the field of public procurement, which is the responsibility of governmental institutions, the same attitude toward the concept of 'sustainability' is emerging. Indeed, focusing on the countries of the Organisation for Economic Co-operation and Development (OECD), it is to be noted that official documents concerning public procurement policies refer to 'green procurement' as a practice to pursue, but in some cases also to the 'social, environmental and economic issues' of the purchasing process, thus highlighting a more comprehensive approach to the ethical aspects related to such a function, at least in some countries, such as Norway, the Netherlands, Belgium and New Zealand (Walker et al., 2012).

4.3 IMPLEMENTING A SUSTAINABLE PROCUREMENT STRATEGY

There are several reasons why organisations are being driven to adopt environmental and social procurement strategies, especially due to external pressures. Environmental regulations and legislation, which cover a broad range of aspects of a company's activities, including Greenhouse Gases (GHG) emissions, ground and water pollution, waste management and take-back processes, represent a major constraint in the design and management of supply chains. In addition, the increasing level of customers' awareness towards sustainability is leading them to prefer more socially and environmentally sound products. If major competitors offer these solutions, the company may start to miss business opportunities. Financial institutions in particular see the potential of investing in companies that are improving their sustainability levels, especially due to the diffusion of international rankings and reporting systems that promote the social and green image of the company. Furthermore, local communities where firms operate, directly or indirectly, show an increasing concern in particular towards the environmental risks associated with the presence of manufacturing sites.

It must also be noted that companies able to embed social and environmental principles into their business processes can enjoy a number of benefits (Gimenez and Tachizawa, 2012; Eltantawy et al., 2009; Day, 2002; Green et al., 1996), ranging from cost reduction to improved inputs efficiency (e.g. if more energy-efficient vehicles are preferred or if physical waste can be reduced through the adoption of reusable packaging), superior product quality (if long-term relationships with suppliers are established to promote their development and learning), enhanced corporate image if evidence of sustainable processes and products can be provided.

In order to achieve these results, companies started adopting the Environmental Management System (EMS), later relabeled as Environmental and Social Management System in order to take into account both dimensions of a company's sustainability. An EMS builds on the principle of continuous improvement and, in particular, on the Plan-Do-Check-Act (PDCA) cycle (also known as Deming's cycle). According to this principle, organisations willing to enhance their performance over time have to 'plan' appropriate actions consistent with the aim to achieve, implement (i.e. 'do') them, monitor (i.e. 'control') the actual results and identify initiatives (i.e. 'act') to fill possible performance gaps. Then the process must be re-started and carried out over time to pursue continuous improvement.

Following this approach, companies that want to address their social and environmental risks must appoint a manager in charge of this process and of its daily duties, define objectives to pursue, design and implement appropriate procedures for the implementation of the continuous improvement cycle. Frequently, the EMS is managed according to the requirements set by ad hoc standards (in the field of environmental management), as ISO 14001 and the Eco-Management and Audit Scheme (EMAS), according to which companies can also certify their EMS.

Focusing on the procurement process, in order to embed the principles of sustainability into its main activities and to deploy company's goals into functional ones, it is necessary to identify its main stages. These can be described as follows (Day, 2002):

- Identifying needs and defining specifications;
- Vendor pre-selection;
- Tender evaluation and vendor selection;
- Vendor control and contract management.

In all of these stages, represented in Figure 4.1, the company has to face specific challenges. In Sections 4.3.1–4.3.4, such stages will be analysed, as well as the different tools and methodologies that can be adopted to achieve a socially and environmentally sound procurement process.

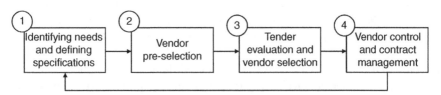

FIGURE 4.1   Main stages in the procurement process. *Source*: Adapted from Day 2002.

4.3.1 Indentifying Needs and Defining Specifications

In this stage companies have to decide what their needs are and how they can be satisfied. These questions and the related possible answers can generate a number of risks, especially from an environmental viewpoint. In this regard, several approaches have been proposed to improve the sustainability of this stage (Day, 2002):

- *Reduce the quantity to buy:* concerning the quantitative dimension of the need (i.e. 'how much to buy'), companies often keep on purchasing the same amount of items without considering variations of the actual needs over time. This can result in overstocking, which ultimately leads to more severe obsolescence rates. From an environmental standpoint, this is a major waste that should be avoided through a more precise computation of the inventory management parameters (Bouchery et al., 2012; Hua et al., 2011).
- *Reconsider conventional purchases and identify alternative solutions:* very often, once a solution to a specific need has been found, it is never challenged, which means that companies keep on buying the same product/service and do not look for more sustainable solutions. In this regard, a systematic monitoring activity of the supply market can be useful to identify alternative products or even different ways in which a given function can be delivered. For instance, companies that switch to reusable packaging enjoy a remarkable reduction of waste management costs. Similarly, there can be cases in which procuring a service rather than a product can be more convenient and environmentally sound (Souza, 2012). When organisations prefer leasing or renting solutions, as in the case of vehicles, they can incur lower expenses, achieving at the same time a better environmental performance due to the fact that these alternatives lead toward a higher exploitation of the potential life of the product (see Section 5.5).
- *Specify green and social products:* when the specifications of a product/service to procure are set, it must be considered that over-specified items, which will deliver a function whose performance will be far beyond the needs of the company, can determine a number of environmental wastes (Coman and Ronen, 2009; Wills, 2009), which will be described in detail in Chapter 5. Thus, during this stage of the procurement process, the company must look for the most fitting solution suitable for satisfying its actual needs, without exceeding them. Furthermore, among the specifications of the product, companies can also mention some 'labels' considered relevant for the product/industry, which provide evidence of the environmental and/or social soundness of the item. Such labels are generally classified into three typologies, according to the ISO 14020 series, which is a set of standards that provides guidelines for companies willing to develop their own labels. In this regard, Type I labels recognise the fulfilment of a set of criteria set by a third party. Type II labels are self-declarations made by the manufacturers concerning the environmental features of their products. Type III labels are based on the adoption of the life cycle approach and provide quantified information about the environmental impact of the product.

- *Redesign the product:* companies should consider the possibility to revise the requirements of the bought-out product, leveraging the so-called waste hierarchy that identifies the following options, most of which are based on the Design for Environment approach (see Chapter 3): *re-think, eliminate, reduce, reuse, recycle, dispose* (CIPS, 2002). In this regard, purchasers can, first of all, 're-think' the way in which a given function is delivered by the product and consider more sustainable options, such as renting and leasing. The 'eliminate' strategy consists of the removal (as much as possible) of hazardous materials in the composition of the product. 'Reduce' concerns not only the already mentioned possibility to reduce the number of pieces to buy, but also to re-design the product so as to use a lesser amount of the materials and components, for instance, through the removal of unnecessary packaging. 'Reuse' involves a re-design of the product (or the search of alternative supply solutions that) so as to extend its life cycle. 'Recycle' calls for a wider adoption of materials such as paper, glass and metals, which can be re-processed at the end of the life cycle of the product, and for a re-design of the product that enables its disassembly into its main constituents. All of these actions can require not only the setting of more sustainable requirements for the bought-out materials, but also a direct commitment of the purchasing company in the co-design of the product together with the supplier, especially in cases where the latter is a small enterprise that needs guidance and support in the adoption of sustainability practices.

4.3.2 Vendor Pre-Selection

In the vendor pre-selection phase, the goal of the company is to define a short list of 'approved' suppliers that possess the conditions necessary for the establishment of a successful commercial relationship. Such an assessment can take several factors into account, which may include the financial soundness of the company, the availability of up-to-date technology and certifications or the adoption of managerial practices that lead towards satisfactory levels of both product and process performance. To accomplish this task, data and information can be collected through questionnaires administered to the target companies and in some cases through site visits, aimed at directly checking the reliability of the information collected and at gaining an in-depth understanding of the overall adequacy of the potential supplier.

Questionnaires are particularly useful when they investigate issues that can be assessed through a 'pass/fail' approach. Focusing on sustainability performance, this may be the case for accreditations based on standards, such as ISO 14001 and EMAS for environmental issues, or SA8000 for social matters. Furthermore, questions may also be asked about the internal organisation, so as to understand whether appropriate processes have been designed and implemented with regard to the establishment of improvement targets and the achievement of adequate results, according to a continuous improvement approach. Thus, questions such as 'Does your organisation have a manager in charge of Environmental Management?'; 'Does your organisation have an Environmental Policy?'; 'Has your organisation adopted an Environmental Management System?' can be asked in order to receive useful feedback. However, although questionnaires can be an efficient way of collecting data about potential suppliers, they can also produce confusing or misleading information if they are designed inappropriately. Some guidelines to prevent these problems are briefly described next (Day, 2002):

- *They should be clear and unambiguous*: in this regard, asking questions on objective aspects of the company and that do not rise any problem of interpretation is crucial.
- *They should be consistent with the aims of the vendor pre-selection process*: this tool is adopted to 'approve' a supplier and not to select it. This means that there will be a further stage of the vendor selection process in which more detailed information will be gathered. Thus, it is important in this stage to distinguish what is a prerequisite, from what is considered an order winner, to investigate further through other tools in a later stage.
- *They should be explained to suppliers*: in order to prevent misinterpretations, it is recommended to explain the aim of this tool, as well as single questions that could rise doubts.
- *Suppliers should be provided with feedback:* even when the supplier is not 'approved', fair conduct involves feedback to the counterpart, so as to illustrate the main areas of weakness that determined the final assessment and, whenever possible, lead toward a process of improvement.

4.3.2.1 Social and Environmental Standards and Certifications

4.3.2.1   Social and Environmental Standards and Certifications   As already mentioned, an important aspect to be analysed in the pre-selection process concerns the accreditation of potential suppliers according to social and environmental standards. Possessing one or more of these certifications demonstrates the commitment of a company to the improvement of specific performance areas. In fact, these standards are based on the continuous improvement approach (or PDCA cycle), which involves the definition of a strategy to be applied to specific targets, the appointment of managers and professionals in charge of the process, the selection of appropriate actions and, finally, the analysis of the results so as to re-start the process. Thus, when an accreditation is obtained, this means that the company is endowed with an organisation and structured processes that support and stimulate its improvement.

In the field of social and environmental sustainability, several standards have been developed, the most relevant of which are reported next:

- *ISO 14000*: this is a series of international standards on environmental management. ISO 14001 is the cornerstone of the ISO 14000 series, which specifies the requirements that an Environmental Management System (EMS) must meet in order for a company to enhance its environmental performance, demonstrate conformance through a third-party certification and achieve compliance with environmental laws and regulations by means of a voluntary accreditation.
- *EMAS (Eco-Management and Audit Scheme)*: this is a management tool suitable for evaluating, reporting and improving environmental performance. It has

been designed so as to enable the acquisition of information about the environmental performance of private and public organisations.

- *ISO 50001*: like ISO 14001, this is a voluntary accreditation according to a standard aimed at improving energy efficiency. By adopting the framework embedded in this standard, companies can make better use of their energy-consuming assets by promoting energy-efficient technology and behaviours, make a remarkable contribution to GHG emissions reduction programs and provide transparent information on their energy policy.
- *Social Accountability 8000*: this standard provides requirements for the ethical behaviour of companies in the following areas: child labour, forced and compulsory labour, health and safety, freedom of association and right to collective bargaining, discrimination, disciplinary practices, working hours and remuneration. Companies accredited with this standard establish and maintain appropriate procedures to evaluate and select suppliers/subcontractors (and, whenever possible, sub-suppliers) based on their ability to meet these requirements, which are in turn compliant with the International Labour Standards (ILO).
- *Occupational Health and Safety Assessment Series (OHSAS) 18001*: this is a standard concerning the occupational health and safety management system and aims to help organisations to control occupational health and safety risks, enhancing their performance in these areas.

4.3.3 Tender Evaluation and Vendor Selection

During this stage of the procurement process, bids are reviewed by buyers and assessed against appropriate criteria, identified on the basis of the specific requirements set for the product/service to be sourced. To identify the most competitive bid, companies perform the Vendor Rating process, which consists of a quantitative assessment of potential suppliers. According to a standard procedure, performance criteria for vendor selection can be grouped into two main performance categories (Dou and Sarkis, 2010; van Weele, 2009), as reported in Table 4.1. The former refers to the strategic factors that distinguish a potential supplier and concern cost, quality, time and flexibility, which are the main areas against which the performance of a manufacturing company is traditionally assessed (Neely et al., 1995). The latter is a bundle of organisational aspects that influence the possibility of establishing a long-term relationship with the supplier.

When a vendor selection process is carried out, the previously mentioned factors, or a sub-group of those considered most relevant, are quantified and summarised in a single value (the 'vendor rate') through a weighting process, which takes the relative importance of each performance factor into account. The standard formula for the Vendor Rate based exclusively on the strategic factors is:

$$Vendor\ Rate = Cost \times \alpha + Quality \times \beta + Time \times \gamma + Flexibility \times \delta$$

In this formula, α, β, γ and δ are the weights associated with the various performance categories. It is apparent that, depending of the type of product/service to be bought (e.g. commodity vs specialty) these weights can be adapted to give

TABLE 4.1 Supplier selection criteria

Strategic performance factors	Organisational factors
Cost:	Culture:
• Low initial price	• Feeling of trust
• Total cost of ownership	• Strategic fit
• Cost reduction activities	• Top management compatibility
• Compliance with sector price	• Compatibility among levels and functions
behaviour	• Suppliers organisational structure and personnel
Quality:	Technology:
• Conformance quality	• Technological compatibility
• Quality philosophy	• Assessment of future manufacturing capabilities
	• Supplier's speed in development
	• Supplier's design and technical capability
	• Current manufacturing facilities/capabilities
Time:	Relationship:
• Delivery speed	• Long-term relationship
• Delivery dependability	• Relationship closeness
• Product development time	• Communication openness
	• Reputation for integrity
Flexibility:	
• Product volume changes	
• Set-up time	

Source: Dou 2010. Reproduced with permission of Taylor & Francis.

more relevance to specific criteria. For instance, if a commodity has to be bought, α would have a higher value than the β, γ and δ.

More recently, companies concerned with social and environmental issues have started to also include these performance areas in the Vendor Rating process (Igarashi et al., 2013; Hassini et al., 2012; Dou and Sarkis, 2010). For example, it is apparent that some cost-reduction objectives can be achieved through outsourcing or off-shoring solutions in low-cost countries, where the company may face environmental and social risks. While in the short term these options can be valuable from an economic standpoint, the reputational risks involved through collaborating with players that do not guarantee satisfactory standards of environmental and social performance can translate into significant losses for the outsourcer, due to most stakeholders being highly concerned with the ethical behaviour of companies.

Table 4.2 reports a classification of the social and environmental areas that must be covered during the vendor selection process.

As can be seen in Table 4.2, social performance can be assessed from two perspectives. The first encompasses initiatives undertaken to support the professional development of employees, as well as their well-being, especially in terms of health and safety. In this regard, the assessment should also consider the results achieved, such as the number of injuries and accidents reported in a given period of time. The second refers to the projects aimed at supporting the local communities, whose well-being can be influenced by the presence of a company's facilities, as well as other stakeholders of the company (mainly customers and suppliers).

TABLE 4.2   Environmental and social factors in vendor selection

Social performance categories	Subcategories	Environmental performance categories	Subcategories
Social sustainability profiles within the company	• Practices related to personnel management • Practices for health and safety at work	*Environmental protection practices*	• Pollution control • Prevention of pollution • Environmental Management System (EMS)
Social sustainability profiles outside the company	• Projects for local communities • Projects related to other stakeholders	*Environmental Performance*	• Consumption of resources • Production of pollution

Source: Dou 2010. Reproduced with permission of Taylor & Francis.

The assessment of the environmental performance of the supplier concerns two main categories. The first refers to initiatives and programs undertaken to prevent pollution and improve the environmental performance of the firm, such as establishing an Environmental Management System. The second is focused on the performance achieved, in terms of the resources consumed in a given period of time (e.g. energy, water, raw materials) and the production of pollution (e.g. CO_2 emissions). A more detailed description of the metrics suitable for quantifying social and environmental performance categories is given in Chapter 8.

4.3.4   Vendor Control and Contract Management

In this stage, the performance of the supplier is reviewed over the lifetime of the contract, in order to check whether initial targets have been met and also to identify improvement opportunities to be discussed with the counterpart. In this regard, vendor control can be exercised through monitoring the actual performance reported in the categories assessed during the vendor rating process. Such a monitoring activity aims to identify critical areas that require improvement initiatives, but also at rewarding good practices. In the field of social and environmental sustainability, the use of structured tools has been suggested to appraise suppliers' performance and progress over time. Table 4.3 gives a brief description of a balanced scorecard that can be used to assess the social performance of a supplier against the 'desired' ethical behaviour that the purchaser is willing to observe.

In order to reach a sounder ex post assessment of the supplier and to trigger improvement programmes, other techniques can be used in addition to the desk activities described previously (Day, 2002):

- *Supplier visits and audits:* these techniques can be used in order to check the reliability of the information provided by the supplier, especially in those areas that cannot be directly measured by the purchasing company. Visiting the

TABLE 4.3 Sustainable components of a supplier-balanced scorecard

Desired behaviour	Indicators
Championing better jobs for workers, good labour standards and having a positive impact on the community	• Staff turnover at production sites • Good human resource management systems (qualitative assessment)
Actively working on a plan to improve standards	• Good labour standards, audit results and management systems (qualitative assessment) • No. of improvement projects carried out with other suppliers to share good practices
Taking pride in steps taken to demonstrate improved working conditions at all times, including when issues arise	• No. of sites with initiatives such as active trade union representation (or worker representation where trade unions are not allowed), steps towards paying a living wage, provision of social benefits (healthcare, schooling, nutrition etc.) • Existence of recognition agreement and Collective Bargaining Agreement • No. of workers with long-term contracts • Ratio of insecure to contracted workers (differentiated by gender) • Analysis of working hours
Stable relationships with own suppliers/subcontractors	• Average length of relationship with suppliers
Transparency about supply chain and production	• Presence of a shared list of all sources of supply, including subcontractors and home workers
Open dialogue on labour standards in subcontracting sites	• Amount of overtime in each production site
Contributing to an enabling environment for improved labour standards within the supply chain	• Level of willingness to work collaboratively to bring about sustainable labour standards improvements on site (qualitative assessment)

Source: Ethical and Sustainable Procurement 2013. Reproduced with permission of The Chartered Institute of Procurement & Supply.

site of the supplier can be a viable solution for gathering indisputable evidence about working conditions and the environmentally soundness of production processes. When such visits are conducted according to structured procedures, they can become part of an *auditing* process, which can be carried out directly by the company or by third parties. The outcomes of these initiatives can trigger the launch of improvement programmes with suppliers, where relevant opportunities are identified. However, due to the amount of resources necessary to carry out visits and audits, these tools should only be used when the purchaser suspects that there is a significant risk of poor environmental and social standards.

- *Supplier workshops and conferences:* these initiatives can be undertaken in particular to stimulate the sharing and dissemination of practices among suppliers, in which their various projects and the results achieved can be described, and also in which discussion can be initiated with other supply chain partners on the viability of these solutions in other contexts.

- *Supplier social and environmental training:* this role is characteristic of larger companies, which can provide support to smaller suppliers in progressing along the path of environmental and social sustainability. This can be achieved through training programmes delivered to suppliers and sub-contractors, in order to stimulate not only the awareness, but also the actual implementation of best practices, the adoption of which requires a significant investment in financial and human resources.

4.4   ETHICS IN PROCUREMENT

Since buyers systematically interact with external organisations, often exerting a relevant bargaining power over their counterparts, the risk of unethical behaviour often arises, which can threaten the reputation of the entire company as well as its operational and economic performance, especially if value-destroying decisions are taken in order to pursue personal interests. This problem has become increasingly significant since Corporate Social Responsibility has emerged as a pillar of a company's strategy and long-term success. Consequently, most professional associations have issued their own codes of ethics and principles, which are to be observed by their members. In addition, individual companies, and larger ones in particular, have adopted their own codes so as to declare the ethical principles that should underlie the conduct of the entire organisation and its employees. Focusing in particular on the role of buyers, the following areas are considered to be of great importance in order to preserve the reputation and the interest of the company (Johnson et al., 2011):

- *Perceptions and conflicts of interest:* the behaviour of buyers, especially during negotiations, must be perceived as fair, correct and appropriate in order to not harm the reputation and the interest of the company. In this regard, it is necessary for the buyer to be and to appear professional and to refrain from abusing his/her position. This implies, for instance, that he/she should not ask for a quote if the potential supplier has not yet been provided with a precise description of the company's needs, that the confidentiality of the information exchanged should be ensured, or that in the event of rejection of the bid, prompt and fair feedback should be provided. However, there may be situations in which the decision-making process of the supply professional can be (or may seem) biased by some specific conditions, such as when family members or friends' interests are involved in the commercial relationship to be established or managed. To prevent such cases, companies should establish specific rules and procedures concerning potential conflicts of interests.
- *Gifts and gratuities:* receiving any sort of gift or gratuity can generate a sense of obligation in the buyer, who may consider it appropriate to return the favour to his/her counterpart. Although the amount and the economic relevance of

such gifts and gratuities can be seen as drivers of possible biased procurement decisions, buyers can become non-objective even in the case of apparently trivial benefits if they can be easily influenced. Therefore, appropriate procedures and rules must be established in the company so as to prevent this from happening. Furthermore, suppliers can try to influence buyers' decisions through contacts with other representatives of the company who, due to their position (not necessarily in the procurement department), can exert an influence on the supply processes. When this risk is perceived as relevant, rules and procedures concerning this area must be extended to all representatives of the company.

- *Bribery*: while small gifts and gratuities can still be considered a fair and legal means for managing a commercial relationship, such as an invitation for dinner aimed at discussing the needs of the client and the conditions of a possible supply contract, bribery is an illegal practice, which is sanctioned with ad hoc laws by most countries. In some industries in particular, bribery is an evil that results in numerous damages for the company, such as poorer product quality, higher prices, low overall performance of the product/service and, generally speaking, higher cost of ownership. Thus, on top of national legislation in this field, companies must prevent and prosecute these crimes through specific norms in their codes of conduct and through internal investigations aimed at identifying such illegal practices.

In the field of supply management, professional associations have issued their own codes of conduct, which must be observed by all their members. These documents play a major role in shaping the culture of supply professionals and in directing how they behave, but these codes are also influential benchmarks for companies willing to introduce and adopt their own codes. Due to the fact that a buyer must be able to detect possible risks of misconduct while carrying out his/her tasks, it is of major importance for a code not only to state how the buyer should behave, but also the principles of ethical conduct. In this regard, for instance, the International Federation of Purchasing and Supply Management (IFPSM) has drawn up a reference document that supports all its members, that is, national associations, in the drafting of their own codes of conduct, which should build on the following values (IFPSM, 2007):

- *Honesty/Integrity*, in all business relationships in which the buyer is engaged inside or outside the company.
- *Professionalism*, which concerns the need for a high competence level of the professional in order to effectively interact with counterparts and pursue the company's interests.
- *Responsible Management*, in particular for company's resources, which must be efficiently used in the interest of the firm.
- *Serving the Public Interest*: this value refers to the risk of corruption and bribery and, more broadly, to all cases in which the professional can benefit from business relationships in the pursuit of personal interests instead of those of the

As a member of CIPS, I will:	
Enhance and protect the standing of the profession, by: • Never engaging in conduct, either professional or personal, which would bring the profession or the Chartered Institute of Purchasing & Supply into disrepute • Not accepting inducements or gifts (other than any declared gifts of nominal value which have been sanctioned by my employer) • Not allowing offers of hospitality or those with vested interests to influence, or be perceived to influence, my business decisions • Being aware that my behaviour outside my professional life may have an effect on how I am perceived as a professional.	**Promote the eradication of unethical business practices, by:** • Fostering awareness of human rights, fraud and corruption issues in all my business relationships • Responsibly managing any business relationships where unethical practices may come to light, and taking appropriate action to report and remedy them • Undertaking due diligence on appropriate supplier relationships in relation to forced labour (modern slavery) and other human rights abuses, fraud and corruption • Continually developing my knowledge of forced labour (modern slavery), human rights, fraud and corruption issues, and applying this in my professional life.
Maintain the highest standard of integrity in all business relationships, by: • Rejecting any business practice which might reasonably be deemed improper • Never using my authority or position for my own financial gain • Declaring to my line manager any personal interest that might affect, or be seen by others to affect, my impartiality in decision making • Ensuring that the information I give in the course of my work is accurate and not misleading • Never breaching the confidentiality of information I receive in a professional capacity • Striving for genuine, fair and transparent competition • Being truthful about my skills, experience and qualifications.	**Enhance the proficiency and stature of the profession, by:** • Continually developing and applying knowledge to increase my personal skills and those of the organisation I work for • Fostering the highest standards of professional competence amongst those for whom I am responsible • Optimising the responsible use of resources which I have influence over for the benefit of my organisation. **Ensure full compliance with laws and regulations, by:** • Adhering to the laws of the countries in which I practise, and in countries where there is no relevant law in place I will apply the standards inherent in this Code • Fulfilling agreed contractual obligations • Following CIPS guidance on professional practice.

FIGURE 4.2 CIPS Code of Conduct. *Source:* Ethical and Sustainable Procurement 2013. Reproduced with permission of The Chartered Institute of Procurement & Supply.

company. The buyer should not only avoid this type of behaviour, but also denounce practices deemed to be improper.

- *Compliance with the Law:* such compliance must be observed not only in relation to national laws, but also with regard to any contractual obligations, as well as the rules and policies of the professional association, to which the buyer belongs.

Figure 4.2 reports the code of conduct issued in 2013 by the Chartered Institute of Purchasing and Supply (CIPS), which is one of the members of IFPSM. It serves as an example of how IFPSM's ethical principles have been effectively deployed into a list of duties for supply professionals.

5

SUSTAINABILITY AND PRODUCTION

5.1 INTRODUCTION

The Goodrich Corporation was a large American company active in the aerospace industry, as well as in the production of tires and chemicals, whose origin can be traced back to the late nineteenth century, a time in which its name was 'B.F. Goodrich'. In the recent years, it has progressively focused on the aerospace industry, leaving the tires sector in the late 1980s and the production of chemicals in 2001, when it was renamed 'Goodrich Corporation'. In 2012 United Technologies Corporation (UTC) bought Goodrich and combined it with Hamilton Sundstrand to form UTC Aerospace Systems, which is now one of the world's largest players in the field of integrated aerospace solutions.

In the mid 1990s, the aerospace division of Goodrich was coping with strong pressures from its main clients, who requested sound improvements in its operational performance, in particular for one if its plants, located in California. One of the solutions proposed was the adoption of a new approach to the management of production activities known as 'Toyota Production System', which in the 1990s was becoming more and more popular. The success of this project at the shop-floor level was so incredible that Goodrich started implementing lean principles in the administrative processes of the plant, then also in all other production sites and, finally, in the overall organization, shaping it according to the 'value-stream' logic and leaving the functional one.

Sustainable Operations and Supply Chain Management, First Edition. Valeria Belvedere and Alberto Grando.
© 2017 John Wiley & Sons Ltd. Published 2017 by John Wiley & Sons Ltd.

Several lean management tools and principles were adopted by the company. First of all, the management strove to identify the 'wastes' of Goodrich's processes, that is, the non-value-adding activities, and to remove them through a series of kaizen events, which were short projects specifically aimed at addressing a single problem with a dedicated time. Then, such principles as visual management, employee involvement, introduction of standard work procedures, one-piece flow, re-design of the layout were introduced. These changes resulted in dramatic operational improvements. For example, the production line of the metal sink for the Boeing 717 enjoyed a reduction 75% of the space covered by the shop floor, a decrease of nearly 85% of the manufacturing lead time, and a remarkable cut to the inventory of finished products and components. The management of the company quickly understood that these improvements could result also in environmental benefits as well as in a more healthy and safe workplace. For example, when introducing the concept of standard working procedures, one effect was the elimination of useless motion and activities (as sorting tools and components) of the workers, which could have exposed them to possible risks. Similarly, the reduction of the stock of materials made obsolescence less frequent, thus reducing scraps and the subsequent waste of materials. The reduction of the batch size (peculiar to lean management) was particularly beneficial when chemical and hazardous materials were concerned. Indeed, the reduction of these substances in the working area reduced the risk of injuries suffered by the production workers. Furthermore, a lower batch size received from the suppliers also reduced the possibility of an expiration of the product before it was used. These solutions led Goodrich to eliminate 5,000 gallon tanks of such substances as methyl ethyl ketone, sulfuric acid, nitric acid, trichloroethane.

Source: UTC Aerospace Systems' website, viewed 1 December 2015, http:// utcaerospacesystems.com/Pages/Default.aspx; EPA, 'Lean Manufacturing and the Environment: Research on Advanced Manufacturing Systems and the Environment and Recommendations for Leveraging Better Environmental Performance', 2003.

As described in the Goodrich case, the way in which the production process is designed and managed determines relevant effects on the social and environmental sustainability of the company. While the need to cope with these aspects is evident, appropriate solutions must be identified to improve the production system. In this regard, several approaches to the design and management of company's operations have been proposed, some of which also seem to be effective as far as social and environmental sustainability is concerned. In particular, Lean Management and Six Sigma share this feature.

In the remainder of this Chapter, we will outline the approaches and logics underlying the design of the production system that have been proposed over time. Then, we will explain why Lean Management and Six Sigma have been suggested as effective approaches to address design requirements that in recent years have been considered mandatory. Finally, we will show how these methodologies can be consistent with the aim of improving the social and environmental standards of a manufacturing company.

5.2   THE DESIGN OF THE PRODUCTION SYSTEM

The design and management of manufacturing systems, as illustrated in Chapter 2, must be based on the principle of *strategic alignment*, which requires strategic and functional goals to be consistent, thus enabling operations management to contribute to the process of creating and maintaining competitive advantage. Functional goals, from the perspective of operations management, refer to performance factors such as cost (or productivity), quality, time (meaning, in particular, dependability and speed of manufacturing and delivery processes) and flexibility, whose importance in relative terms must be defined taking the competitive strategy pursued by the company into account.

Nevertheless, over time we have witnessed a series of technological and managerial innovations, as well as stimuli coming from the market, that have urged companies to pursue different improvement goals in the field of manufacturing, which highlight the importance of each individual performance factor and the possibility of exploiting synergies between them.

The productivity of the manufacturing system, and therefore its ability to be cost-effective, is traditionally considered by the management of production departments to be a priority (Cigolini and Grando, 2009; Grando and Turco, 2005; Hayes et al., 1988; Hayes and Clark, 1985). At the end of the nineteenth century, with the dissemination of scientific management principles, the efficient use of production inputs (namely workforce) was considered a key objective in process design, which was achievable through the standardisation of activities and the parcelling out of tasks (Sprague, 2007). This, in fact, made it possible to rapidly insert new manpower in production lines and to quickly reach an adequate level of efficiency – essential for achieving economies of scale. These first experiences, which in fact marked the birth of operations management as a discipline, strongly influenced the management culture in manufacturing sectors, where for a long time the ability to reduce costs was seen as the key priority of a factory (Skinner, 1969). This paradigm was called into question only from the 1970s, most of all due to the competition posed by Japanese companies, which demonstrated that market success was the result of a series of actions aimed at improving performance areas such as quality, logistic service and product innovation (Skinner, 1986; Abernathy, 1978; Skinner, 1974). By contrast, too much focus on cost-reduction goals gave rise to the so-called productivity paradox (Skinner, 1986), namely economic results that were out of line with improvement efforts, due to the inability of the management to identify the real demands for change when managing manufacturing processes (Adler et al., 2009). Empirical studies had in fact highlighted a correlation between productivity and economic decline in the automobile sector, since improvement plans that focused on efficiency gains compromised the ability to innovate both the product and the process (Adler et al., 2009; Abernathy, 1978). Furthermore, in the 1980s the success of the theory of constraints had further called into question the opportunity of focusing improvement programmes on cost-reduction goals, and in particular the saturation of production lines (Goldratt and Cox, 1984). This choice, in fact, prompted also by inadequate product costing systems (Johnson and Kaplan, 1987), resulted in a series of inefficiencies typical of excessively saturated production lines, namely long production lead times, poor quality rates, high stocks of semi-finished and finished products and, finally, a low level of customer service due to frequent stock-outs (Goldratt and Cox, 1984).

During the same period, the dissemination of Japanese production techniques had shown that operational performance was not bound by a trade-off relationship, which imposes the identification of a primary performance area to invest in, but that the individual performance factors supported one another, producing important synergies (Schonberger, 1986). This new awareness led to the development (and the validation through empirical studies) of the idea that there may be a 'virtuous cycle' in the improvement of manufacturing performance (Ferdows and De Meyer, 1990), which begins with the need to invest in the improvement of product quality, without which high performance levels related to other aspects become less relevant. Once this result has been consolidated, the subsequent areas to be dealt with are dependability and reliability, with the aim of stabilising the length of manufacturing and delivery processes. This is precursory to actions aimed at reducing lead times and improving speed performance. Only at this point can manufacturing costs be efficiently reduced. From this perspective, therefore, productivity is the final outcome of a long improvement process and certainly not the departure point, nor the only goal.

In this scenario, in which production and logistic performances are in fact considered to complement one another, it became widely acknowledged that environmental and social performance must also contribute to the overall evaluation of the results of manufacturing enterprises. This is not only due to the importance attributed by the customer to the sustainability of a product and the company processes of the manufacturers, but also (once again) to the synergic relationship that links industrial performance factors – namely cost, quality, time and flexibility – to environmental and social performance (Walker et al., 2014; Kleindorfer et al., 2005; de Ron, 1998). The most recent experience of many companies in this regard has, in fact, shown that in the search for increasing levels of sustainability in the fields of manufacturing and logistics it is necessary to implement practices and methodologies that have a positive impact on other performance areas, such as efficiency in the use of production input, product quality rates, and the speed and dependability of delivery processes, to quote but a few (Drake and Spinler, 2013).

On the basis of this analysis, in this Chapter we will illustrate the two most common approaches that enable the sustainability of industrial manufacturing processes to be improved, namely Lean Management and Six Sigma. For each of these approaches we will discuss the reasons why they were developed, how they work and the implications of their adoption for the sustainability of manufacturing and logistic activities.

5.3 LEVERAGING LEAN MANAGEMENT FOR A SUSTAINABLE PRODUCTION

Although the word *lean* was used for the first time by Womack et al. (1990) to refer to the numerous principles and techniques currently known as Lean Management, the first experience that lead to the development of this paradigm can be traced back to the 1950s, when Taiichi Ohno, production engineer at Toyota Motors, started revising several aspects of the production system of the company (Holweg, 2007). In his view, most car manufacturers, namely the western ones, although aware of the necessity to satisfy customers' need of product variety, still had a mass production system, based on large batches and a rather narrow product range, in order to mini-mise the time spent in setups and achieve economies of scale. Taiichi Ohno had been working for years in order to remove those 'wastes' that kept Toyota, as its compet-itors, from combing satisfactory efficiency rates with a wider and more responsive product offering, through the development of several managerial tools and tech-niques known as Toyota Production System (TPS), which will be described later in this Chapter.

Such a set of tools and techniques became popular in the 1980s at a worldwide level, when speed and flexibility of the manufacturing and logistic systems started gaining higher and higher importance, as a result of competitive pressures exerted mainly from Japanese companies. The latter, using innovative practices to organise and manage manufacturing processes, using *just-in-time* logics, were in a position to rapidly bring a wide variety of innovative and high performance products to the market, guaranteeing very quick response times (Blackburn, 1991; Stalk, 1988). Since then, the combination of variety and speed, specific to *time-based competition*, has been one of the cornerstones of the competitiveness of many companies, becoming even more important in recent years due to the establishment of new organisational paradigms of the supply chain based on the concept of 'agility', according to which the ability to respond to the market is the primary objective on which to base design and management choices (Bernardes and Hanna, 2009; Reichhart and Holweg, 2007; Christopher, 2000; 2005). However, the use of *time-based* strategies showed companies that it was impossible to achieve fast delivery times, high levels of product customisation and a wide range of constantly evolving products without a high degree of flexibility in the manufacturing system.

Traditionally, it was believed that the choices concerning the size of a product range were conditioned by the trade-off between the variety of the products on offer and their manufacturing cost. The latter is inversely related to the production vol-umes, but increases as the size of the product range grows. Formally, an 'optimal' level of variety can be identified, at which costs are minimised. This threshold is influenced by the cost curve of the variety of products on offer, whose shape depends on the degree of flexibility of the manufacturing system. The experience gained since the 1980s in flexible manufacturing systems – FMS – in fact showed that it is pos-sible to combine a large product range with low manufacturing costs, by dealing with aspects such as the use of flexible automation, the size of production batches, the layout of the factory and the application of production planning logics (Stalk, 1988).

These aspects are the levers to be taken into consideration when attempting to reduce manufacturing lead times and stabilising their variability, with evident positive effects on the speed of transformation processes, production plans adherence, and last, the dependability and timeliness of deliveries.

Manufacturing flexibility, therefore, becomes essential for product variety and, more generally, the responsiveness of the transformation system, regarded as the ability to respond quickly to the market, renewing the range of products on offer more often and delivering the requested products on time (Bernardes and Hanna, 2009).

In the 1990s, the set of management techniques and logics adopted by the most innovative companies to confront these new challenges were codified and harmonised within a new manufacturing paradigm, called *Lean Management*, which has had a positive impact on a wide variety of performance areas, thus also generating benefits for the social and environmental sustainability of industrial enterprises.

Lean Management is the set of practices and tools aimed at improving the manufacturing processes of goods and the provision of services, based on the experience accumulated mainly in Japanese companies and, in particular, in Toyota Motors (Holweg, 2007; Womack et al., 1990). These experiences are based on the constant search for 'waste' (also called *muda* in Japanese), namely all the improper uses of company resources that do not generate 'value' for the customer (Womack et al., 1990). The different types of waste that are typically found in manufacturing processes can be grouped into the following categories (Wills, 2009):

- *Over-production*: it occurs in particular where batch sizes are large, making it impossible to align production volumes with actual market demands. Sometimes excess quantities are not reusable due to their physical and/or commercial obsolescence, causing a rapid reduction in the value of the product or even its physical deterioration. In cases where it is possible to use these quantities to meet future market demands, the products must be stored in warehouses as product inventories that, in turn, are the source of further waste, such as the space to be used for storage, the energy required for heating/cooling the warehouses and so on.

- *Excess inventory*: especially in environments where the production planning process is managed using a *push* approach, the company keeps stocks of finished products, which are duly sized to meet demand. Nevertheless, particularly in sectors characterised by products with short life cycles and a large range of products, the push approach may not be reliable, thus making it difficult to align stock with the requests of the market. Therefore, in cases where sales forecasts exceed actual demand, the stock of products is too large, meaning the unnecessary use of the spaces required for storage, as well as production resources used to manufacture the products (materials, energy and labour in particular).

- *Over-processing*: this consists of production activities aimed at providing the product with several functions or performance features that the customers have not requested (and for which they are not willing to pay). This is typically the case in tight tolerances – for example, those connected to some dimensional specifications of the product, or the addition of unrequested attributes, for example the finishings of components inside the product that are invisible to the customer.

- *Defects*: the manufacturing of items that do not comply with design requirements by definition constitutes waste. These items may in fact need remanufacturing in order to correct the defect, whereas in other cases they must even be disposed of. In both cases the company incurs 'un-quality' costs.

- *Waiting* (idle people and machines): industrial equipment is often idle for multiple reasons. This means that production resources that are theoretically available, but not in a condition to work, are not used – for example, due to the lack of customer orders or due to idleness caused by breakdowns and maintenance.

- *Unnecessary transport*: the transportation of materials (within the production plant or between different sites) is a waste since during transportation the product does not undergo any useful transformation from the point of view of the customer; consequently, it is appropriate to consider it a *muda*.

- *Unnecessary motion*: as in the case of products, the unnecessary movement of production-related employees is also a waste, deriving from an inappropriate process design or the inefficiencies that force employees to frequently move along production lines.

In the *lean* philosophy, the elimination of these types of waste means that the various performance areas in manufacturing, such as efficiency, product quality and the logistic service provided to the customer, can all be improved (Womack et al., 1990). Furthermore, since lean management assigns an important role to employees as the drivers of ongoing improvement processes, the use of this management philosophy also envisages an improvement in the working conditions of production-related employees, most of all thanks to job enlargement and enrichment and the improvement of industrial safety standards.

The emphasis placed on the elimination of waste, on the one hand, and the enhancement of human resources, on the other hand, has led to the suggestion that Lean Management is also useful for improving sustainability performance, thanks to the beneficial effect that its techniques may also have on the environmental and social 'wastes' peculiar to manufacturing processes. These, even in the different classifications proposed until now (Zokaei et al., 2013; Emmett and Sood, 2010; Pusavec et al., 2010a, 2010b; Wills, 2009; Driussi and Jansz, 2006), can be grouped into the following types, which will be illustrated in the next sections:

- Energy.
- Water.
- Physical waste.
- Emissions.
- Noise.
- Land contamination and biodiversity.

5.3.1   Overview of Environmental and Social 'Wastes'

5.3.1.1   Energy Waste   Industrial activities necessarily imply the consumption of energy, thus giving rise to significant environmental effects, especially in the case of the use of fossil fuels (such as oil, gas and coal), which produce polluting emissions when burnt and use land and generate waste at the time of their extraction/processing. Approximately 25% of the total energy consumption in Europe in 2013 (EUROSTAT data) was caused by the manufacturing sector and 31.6% by transportation. This data highlights the importance of monitoring the saving of energy in these fields. This is all the more important if it we consider that 70% of the energy consumed comes from oil, gas and coal, 14% from nuclear power stations and only 9% from renewable sources. Even if the latter percentage is growing rapidly, especially thanks to the dissemination of solar photovoltaics, in order to have an impact on the environmental energy footprint of a company it is necessary not only to change the mix of the energy sources in favour of renewable ones, but also to reduce their overall consumption. In this setting, it is evident that industrial inefficiencies, such as over-production, over-processing or the scrap rate, affect the quantity of energy used, causing the unjustified increase in the consumption thereof. The same occurs due to the ways that services are used (such as the heating/cooling of company premises), which are excessive compared to actual demands. In order to quantify the magnitude of this waste, it is necessary to estimate the quantity of energy used due to the various inefficiencies that may be identified in a manufacturing process and check its origin based on the different polluting potential of fossil fuels compared to the energy obtained from renewable sources.

5.3.1.2   Water Waste   The impact that industrial manufacturing has on water is twofold. On the one hand, it is often the cause of water pollution, for example in the form of the emission/release of heavy metals or chemical substances. On the other hand, industry uses water as input for its manufacturing processes. As far as the first aspect is concerned, refer to Section 5.3.1.4 for more details on the most harmful emissions. However, in recent years the polluting potential of industrial sectors has been reduced, thus recording negative rates of change in the intensity of water emissions, especially if we consider that manufacturing activities on the whole are constantly growing. On a European level, for example, the majority of countries recorded a reduction in the emissions of heavy metals in the period from 2004 to 2012, while enjoying an increase in the Gross Value Added. This is the case for Slovenia, which saw the first indicator reduced by 90.52% and the second indicator grown by 11.96%. Even in the countries that reported a decrease in the Gross Value Added during this time interval, such as in Italy and the United Kingdom, the reduction of the intensity of heavy metals was greater than the decrease in Gross Value Added. Similar evidence stems from the analysis of the EUROSTAT data on the total organic carbon emissions intensity of the chemical industry and the heavy metal emissions intensity of the metal industry, which have witnessed a clear decoupling process of the water-polluting potential from economic growth due to technological innovation of machinery and equipment.

Furthermore, as far as the use of water as an input of manufacturing processes is concerned, in the last two decades there has been steady improvement in this area, in this case due to the upgrading of machinery, to the adoption of new technology in the manufacturing sector and to the constant search for higher levels of efficiency during the manufacturing phase. This has resulted in an average reduction in the consumption of water of 81.8% in Eastern European countries and 9.9% in Western European countries during the period from 1990 to 2007 (EEA, 2009). Despite these significant improvements, the subject of water consumption remains a clear priority in environmental management policies, to be monitored through the use of state-of-the-art equipment, which guarantees higher standards of efficiency, and regeneration systems that enable the overall quantity of water consumed to be reduced, with beneficial effects on cost and environmental performance. In this case, it is also evident how the different types of waste, dealt with using lean management, may affect water consumption. Take, for example, how much a phenomenon such as over-production can become critical from this point of view and even more so in sectors such as paper manufacturing or several sectors of the food industry, in which the consumption of water per unit of product is particularly high.

5.3.1.3 Physical Waste   This type of waste concerns (solid or liquid) substances that cannot be reused at the end of their life cycle and whose disposal has a negative impact on the environment. This is particularly critical in the case of products that have not been designed according to Cradle-to-Cradle logics, as described in Chapter 3. Nevertheless, manufacturing inefficiencies can also be a significant source of the waste of both direct and indirect materials. In order to deal with this type of waste, it is necessary to identify the type and quantity of input and output in the transformation processes, which are to be used as the starting point for planning improvements. Compared to the case of water and energy, the analysis of the *as-is* situation is more complex due to the variety of components and materials used in industrial manufacturing processes. In this case, the direct input of manufacturing, which is the main source of this type of waste, can be identified by studying the bill of materials first of all, thus identifying the single parts that the product is made up of and its constituent materials, which are usually distinguished by different levels of danger. If the guidelines of the Cradle-to-Cradle certification are to be followed, it is necessary to describe the chemical composition of individual materials in order to assess their level of danger, going as far as identifying the substances that represent at least 0.0001% of the product (the so-called 100 ppm level). The danger that each of these substances poses for human beings and the environment must be assessed in order to classify the material as one of three different types – Green, Yellow and Red, which express increasing danger levels. If a company manufactures products that, in Cradle-to-Cradle terminology, are *Technical Nutrients* or *Biological Nutrients*, the elimination or the reduction of the possible 'waste' of materials during manufacturing has a rather insignificant effect. The former in fact, according to the definition of McDonough Braungart Design Chemistry, are 'materials of human artifice designed to circulate within technical metabolism (industrial cycles) forever', namely non-biodegradable materials, but that can be recycled and reintroduced to a new production cycle, such as glass, iron or several types of nylon at the end of their life cycle. The latter, on the other hand, are defined as 'materials used by living organisms or cells to carry on life processes such as growth, cell division, synthesis of carbohydrates and other complex functions. Biological nutrients are often carbon-based compounds that can be safely composed and returned to'. Therefore, these are biodegradable materials. Any item that does not fall into one of these categories, because it is non-recyclable and non-biodegradable, belongs to a *Cradle-to-Grave* cycle and thus has to be disposed of.

Consequently, the elimination of the waste of direct and indirect materials is particularly important in manufacturing processes that use input and/or generate output characterised by *Cradle-to-Grave* cycles (or also in the single phases of these processes).

5.3.1.4 Emissions

5.3.1.4 Emissions The manufacturing activities typically carried out in industrial enterprises are among the main sources of pollution, due to the release of a high number of substances, which include among others (EEA, 2011):

- *Air pollutants*: ammonia (NH_3), nitrogen oxides (NO_x), non-methane volatile organic compounds (NMVOCs), particulate matter (PM_{10}) and sulfur oxides (So_x). These pollutants are generated by industrial, agricultural and transportation activities, but can also be emitted by several products, such as paints, glues and solvents. They can be harmful for both human health and the environment, causing (among other problems and depending on the specific pollutant under analysis) such phenomena as acidification, eutrophication and several human diseases.
- *Heavy metals*: this category encompasses arsenic (As), cadmium (Cd), chromium (Cr), lead (Pb), mercury (Hg) and nickel (Ni), which are toxic for a number of eco-systems.
- *Organic micro-pollutants*: these include benzene, dioxins and furans, and polycyclic aromatic hydrocarbons (PAHs). Such pollutants can have severe effects on human health, being carcinogenic, as well as on the environment;
- *Carbon dioxide (CO_2)*: it is emitted primarily by fuel combustion (oil, coal, natural gases and biomasses) and originates from industrial and domestic activities as well as from transportation. It is the most relevant driver of climate change.

The polluting potential of a production plant, in absolute terms, depends on its size, but also on the sector in which it operates and the degree of efficiency of its equipment. For example, on a European level it has been shown that approximately 50% of the pollution generated by industrial activities is produced by 2% of registered factories and that the sector that makes the biggest contribution to the production of emissions is that of power generation (EEA, 2011). Furthermore, to obtain a measurement capable of expressing the efficiency of manufacturing processes it is necessary to standardise emissions in relation to the national GDP of a country.

Western countries in Europe, which on average have more modern equipment, fare better in this regard. This, once again, demonstrates the need to address manufacturing processes in order to reduce polluting potential.

It must also be taken into consideration that the emission of hazardous substances originates not only from transformation activities, but also from input and output, as is the case with glues, solvents, paints and all the items that contain these substances, for example furniture and domestic appliances. The correct organisation and management of manufacturing activities, therefore, may have a positive impact on the amount of emissions produced, not only due to equipment that is more efficient, but also by reducing the waste of materials associated with these activities. To plan improvement actions, also in this case, it is necessary to start with the quantification of the total emissions produced, which in turn requires making a choice in relation to the unit of analysis chosen (Wills, 2009). The latter may concern transformation processes alone, or may also include the materials used and produced, extending even to the buildings that house the manufacturing activities. In the first case, the estimate of emissions can be relatively easy if the production plant is obliged to provide regular reports in order to fulfil legal obligations, or as a result of certifications, such as ISO14001 or EMAS, which require a self-certification of the quantity of emissions produced. If these conditions do not exist, a qualified third-party tester can be used to obtain a voluntary certification. The same solution can be adopted for the assessment of materials (input and output), in the case where material safety data sheets are not available. The latter are documents provided by manufacturers that illustrate the characteristics of the products in terms of their toxicity or danger level, as well as the most appropriate ways to treat, use or dispose of them in order to safeguard the health and safety of anyone that may come into contact with them.

5.3.1.5 *Noise*

Although the main source of noise is indisputably linked to the transportation system of goods and passengers and, to a lesser extent, the performance of manufacturing activities, the phenomenon of noise disturbance is highly significant due to the number of persons affected. Indeed, it is estimated that in European cities with more than 250,000 inhabitants, at least 67 million people are exposed to average intensity noise of more than 50 dB within the timeframe of 24 hours. By extending the analysis to smaller cities, this number increases by a further 33 million (EEA, 2014a). The choices on where to locate logistic facilities (namely warehouses and distribution centres) and production plants, determining the size of the flow of goods and the related traffic, affect the quality of life of the people resident in the areas in question, who, due to the persistence and intensity of the noise produced, may suffer from pathological illnesses, such as anxiety, sleep disturbances and even forms of serious hypertension and cardiovascular problems (Bodin et al., 2015; Sygna et al., 2014; Van Kempen et al., 2002).

The noise produced in manufacturing processes in particular affects the well-being of employees, especially those working in production. Even if policies on safety at work in some cases impose the use of devices capable of limiting the effects of increased audio stimulation (such as the use of hearing-protection tools), the need to use technical solutions capable of reducing noise pollution is abundantly clear and is being assessed more and more often by many companies (Calabriso et al., 2015; Ahmed et al., 2014).

5.3.1.6 *Land Contamination and Biodiversity*   This type of waste is caused in particular by demographic trends that lead to the steady growth in so-called *land take*, which refers to urbanised areas and the areas used to meet food requirements through farming and livestock-breeding. These phenomena are causing a reduction in both the overall quantity of uncultivated land in favour of artificial surfaces, and animal and plant biodiversity. On a European level, it is estimated that the total land take in the period 2000–2006 was reduced by 9% compared to the previous decade. Nevertheless, its composition has undergone a significant change, in favour of more arable land and permanent crops and fewer pastures and less mosaic farmland (EEA, 2013). These trends produce harmful effects not only on flora, but also on fauna, gradually reducing the natural habitat of many species.

Excluding agricultural activities in the broad sense from this analysis and focusing, on the other hand, on the construction of new buildings in recent years in Europe, manufacturing and logistic facilities represent 15.5% of the total of new builds. Infrastructures for transportation (7.1%) are to be added to this figure, making a total of 22.6% (EEA, 2013). These plants are also a cause for the emission of polluting substances – mineral oils and heavy metals in particular – which give rise to forms of soil contamination, the seriousness of which varies depending on the sector and reaches its highest levels in metal production. The number of contaminated plants or those potentially exposed to this risk remains high, bearing witness to the pervasiveness of the problem. It is estimated in Europe that there are approximately 2.5 million of these plants and decontamination programmes have been adopted in only approximately 2% of cases, the majority of which are attributable to excavation and off-site disposal. These activities, nevertheless, are an ex-post remedy to the problem of soil contamination and produce substantial expenses not only for private organisations, but also for government bodies, which on average cover 42% of the total budget allocated to these projects (EEA, 2014b). Therefore, it is necessary to deal with this type of waste not only through ex-post solutions, but also with a prevention approach, which requires taking the numerous technological and managerial aspects of manufacturing processes into consideration.

5.3.2   The Lean Principles and Toolkit

The link between the typical waste found in manufacturing processes and environmental and social waste, which is described in the previous sections, is summarised in Table 5.1. The possibility of increasing the degree of sustainability of a factory, therefore, requires the use of management practices and solutions capable of dealing with this waste and that define improvement strategies whose priorities must also take the benefits that can be achieved socially and environmentally into account. From this perspective, Lean Management, on the one hand, appears to be a philosophy that is consistent with these goals, and on the other hand, provides a wide variety of tools and management principles that make the identification of an improvement strategy relatively easy.

TABLE 5.1   The environmental and social impact of waste in manufacturing processes

Waste	Environmental and social impact
Over-production	• More raw materials, energy and water consumed in making unnecessary products • Extra products may spoil or become obsolete requiring disposal of physical waste • Extra-hazardous materials resulting in extra emissions, waste disposal, land contamination, workers' exposure to risk of injury • Noise deriving from the production of unnecessary products affects the local community and employees
Inventory	• More packaging to store works-in-progress (WIP) • Waste from deterioration or damage to store (WIP) • More energy used for heating, cooling and lighting of inventory space • Increased land take due to the need for bigger warehouses/factories
Transportation and motion	• More energy and emissions from transportation • More packaging required to protect components during movement and transportation • Damage and spills during transportation • Higher risk of accidents and injuries to employees during transportation and movement
Defects	• More raw materials, energy and water consumed in making defective products • Scraps can require disposal of physical waste • Defective products may require reworking, which results in the same problems as over-production • Extra-hazardous materials embedded in defective products result in extra emissions, waste disposal, land contamination, workers' exposure to risk of injury • Noise deriving from the production of defective products affects the local community and employees
Over-processing	• More energy and water used to carry out unnecessary processing • More emissions, noise and land contamination due to unnecessary processing • More parts and raw materials used to enrich the product with unnecessary features and functions
Waiting	• Potential material spoilage or component damage causing physical waste and need for disposal • Wasted energy from heating, cooling and lighting during production downtimes

Source: adapted from the lean and environmental toolkit, EPA.

This also explains why many contributions to the topic of sustainability in industrial manufacturing processes pay great attention to how significant and long-lasting results can be achieved if Lean Management principles are adopted. And it is not surprising that national and international bodies, such as the Environmental Protection Agency (EPA) in the United States and the Organisation for Economic

Co-operation and Development (OECD), have drawn up manuals to improve social and environmental sustainability in manufacturing drawing on the principles of Lean Management. Furthermore, many companies that have adopted these principles have had numerous benefits related to levels of efficiency, the logistic service provided to the customer and also environmental protection and the safety of workers, thus demonstrating the compatibility of the three different forms of sustainability, namely economic, social and environmental sustainability.

In order to eliminate the waste typically produced in manufacturing processes managed using traditional approaches, therein including environmental and social waste, Lean Management proposes the reorganisation of transformation activities using the following criteria (Womack et al., 1990):

- *Value:* first of all, it is necessary to understand which activities in the process of manufacturing and delivery of a product create value for the customer, in order to eliminate all the others. Non-value-adding activities, in fact, are the cause of many kinds of waste, such as the use of resources for unproductive purposes and the lengthening of manufacturing and delivery times.
- *Flow:* once the non-value-adding activities are eliminated, it is necessary to ensure that the manufacturing and logistics system functions without any interruptions that may be caused due to various circumstances. For example, unexpected downtimes due to machine breakdowns or the sudden unavailability of materials due to delays from suppliers cause inefficiencies and waste, especially waiting and the excessive accumulation of stocks of work-in-progress. From the perspective of Lean Management, it is necessary to identify and implement practices and solutions that enable processes to run smoothly and in tight sequence.
- *Pull:* once the processes have been redesigned using the above criteria, it is necessary to ensure that each phase of the process is carried out using pull logics, that is, only if a specific request/order has been made by the customer. In the case of final product the customer is by definition external; for other manufacturing stages, the customer is represented by the department that is immediately downstream. This principle implies that nothing may be manufactured (neither finished nor semi-finished products) in the absence of demand, as in a *just-in-time* system.
- *Perfection:* Lean Management states the need to strive for continuous improvement, also called *kaizen* in Japanese, through the systematic analysis of value flows and the elimination of inefficiencies that may arise in the performance of manufacturing and logistic activities.

The logics and the tools that make it possible to implement these principles in practice are illustrated in the following sections.

5.3.2.1 *Value Stream Mapping and Pull Processes*   Value Stream Mapping is the process-mapping method used to describe the current ('as-is') and future ('to-be') state of a process (Rother and Shook, 1999). More specifically, the former is the

description of the way in which the process is currently managed, enriched with information suitable for identifying improvement actions. The latter is the description of how the process will look after the implementation of these actions. Value streams are generally drawn up using standard symbols, some of which are shown in Figure 5.1.

A Value Stream Map is a graphical representation of the activities carried out in order to produce an item or to deliver a service. They can be classified as follows (Souza, 2012):

- *Value-added activities*, for which clients are willing to pay. For instance, a transformation phase along the production process, such as the cutting of a layer of cloth aimed at producing a garment, belongs to this type of activities.

- *Non-value-added*, for which clients are not willing to pay because these activities make no change to the product. This is the case in transportation and quality control, as well as waiting, which may occur if an item (be it a finished product, a component or a raw material) stops during a stage of the production/distribution system due to an imbalance among the transformation activities or the adoption of a *push* production planning approach.

- *Business non-value-added activities*, for which clients are not willing to pay, but necessary for legal, accounting and regulatory purposes, such as the drawing up of financial statements.

As explained here, the value stream includes both manufacturing activities and administrative ones, such as marketing and sales, administration and accounting, which support the production activities. A company may have several value streams, depending in particular on the processes carried out and the types of products that are manufactured.

This approach to process analysis is particularly helpful when companies wish to address the environmental issues caused by production activities or to improve the working conditions of production-related employees. In these cases, the expression 'Green Value Stream' is also used, even though this tool can be suitable also for identifying and addressing social sustainability issues, namely those concerning health and safety.

A Green Value Stream focuses on the negative environmental and social impact of value stream activities, such as the emissions caused by the transportation of goods being received or shipped, the energy used to run the machines, the physical waste generated in various steps of the transformation process due, for example, to the production of scraps, the injuries reported in a given period of time on the shop floor, and so on. The production facilities and, generally speaking, any company's premises may also affect the environment because of the energy required to run computers and printers, the use of paper instead of electronic devices for mailing, the emissions from transportation due to business trips or commuting, and so on.

In order to improve the sustainability of its production processes, the value stream can be drawn up so as to describe the current state of the process and complement it

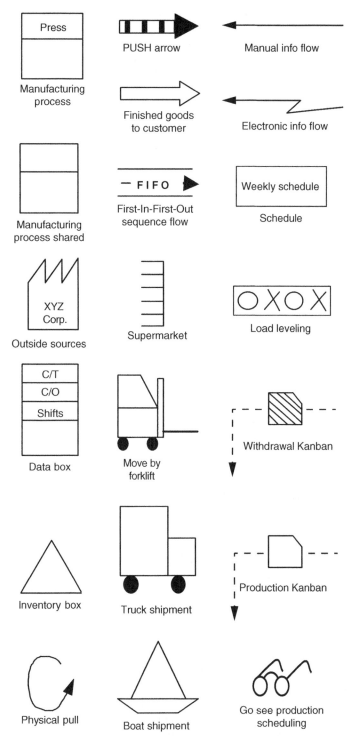

FIGURE 5.1 Standard symbols in Value Stream Mapping. *Source:* Rother 1999. Reproduced with permission of Lean Enterprise Institute.

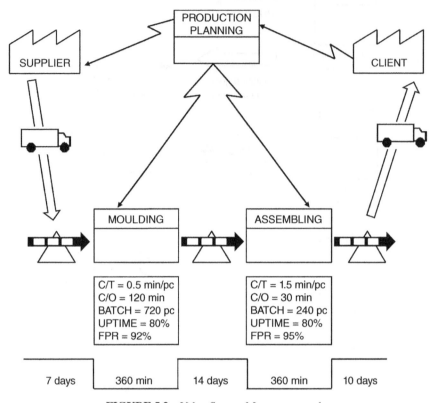

FIGURE 5.2   Value Stream Map: an example.

with its specific areas of performance. Figure 5.2 depicts the Value Stream of a company that produces small plastic toys through a moulding operation, using plastic grains bought from an external supplier, and the subsequent assembly of the toys, after which the finished product is stored in the warehouse until an order from the customer is received. Assuming that a push production planning approach is adopted, the 'as-is' could look like the one in Figure 5.2.

As can be seen in Figure 5.2, namely in the data boxes below the two production steps, several inefficiencies characterise the 'as-is' state of this process, some of which refer to sustainability profiles. Indeed, the two departments show a first pass rate (FPR) equal to 92% (moulding) and 95% (assembling), which result in a waste of materials and of the energy necessary to run the machines during the moulding and assembly of defective products. Furthermore, because of the long change-over (C/O) times especially in the moulding phase (120 minutes at moulding and 30 minutes at assembling), the company produces large batches, namely 720 pieces during mould- ing and 240 pieces during assembly. This choice, coupled with a rather high product variety, results in a large inventory of components downstream to moulding (equal to 14 days of coverage) and finished products after the final assembly (equal to 10 days of coverage), as pointed out by the *time line* at the bottom of the diagram. Furthermore, because the shipments from the supplier of plastic grains are on a weekly basis, the stock of incoming goods is also rather high.

It must also be considered that both operations do not enjoy a high level of saturation (uptime equal to 80% in both cases) because of frequent delays from suppliers, breakdowns, missing parts and minor inefficiencies due to the poor organisation of the shop floor. All of these events cause waiting, over-production (due to the need to cope with unexpected events) and motion waste, which in turn result in several types of environmental and social waste, such as higher energy consumption and a higher risk of injuries.

Looking at the *time line* at the bottom of the value stream represented in Figure 5.2, it can be seen that in this production process the total manufacturing lead time is nearly 15 days, which encompass the time necessary to complete a batch in the moulding department (360 minutes), the days of coverage of the decoupling buffer (14 days) and finally the time needed to complete one batch in the assembly phase (360 minutes). However, assuming that one finished product is made up of five components on average, its total processing time is only 4 minutes (i.e. 0.5 min/pc at moulding for each component and 1.5 min/pc at assembly), which means that only a very small portion of the whole process is able to add value to the product. This data leads to the following Flow Rate:

$$Flow\,Rate = \frac{Value\,Added\,Time}{Total\,Lead\,Time} = \frac{4\,minutes}{15\,days}$$

If the waiting times at the incoming goods warehouse and the finished products warehouse are also taken into consideration (7 days and 10 days), the Flow Rate becomes much worse:

$$Flow\,Rate = \frac{4\,minutes}{32\,days}$$

Ultimately, because the client is willing to wait no more than two days for the order to be fulfilled (much shorter than the manufacturing lead time), the company has adopted the make to stock (*push*) production planning approach that results in a stock of finished products and in all the waste associated with it.

In this kind of environment, several environmental, health and safety (EHS) problems can be observed, since the current state is characterised by different types of 'waste' (see Table 5.1). In order to clearly highlight the EHS performance of the 'as-is' value stream, some other pieces of information must be added.

With regard to *energy* consumption, it must be considered that several sources of energy can be used in a manufacturing facility, ranging from natural gas, to electricity, coal, fuel, oil and many others. Thus, it is necessary first of all to collect information regarding the composition of the energy use, since its source is an important driver of the environmental footprint of the company. Second, the total amount of energy used must be split among the various steps of the manufacturing process. Focusing only on transformation phases (energy consumption for transportation will be addressed in Chapter 6), such an activity is not always straightforward and can be carried out using direct and indirect measurement techniques, as:

- *Metering:* this technique consists of installing meters in specific production stages to directly measure the consumption of energy (e.g. electricity or gas) by a given piece of equipment.
- *Estimating:* this indirect approach relies on the attempt to estimate energy use on the basis of manufacturers' information concerning the hourly energy consumption of the machine and of the actual uptime of such machine over a certain period of time.

This (direct or indirect) calculation provides the baseline to be used for the definition of improvement goals. In order to facilitate comparisons between different steps of the production process and to make it easier to identify the most relevant improvement areas, it is worthwhile reporting the energy use data in the current and future state value stream maps in terms of the product's energy intensity, which can be calculated as follows:

$$Product\ Energy\ Intensity = Total\ kWh/Total\ Output$$

Once this information has been obtained, it is possible to start identifying possible solutions, carrying out, first of all, an assessment aimed at understanding whether major inefficiencies exist and, then, identifying improvement opportunities based on the adoption of technological solutions or best practices. With regard to the initial assessment, *kaizen* events can be carried out in order to discover whether the production process suffers from major sources of inefficiencies, such as those summarised in Table 5.2.

TABLE 5.2   Identifying major inefficiencies in energy use

Motors and machines
- Are machines left running when not in operation? If so, why?
- Are energy-efficient motors, pumps and equipment used?
- Are motors, pumps and equipment sized according to their loads?
- Do motor systems use variable-speed drive controls?

Lighting
- Is lighting focused where workers need it?
- Is lighting controlled by motion sensors in warehouses, storage areas and other areas that are intermittently used?
- Is energy-efficient lighting used?

Process heating
- Are oven and process heating temperatures maintained at higher levels than necessary?

Facility heating and cooling
- Are work areas heated or cooled more than necessary?
- Do employees have control over heating and cooling in their work areas?
- Are exterior windows or doors opened or closed to adjust heating and cooling?

Source: based on Lean Energy & Climate Toolkit, EPA.

Once the most relevant sources of inefficiencies have been identified, it is possible to select and implement the most appropriate bundle of technological and managerial solutions. As will be explained later in this Chapter, several lean tools are fully in line with the aim of reducing energy use. In particular, actions undertaken to improve the factory layout and streamline the product flow (Section 5.3.2.2), to reduce the amount of stock (Sections 5.3.2.2 and 5.3.2.3) and to improve the machine availability through the Total Product Maintenance (Section 5.3.2.5) are clear examples of the positive effects that Lean Management can bring to energy efficiency.

Similar comments as those made for energy can be also made for *water*. Indeed, also in this case it is necessary to start measuring the total amount of water used in each step of the production process in a given period of time and report it in the current value stream map (e.g. in terms of thousands of litres per day). To obtain this data it may be necessary to use a metering technique, like the one for measuring energy. However, the actual water usage of each production step must be based on the calculation of the *water balance*, which can be obtained as follows:

$$Water\ Balance = Input - (Water\ Loss + Output)$$

Whereas *input* is the total amount entering the production step, water losses can be problems like evaporation and leaks, and output is the quantity of water leaving the production step in the form of wastewater discharge. The water balance is the amount to be reported in the value stream map, which consequently leads to the detection of the most critical areas and enables the identification of their root causes. Besides water balance, product water intensity can also be calculated and reported, following an approach similar to the one explained for energy.

With regard to *physical waste*, its overall amount, which can vary depending on the production step under analysis, can be reported in the data boxes of both the current and future value stream maps in terms of *first pass rate* (or *scrap rate*) or through the *input-output line* (also called *materials line*), whose upper segments, as for the *time line*, describe the amount of input treated during each production step, while the lower ones report the amount of output downstream to each transformation phase. The ratio between the latter and the former measures the efficiency of the process as far the physical waste of direct materials and components is concerned.

When reporting and analysing physical waste, its composition must be taken into account, since some materials and substances can be more harmful than others for human health and the environment, especially chemicals and metals. When these kinds of *hazardous waste* occur, they must be recorded in the data boxes of the value stream maps, highlighting the average quantity produced in a given period of time (e.g. kg of hazardous waste per day).

Emissions, as described in Section 5.3.1.4., derive from the harmful substances released primarily into the air as a consequence of transportation and production activities, as well as onto the land and into the water. The calculation of these emissions will be extensively addressed in Chapter 6. Given the wide number of sources of this kind of waste (i.e. transportation and production activities, as well as the items entering the production process as input or leaving it as output), it is difficult to split the total amount of emissions generated by a manufacturing plant into the individual steps of the production process. However, because of the high polluting potential of this waste, the total amount of emissions (possibly split at least between two macro groups, i.e., transportation and production activities) is one of the most widely reported environmental metrics in manufacturing companies.

As far as *noise* is concerned, it must be measured from an external perspective, so as to understand the level of disturbance that the company's facilities produce on the outer environment and its inhabitants. Furthermore, because some production activities are inherently noisy (such as some moulding processes), the number of dB reached in each department of the shop floor must be measured in order to enable the proper use of ear-protecting devices. The noise specific to each production step can be reported in the data boxes of the value stream in terms of average dB produced.

Finally, *land contamination* (in relation to land use) can be reported in value stream maps in terms of the size of the manufacturing facilities (e.g. square metres occupied), which can be split into the different departments and warehouses.

Once the 'as-is' value stream map has been drawn up and the different kinds of waste highlighted, it is possible to start thinking of a possible 'future state' (or 'to-be'), identifying the tools and managerial practices suitable for improving current performance. In this regard, the lean toolkit is a useful starting point, providing managers with a wide variety of solutions likely to bring about sound improvements, enabling the implementation of a *pull* production system, where transformation and distribution activities are carried out only when an actual order from the (internal or external) client is received. A pull production system is a key lever to achieve a higher degree of sustainability, especially from the environmental viewpoint. Indeed, when products are manufactured only when an actual order is received, those types of waste as *excess inventory* and *waiting* are eliminated (or at least sharply reduced), as well as the *defects* due to the physical obsolescence of some products stored in the warehouses. Furthermore, as will be explained later in this Chapter, the enabling factors of a pull production approach refer to several operating conditions, all of which can produce beneficial outcomes on the other types of waste and on the environmental and social sustainability of the production system.

5.3.2.2   *Lay-Out Re-Design and Balancing*

In order to achieve a pull production system it is necessary to be endowed with flexible production resources. Therefore, where necessary, it is important to be able to supplement the manpower used in a production line with other employees, thus enabling production capacity to be increased quickly, and vice-versa. Highly flexible employees are needed in order to achieve this, namely employees capable of performing a high number of different operations so that tasks within a production line may be easily reallocated.

To achieve a high level of workforce flexibility, companies must set up training programmes for production-related employees with the aim of enriching and enlarging skills so that they can carry out a wide range of tasks. This is often done by launching job rotation programmes. Furthermore, it is necessary to rethink the layout of the production line, in order to place the machines in the best position to allow for

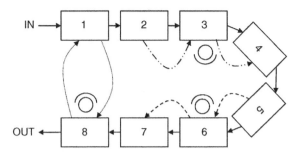

FIGURE 5.3   U-shape production line.

the reallocation of tasks. The layout that best satisfies this requirement is a 'U-shape' production line, shown in Figure 5.3.

The advantage of this type of layout consists in the fact that the various employees work in close contact with one another, thus facilitating a reciprocal learning process and the broadening of skills.

Therefore, if, for example, it is necessary to produce a lower quantity of output due to a downturn in demand, it is possible to reduce the number of workers on the production line, broadening the tasks of those that remain. The example in Figure 5.3 depicts a situation in which three workers perform the tasks in a production line made up of eight workstations.

Furthermore, the U-shape layout in general implies that each production line specialises in a product (or family of products), in order to simplify the materials management processes and minimise setups, which have a negative impact on the pace of production. This type of layout, combined with the specialisation of production lines per type of product, is also known as *cellular manufacturing*.

The adoption of this approach may expose the company to the risk of excessive variability in demand and therefore to obvious difficulty in managing the production capacity of its departments. In order to overcome this difficulty, it is necessary to level out production at the workstation further downstream (i.e. at the workstation where the last manufacturing step is carried out) because it 'pulls' the other departments and affects their workload. This involves the drawing up of a production plan that, on the basis of the total volumes to be manufactured, levels out production on a daily basis. Daily production, in addition, is planned using the so-called *mixed model* approach.

In order to understand the rationale behind mixed model scheduling, suppose that a company has to produce a total of 100 units in the next month. Suppose also that the company will manufacture only three different types of finished product (A, B, C) and that the overall sales will be divided up as follows: A 50%, B 25%, C 25%. The application of the *mixed model* approach, in this case, would mean planning the production of these three articles on a daily basis as follows: A, B, A, C. In other words, every day the company will produce a mix that corresponds with demand. Furthermore, the decision to not manufacture the two units of A in a single batch keeps the company from accumulating stock.

(a)

Models	Weeks						
	1	2	3	4	5	6	Total
A	100			100			200
B		50			50		100
C			50			50	100
Total	100	50	50	100	50	50	400

(b)

Models	Weeks						
	1	2	3	4	5	6	Total
A	33	33	33	33	33	35	200
B	17	17	17	17	17	15	100
C	17	17	17	17	17	15	100
Total	67	67	67	67	67	65	400

FIGURE 5.4 MPS based on a fixed production batch (a) versus MPS based on the mixed model logic (b).

Mixed model scheduling creates an important benefit for the customer. Indeed, if the company frequently manufactures all the articles, it can guarantee a better response time to the market.

Furthermore, the company also benefits directly from using this scheduling method. If it were to manufacture products according to the traditional method, which involves large production batches, it would accumulate a significant amount of stock of finished products, which in turn causes various types of waste.

On the contrary, by producing a mix that corresponds with demand, stock levels are kept under control.

Figure 5.4 compares a Master Production Schedule (MPS) drawn up using the mixed model logic with an MPS drawn up (under the same conditions) using the traditional logic of large batches.

The production pace of a factory able to fully leverage this approach is expressed by the so-called *takt-time*, calculated as follows:

$$Takt\,Time = \frac{Available\,Production\,Time\,per\,day}{Daily\,Sales}$$

This scheduling method exclusively involves the department that is the furthest downstream in the entire manufacturing process. In the upstream ones, the *kanban system* is used, illustrated in Section 5.3.2.3.

Last, it should be considered that in order to implement the *mixed model* approach it is necessary to enjoy quick setup times for the equipment and machinery, since this scheduling system involves a much higher number of change-overs. This issue will be discussed in Section 5.3.2.4.

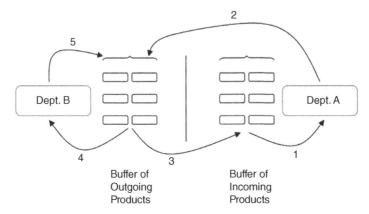

FIGURE 5.5 Kanban system: An example.

5.3.2.3 The Kanban System The *kanban* (a Japanese word whose meaning is *card*) is the scheduling system peculiar to just-in-time environments, which enables the implementation of a pull production approach in the upstream departments of a factory. According to this system, each department may start producing an item only if the department downstream requests the manufacturing of a certain number pieces of that specific product. This 'pull' method is put into practice with the use of *kanbans*, which are divided into two main categories:

1. *Withdrawal kanban:* it requires the transfer of a set of items, which can be placed inside a standard bin, from the buffer of outgoing products of a department to the buffer of incoming products of another department.
2. *Production kanban:* it requires the production of a bin of items, in order to replenish the materials that have been moved downstream.

In order to understand how the kanban system triggers the information flow between the different departments pulling their production activities, please refer to Figure 5.5.

The system is divided into the following phases:

1. A worker in the department downstream (A), having received the order to manufacture a certain quantity of an item, picks a standard bin from the buffer of incoming goods (where the components that represent the input of the operation carried out in A are stored), which in this phase holds a *withdrawal kanban*.
2. The worker, after having used all the items in the bin, removes the *withdrawal kanban* from the bin, which is taken to the buffer of outgoing goods of department B.
3. The *withdrawal kanban*, at this point, is placed in a new full bin (located in the buffer of outgoing products of department B), from which the *production kanban* is removed; now, this bin can be transferred from the buffer of outgoing products of department B to the buffer of department A.

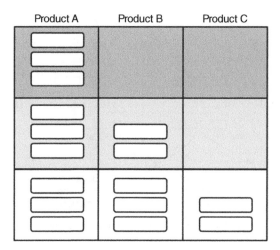

FIGURE 5.6   Kanban board.

4. The *production kanban* (which in the previous phase was removed from the full bin) is placed in a kanban board; in this way the workers in department B are informed of the need to manufacture the semi-finished products in order to replenish the buffer of outgoing goods with the same quantity that has just been transferred (namely, one bin).

5. Once the semi-finished products have been manufactured and a new bin has been filled, a *production kanban* is removed from the board and placed in the bin, which is then transferred to the buffer of outgoing goods of department B.

In the majority of cases each department is in charge of producing numerous items and therefore the *production kanbans* for different products are placed on the same board. Workers must therefore be able to quickly understand which item to prioritise. In order to simplify this activity, the boards are made in such a way as to visually guide the actions of the worker. In fact, the boards are generally divided into several columns, each one for a specific item, and with different colours associated with a given degree of urgency. For example, in Figure 5.6, it is envisaged that the department manufactures three items (1, 2, 3) and therefore the board is divided into the same number of columns.

Each column is divided into three areas characterised by different colours with increasing levels of urgency. This means that if the worker has to decide what to manufacture, he/she must opt for product 1, which has accumulated a number of *kanbans* that have reached the area of maximum urgency.

In practice, the presence of a certain number of *kanbans* for item 1 on the board indicates that the same number of bins full of item 1 have been taken from the outgoing goods buffer of the department in question and moved to the production centre downstream. This means that the buffer is being emptied and therefore must be replenished.

It is apparent that production activities in the *kanban* system are managed according to a pull logic, since each department is allowed to manufacture a product only if requested by a production centre downstream.

5.3.2.4 Setup Time Reduction   As already highlighted in the previous section, an essential condition for achieving a pull production system is the reduction of setup times. This determines two important benefits, linked to the possibility of reducing the batch size and of improving the degree of saturation of the production capacity.

The total setup time can be reduced using two different methods. The first consists in the reduction of the total number of change-overs carried out in a certain time interval, designing modular products. If, in fact, the degree of variety is reduced during the design phase, and especially the number of components, a lower degree of mix flexibility will be required in the production process.

The second method consists in dealing with the unit setup time, trying to reduce the interval during which the machine is idle due to preparations for the manufacture of a new item. In this case, if a certain mix of products is to be manufactured, the goal is to keep the time during which the equipment is idle and unproductive due to setup operations as low as possible. In this regard it is to be remembered that the setup of equipment can be divided into two components:

1. *Internal setup*: it refers to preparatory operations for the production of a new item, which are performed when the machine is idle.
2. *External setup*: it is the set of activities that can be carried out while the machine is working.

Therefore, organisational and technical solutions that limit the number of internal setup operations must be found, possibly increasing the weight of external setup activities. The techniques employed to reduce the unit setup time are generally called SMED, namely *Single Minute Exchange of Die*. If these actions enable the unit setup time to be reduced in such a way as to make it substantially irrelevant, it is possible to manufacture goods according to the so-called *one-piece-flow* principle, namely by manufacturing, if necessary, a sequence of products that differ from one another, as may be requested in a *mixed model* production line.

5.3.2.5 Total Productive Maintenance   One of the enabling factors of a pull production system is the full *availability* of equipment, necessary for guaranteeing a reliable production flow that is constantly able to meet demand from the perspective of both time and quantities. This condition may be compromised by the occurrence of downtimes and the subsequent maintenance activity.

Total Productive Maintenance (TPM) is an approach aimed at maximising the availability of equipment using maintenance plans based on the principle of prevention and the delegation of ordinary maintenance to the workers controlling the equipment (Nakajima, 1988). This approach, which became popular starting from the end of the 1980s, is particularly widespread in industrial environments in which production is managed using a *just in time* approach, where the possibility to respond

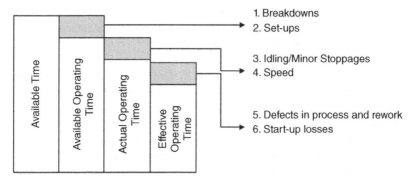

FIGURE 5.7 Deployment of machine downtime in the OEE calculation. *Source:* Muchiri 2008. Reproduced with permission of Taylor & Francis.

quickly to market demand without drawing on stocks of finished and semi-finished products requires equipment to be highly reliable, namely by substantially eliminating downtime due to breakdowns and unplanned maintenance.

In order to assess the efficiency of the implementation of the TPM techniques, the indicator called the Overall Equipment Effectiveness (OEE) is calculated.

From a formal point of view, this requires the availability of data on the operating conditions of the equipment, which can be described as in Figure 5.7.

Looking back at Figure 5.7, the calculation of the OEE first of all requires the determination of the *available time*, namely the time (normally measured in number of hours) during which the equipment could have been operative in the period in question, taking into account the work calendar of the factory and its daily hours of operation. Nevertheless, during the aforesaid available time the equipment may remain idle or may not be producing according to the standard pace or, even, may be manufacturing products that cannot be sold due to defects (Muchiri et al., 2008; Nakajima, 1988). Along these lines, it is possible to identify six main 'losses' that have an impact on the performance of equipment, namely:

1. *Breakdowns*, due to malfunctioning and subsequent maintenance activities, whose duration depends on the effectiveness of such interventions, especially if managed using prevention logics.
2. *Setups*, which refer to the change-overs that make it possible to produce a mix of different products on one machine.
3. *Idling/minor stoppages*, due mainly to temporary, short-term malfunctions caused by errors in managing the machine, which in any case affect production pace.
4. *Speed*, whose reduction occurs when the actual production time exceeds the standard time, that is, the amount of time required on average for a machine that is working and maintained properly to carry out the envisaged operation.
5. *Defects in process and rework*, due to the production of non-conforming products.

6. *Start-up losses*, which consist in the production of lower quantities than the nominal value expected from the process, or due to defects that are discovered once production has started, for example after a change of shift.

As shown in Figure 5.7, these losses can ideally be divided into three categories. The first is influenced by the effectiveness of maintenance programmes; the second expresses the effectiveness of the production activities in the strict sense; the third one refers to quality management.

Starting with this classification of time, the OEE can be obtained as a product of the three indices, namely:

$$OEE = A \times \eta \times Qr$$

where:

$$A = \frac{Available\ Operating\ Time}{Available\ Time}$$

$$\eta = \frac{Actual\ Operating\ Time}{Available\ Operating\ Time}$$

$$Qr = \frac{Effective\ Operating\ Time}{Actual\ Operating\ Time}$$

The OEE value obtained in this way expresses the percentage of hours during which the equipment has been in operation (A, i.e. availability), guaranteeing the expected speed (η, i.e. efficiency), and quality standards (Qr, i.e. quality rate), compared to the available time. As a result, low values of this indicator highlight the need to take action in order to reduce the 'losses' illustrated previously, attempting to identify and remove any problems in the system.

5.3.2.6   5S   The expression *5S* refers to a bundle of principles that eliminates waste and improves productivity based on the correct organisation of workplaces. This system originates from the observation that many errors, inefficiencies and also accidents involving employees are caused by objects or materials that should not be in the workstation, the irrational and disorganised arrangement of what, on the other hand, is required in order to perform value-added operations and, more generally, the absence of standardised routines that enable workers to work quickly, safely and efficiently.

In order to achieve the latter result, the 5S methods suggest the following path of improvement:

1. *Sort (seiri)*: this activity is aimed at eliminating everything that is irrelevant to the performance of the production activities from the workplace, through the correct description of the work and the identification of the input materials and equipment to be used.
2. *Set in order (seiton)*: the materials and equipment chosen in the previous activity must be arranged and organised in such a way that they can be easily

detected, in order to avoid waiting and motion waste. This result is often achieved through the creation of shaped tables that hold the components to be assembled, with which it is possible, on the one hand, to check that the kit necessary for the completion of the manufacturing is complete and, on the other hand, to quickly identify the pieces to be used each time. Similar solutions, based on *visual management*, are used to organise equipment.

3. *Shine (seiso)*: keeping the workplace clean is necessary in order to prevent breakdowns and the malfunctioning of the equipment, accidents in the workplace and defects in the product that may be caused by contamination or contact with substances and materials, such as oil, chips, dust and so on.

4. *Standardise (seiketsu)*: this principle concerns the need to identify standard working procedures, to be applied repetitively in order to guarantee high levels of efficiency.

5. *Sustain (shitsuke)*: finally, it is necessary to sustain excellent practices for organising the workplaces and the performance of production activities, in order to guarantee the consolidation of new procedures and the benefits that these bring.

The 5S method is widely used in all organisations that intend to adopt lean management principles. Its implementation in fact requires a modest allocation of resources, but produces quick, significant results related to the effectiveness of machinery, quality rates in products, downtime due to defects, accidents and the amount of space occupied by production departments. This set of benefits ensures that the use of the 5S method is often a necessary condition to the implementation of more sophisticated practices, in particular Total Productive Maintenance.

5.4   LEVERAGING SIX-SIGMA FOR A SUSTAINABLE PRODUCTION

Six Sigma is a quality management methodology that became popular in the 1990s through the success experienced in large international firms, like Motorola, General Electric and Honeywell, which widely demonstrated the positive effects they had on a number of operational and economic performance factors. The distinctive features of this methodology, grounded in the stream of quality management studies and initially being considered an evolution of Total Quality Management, are its focus on measurement, which is necessary for launching improvement projects, its search for perfection, regarded as the ability to fully meet customer needs and, finally, the importance it gives to change management practices as a lever for lasting improvement. An exhaustive definition of Six Sigma, which encompasses this variety of features, is given by Pande et al. (2000, p. xi):

A comprehensive and flexible system for achieving, sustaining and maximising business success. Six Sigma is uniquely driven by close understanding of customer needs, disciplined use of facts, data, and statistical analysis, and diligent attention to managing, improving, and reinventing business processes.

In order to understand the goals and tools that are characteristic of Six Sigma and the reasons why this methodology can lead to sound improvements of manufacturing processes, it is worth briefly underlining the main contributions to the field of quality management. In fact there is a wide range of literature on the subject, linked to the work of many authors who, by studying the various aspects of this phenomenon in depth, have come up with a variety of definitions of the term 'quality' and of solutions suitable for improving it. From the various definitions offered, the most significant are the following:

- *Conformance to requirements* (Crosby, 1984a).
- *Predictable degree of uniformity and dependability with a quality standard suited to the customer* (Deming, 1986).
- *The total composite product and service characteristics of marketing, engineering, manufacturing, and maintenance through which the product and service in use will meet the expectations of the customer* (Feigenbaum, 1991).
- *Fitness for use* (Juran, 1988).
- *Meeting customer requirements* (Ishikawa, 1985).
- *(Un)quality, as the set of losses incurred by the community when the product leaves the factory* (Taguchi, 1986).

Each of these definitions highlights different quality features, starting with the approach of Crosby, which is more restrictive and focused only on technical and production aspects, and arriving at the definitions provided by Ishikawa and Taguchi, who, in order to define the phenomenon in question, use the concepts of 'customer satisfaction' and the 'loss incurred by the community' due to shortcomings in product quality.

In manufacturing, however, the main approach to quality management and improvement is based on Crosby's proposal, which best highlights the real contribution made by industrial transformation processes to the manufacturing of a product capable of guaranteeing high performance levels and customer satisfaction.

In an industrial production system, in fact, the role of operations consists of making products that conform to specification limits, whose effectiveness depends on the actions of a large number of organisational units involved in the new product development process, and in particular Marketing, Design and Engineering, which are responsible for market analysis, the identification of the needs of target customers and the transformation of the latter into technical requirements. Consistent with Crosby's approach, based on the concept of conformance, a product is considered defective if, taking a certain feature into consideration, the corresponding value observed for the individual unit of product does not fall within the interval of tolerance envisaged in the project. In this regard, refer to Figure 5.8, which shows the case of one feature measurable in centimetres, with a nominal value of 100 and interval of tolerance ± 1.

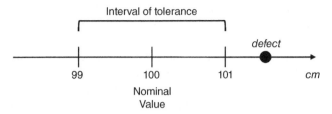

FIGURE 5.8 Conformance to specification limits: An example.

By adopting this perspective, a synthetic indicator of the product quality along the production line is represented by the First Time Pass Yield Rate, which expresses the percentage of compliant products out of the total number of manufactured items:

$$First\ Time\ Pass\ Yield\ Rate = \frac{Number\ of\ conformant\ products}{Total\ production\ volumes}$$

Starting from the 1980s, the growth in popularity of management philosophies and practices specifically focusing on the subject of quality, or in the context of which quality plays a crucial role (e.g. Total Quality Management, first of all, and then Lean Management and Six Sigma itself), determined a greater attention toward the prevention of defects. In particular, Six Sigma, even though suitable for a wide range of business processes, is mainly applied to product quality improvement projects, in order to prevent defects through the continuous reduction of variability in manufacturing processes. This leads to measuring conformance in 'ppm', that is, parts per million (Pande et al., 2000), since in a Six Sigma environment the amount of scraps is so low that an indicator expressed as a percentage would be no longer adequate. In these cases the output of manufacturing processes has a very low variability rate compared to the nominal value (for each feature of the product). In particular, according to Six Sigma principles, perfection is reached when the interval of tolerance may contain six times the *sigma* (i.e. the standard deviation) of a process. In these cases, assuming a normal distribution of the values observed in relation to a given feature, the defects are 3.4 ppm and the conformity rate, if expressed as a percentage, would be 99.9997%. Table 5.3 shows the conversion of the various sigma levels (namely the size of the interval of tolerance expressed in multiples of the sigma identified in the process), as well as the related conformance rates and ppm.

In order to reduce variability in manufacturing processes, Six Sigma proposes the use of an improvement process called DMAIC, managed by an ad hoc team (generally with a minimum of five and a maximum of ten members) and divided into the following phases:

- *Define (D)*: in this phase the problem is identified by defining its scope, nature and size, in order to set improvement targets.
- *Measure (M)*: concerns the need to collect all data necessary for calculating indicators to be used to quantify the current performance of the process and the improvement target.

TABLE 5.3   Relationship between conformity, ppm and sigma

Sigma	Conformance rate	PPM
1	30.9%	690,000
2	69.2%	308,000
3	93.3%	66,800
4	99.4%	6210
5	99.98%	320
6	99.9997%	3.4

- *Analyse (A)*: in this phase the data collected is analysed using tools that highlight forms of variability or trends considered critical and that identify the main causes thereof. To this end, Six Sigma proposes the use of a number of tools mainly borrowed from Statistical Process Control and illustrated in Section 5.4.1. In this phase, the Design of Experiments (DOE) method is widely used, a statistical technique for planning experiments capable of identifying the external and internal factors of a process that produce the main forms of variability in its performance, the weight of each of these factors and, finally, the mathematical model that expresses the relationship between each parameter and the observed area of performance.
- *Improve (I)*: to achieve improvement targets, it is necessary to use different tools and approaches that are appropriate for the observed environment, depending on the nature of the problem and the type of process involved. Often these tools are those used in Lean Management.
- *Control (C)*: after having implemented the improvement plan, or at the end of relevant phases of the project, the team must evaluate the achieved results by analysing the indicators defined in the second phase of the DMAIC process, in order to enable a feedback mechanism aimed at undertaking new corrective measures in the case where significant gaps are discovered between targets and results.

A characteristic feature of Six Sigma is the identification of specific people in charge of the management of improvement plans. Depending on the degree of training and responsibility, a distinction can be made between:

- *Green Belts*: usually people that perform their normal functional activities and are also involved in Six Sigma projects.
- *Black Belts*: people dedicated full-time to the management and implementation of Six Sigma projects, under the coordination of Master Black Belts.
- *Master Black Belts*: their role consists mainly of identifying new improvement areas, proposing Six Sigma projects in line with targets and monitoring those in progress.

Today, Six Sigma is considered to be an approach suitable for achieving more sustainable manufacturing processes since, enabling scrap rates to be minimised, it helps in coping with the waste associated with this phenomenon, as already illustrated in earlier sections of this Chapter. Furthermore, this approach, focusing on continuous improvement, may be a roadmap for enhancing environmental performance, as has occurred in a number of cases, mainly related to the reduction of greenhouse gases (Souza, 2012; Olson, 2010). For this kind of applications, the expression Green Six Sigma has been used (Olson, 2010), to highlight the relevance of this approach, especially in environmental performance improvement strategies.

5.4.1 Six Sigma and Statistical Process Control

The popularity of the Six Sigma approach in recent years has led to a renewed interest in the Statistical Process Control. Statistical Process Control (SPC) is based on the work of Shewhart (1931), which was conducted at the Bell Laboratories, and is directed at the identification of 'out-of-control' manufacturing processes, namely those that produce items with values that deviate from the tolerances envisaged during the design phase. During the Second World War these techniques were used by US industry to guarantee adequate quality standards for military equipment and, subsequently, were adopted in civil environments in many Japanese companies, which based their success also on an innovative approach to quality management (Dale et al., 2013).

SPC, in particular, aims at guaranteeing the control of manufacturing processes using statistical tools, which provide managers with useful information for planning actions to reduce variability (Dale et al., 2013; Oakland, 2008). The deviation between actual and nominal values, in fact, may be caused by various factors. In some cases, it is the input that produces different outcomes of a transformation process. Take, for example, food production (like wine or olive oil), in which the characteristics of the raw materials can be influenced by the environmental and climatic conditions of the place of harvest, among other factors, which can lead to significant variations of the yield.

Further causes of variability are due to the equipment used in the manufacturing processes. Sometimes, an inadequate maintenance programme, or even a simple problem related to the cleaning of a machine, may produce differences in the characteristics of the goods produced. Take, for example, processes for dyeing clothing, in which improper cleaning of the machine when moving from one batch to the next may produce contaminations that compromise colour. Obviously, malfunctioning of a machine can be a reason for high variability.

Sometimes, the variability in the process is caused by the lack of skill of the operator and degree of experience, as well as working conditions. If the workplace is badly illuminated, non-ergonomic or lacks the materials and tools that the worker needs to perform the manufacturing activities properly, the stability of the process will tend to be reduced, as well as its conformance rates.

High variability is a pathology that the company must try to eliminate, or at least reduce. For this purpose, it is appropriate to use a set of tools based on statistical methods, which make it possible to highlight possible critical areas and to guide the company during the improvement process.

Suppose that a sample of n items manufactured in a certain period of time is subject to control and that the measurement x of a certain feature is taken (take, for example, the weight of a can, the thickness of a metal sheet etc.). The values corresponding to these measurements will be identified as follows:

$$x_1, x_2, x_3, \ldots, x_{n-1}, x_n$$

The first calculation to be made is obviously linked to the simple average of the values recorded, which makes it possible to position the performance of the process in relation to the interval of tolerance defined during the design phase. Second, in order to assess the variability of the process compared to the average, the *range* (namely the difference between the highest value and the lowest value recorded) and the *sigma* (or standard deviation) are calculated. With regard to the sample of n items being checked, the three indicators are calculated as follows:

$$\bar{x} = \frac{\sum_{i=1}^{n} x_i}{n}$$

$$R = x_{max} - x_{min}$$

$$S = \sqrt{\frac{\sum_{i=1}^{n} (x_i - \bar{x})^2}{n-1}}$$

These calculations need to be made in order to obtain the main tool of SPC, the control chart: see Figure 5.9.

The horizontal axis shows the samples according to the time sequence in which they are checked. The vertical axis, on the other hand, has the same unit of

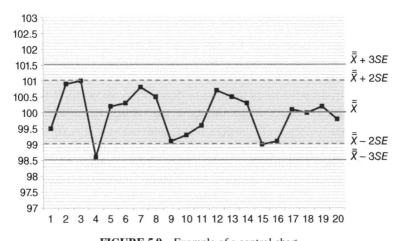

FIGURE 5.9 Example of a control chart.

measurement as the feature being observed (e.g. millimetres in the case of thickness). On this second axis, the average $\overline{\overline{X}}$ is shown (in the example in Figure 5.9, this is 100), which is calculated using the $\overline{x}$ values recorded in the k samples analysed, obtained as follows:

$$\overline{\overline{X}} = \frac{\sum_{j=1}^{k} \overline{x}_j}{k}$$

A process is considered to be under control if the $\overline{x}$ values fall within a range equal to 6 times the sigma of the observed phenomenon, centred on the average value $\overline{\overline{X}}$. Since in this case the observed data is not referred to the individual items that undergo quality control, but to the averages recorded in each sample, the sigma is replaced with the standard error, which is calculated as follows:

$$SE = \frac{s}{\sqrt{n}}$$

If the process is stable, supposing that the values are normally distributed, more than 99% of the $\overline{x}$ averages must fall within the interval equal to $\overline{\overline{X}} \pm 3SE$, with a high concentration around $\overline{\overline{X}}$. This is in line with the requirements of the Six Sigma approach, according to which a process under control is characterised by a number of defective products equal to 3.4 ppm, equivalent to 99.9997% of the volumes produced (please see Table 5.3).

In a situation such as the one shown in Figure 5.9, only one out of forty average values would fall in the area outside the interval $\overline{\overline{X}} \pm 2SE$ (Oakland, 2008). The example shown in Figure 5.9 assumes that the average value $\overline{\overline{X}}$ is 100 and SE is 0.5. Therefore, the threshold values are, respectively, 98.5 ($\overline{\overline{X}} - 3SE$), 99 ($\overline{\overline{X}} - 2SE$), 101 ($\overline{\overline{X}} + 2SE$) and 101.5 ($\overline{\overline{X}} \pm 3SE$). Thus, the data shown in Figure 5.9 represents a situation of substantial stability in the process. This example reveals the big potential of a control chart. Indeed, the probability that the average values of two consecutive samples fall outside the interval $\overline{\overline{X}} \pm 2SE$ is so low ($1/40 \times 1/40 = 1/1600$) that this event deserves attention, because it is most likely connected to a pathology of the production system.

More broadly, the presence of (positive or negative) trends or values that are systematically higher or lower than the average $\overline{\overline{X}}$, even if they fall within the interval $\overline{\overline{X}} \pm 3SE$, are clear evidence of situations that require analysis in order to check for the existence of any pathology of the system. The study of the stability level of the process is also crucial for the calculation of the process capability, which expresses the ability of a process to produce items that conform with design specifications. In this regard, suppose that the interval of tolerance is equal to $x_0 \pm \varepsilon$ for a product feature, where x_0 is the nominal value. The range of the interval of tolerance is 2ε. During the design phase, it is first of all worth checking whether the machinery used in production will be able to guarantee compliance with this tolerance, which requires that the variability range of the actual values reported during the quality control be no greater than the size of the interval 2ε. If the process is under control, with a standard deviation of σ, more than 99% of its products will fall within the interval equal to 6σ. Therefore, it is possible to guide the aforesaid check during the design phase by calculating the following process capability index (Cp):

$$Cp = 2\varepsilon/6\sigma$$

In the cases where this indicator is greater than 1, the interval of tolerance is wider than the range of variability of the process. Therefore, upon first analysis, no problems should arise during the production phase. In contrast, if the value obtained is lower than 1, it can be said that the interval of tolerance being defined during the design phase is too narrow and that, therefore, the process will be characterised by the systematic production of non-conforming items. In this regard, refer to Figure 5.10. This situation, also known as over-specification, usually leads to

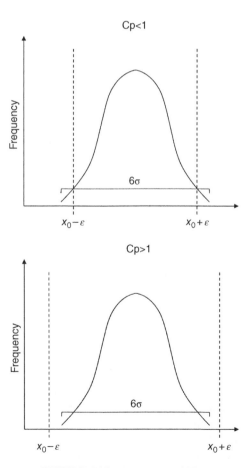

FIGURE 5.10 Process capability.

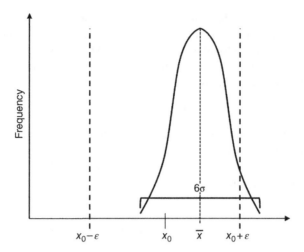

FIGURE 5.11   Process capability with off-centre processes.

unsatisfactory economic results, due to the high production cost of items characterised by tolerances that are excessively tight and whose market does not recognise
their value (Coman and Ronen, 2010).

Even when the *Cp* is greater than 1, it can still be difficult to meet design specifications if the two variability margins are centred differently, as shown in Figure 5.11.
The graph shows a situation in which the range of variability of the process (6σ) is
narrower than the interval of tolerance. Nevertheless, the output values of the process
are distributed normally with an average of $\bar{x}$, which is higher than the nominal value x_0.
Therefore, the process is more precise than required, but reports values that are distributed around an average that differs from the target.

Therefore, the *Cp* indicator cannot highlight this type of situation. It is necessary
to use a second indicator, the *Cpk*, which takes not only the variability of the process
into consideration, but also its centring. The *Cpk* of a process, in particular, is the
lower of the following two indicators:

$$Cpk_u = \frac{(x_0 + \varepsilon) - \bar{x}}{3\sigma}$$

$$Cpk_1 = \frac{\bar{x} - (x_0 + \varepsilon)}{3\sigma}$$

A *Cpk* of lower than 1 highlights the fact that the variability of the process and its
centring are such as to not allow compliance with at least one of the two extremes of
the interval of tolerance. In this case, the solution to the problem may lie not only in
reducing the variability of the process, but also in centring it differently, which sometimes can be easily achieved by regulating the equipment.

5.5 SERVITISATION AND LEASING

A way to further improve the environmental performance of a production process consists of designing the product offering of the company so as to ensure that the product will be properly used and disposed of at the end of its life cycle. This can have remarkable implications in particular on the design phase and on the recovery one, which must be supported by an effective reverse logistic process. However, the potentialities of such solutions can be further exploited if a servitisation strategy is adopted by the manufacturer. 'Servitisation' has been defined as 'the increased offering of fuller market packages or bundles of customers focussed combinations of goods, services, support, self-service and knowledge in order to add value to the core product offerings' (Vandermerwe and Rada, 1988). This strategy became popular in the late 1990s, when manufacturing companies 'went downstream' (Wise and Baumgartner, 1999) through the provision not only of physical goods, but also of a number of profitable after-sales services, as spare parts supply, maintenance and assistance activities, which are valuable for the customer especially when the product life cycle is long – for instance, home appliances or capital equipment. A further evolution of this strategy consists of the possibility to adopt new businesses models in which the ownership of the product is no longer a condition for the customer to use it, and solutions such as rental or leasing can be seen as an alternative to sale (Tukker, 2004).

The adoption of these business models can result in opportunities to improve the environmental performance of the product/service (Souza, 2012). Indeed, end-of-lease (rent) products are still functioning and can be reused as they are or through a refurbishing process. Thus, leasing companies can ensure a higher degree of exploitation of the product and of its materials and components, while in the case of sale the customer could dispose of the item, even though it (or some of its parts) could still be used. This opportunity can be further improved if the product has been designed through a modular approach, which enables an efficient disassembly and rework at the end of the leasing period. This is actually a key condition for making lease and rental environmentally sound practices. In fact, when the recovery process of a used product is complex and expensive, the company could consider it more convenient to dispose of the product rather than to refurbish and/or disassemble it, and solutions such as a premature disposal could be seen as preferable.

6

SUSTAINABILITY AND LOGISTICS, PHYSICAL DISTRIBUTION AND PACKAGING

6.1 INTRODUCTION

Nestlé is a multinational company engaged in the fast-moving consumer goods industry, which in the recent years has strived to embed the principles of Corporate Social Responsibility (CSR) in its business processes, especially in the production and distribution of mineral water.

The degree of environmental sustainability of products and processes in the mineral water industry has recently become a relevant issue. Indeed, producing and distributing water in plastic bottles involves a number of choices that, from a life cycle perspective, can produce a wide range of negative environmental impacts. Indeed, several inputs (mainly energy, oil and other raw materials) are used to manufacture plastic bottles, which, at the end of their (short) life cycle, must be disposed of or recycled. Furthermore, production and distribution activities produce several negative effects on the environment, for example, due to emissions (mainly caused by transportation) and soil contamination (caused by production activities). Local communities are also significantly affected, especially for the municipalities in which distribution hubs are located (in terms of traffic congestion and air pollution if trucks are used for distribution).

All of these problems are a reason for widespread concern among final consumers, due to the fact the people can easily drink tap water as an alternative to mineral water, thus enjoying at least two benefits. On the one hand, they can save money given that tap water is much cheaper than bottled water and, on the other hand, they can contribute to the reduction of the negative environmental impacts caused by mineral water during its life cycle.

In order to cope with the threats that are emerging from the recent concerns about the actual benefits of the mineral water and its environmental sustainability, Nestlé has started investing in its own sustainability model, which is based on three pillars:

1. Health.
2. Quality.
3. Environment.

With regard to the first aspect, the company is working on the concept of 'hydration', which is the primary reason for water consumption. Nestlé is invest-ing in R&D activities and in scientific initiatives in order to improve its product and its capabilities in this field of research by taking part in scientific committees, clinical trials and medical conferences, and so on.

As far as the second aspect is concerned, Nestlé is striving to enhance the quality of its mineral water through a strict control of all the steps in the produc-tion process. In this regard, major importance is attached to the sourcing process, and namely to the selection of springs where specific tastes and mineral char-acteristics can be obtained. In the manufacturing process, social sustainability is pursued in Nestlé factories through compliance with international standards (such as ISO 18001 and OHSAS). Furthermore, the selection of the treatments that the product can undergo is a major concern. Indeed, while chemical treat-ments are avoided to preserve water's purity, some physical ones are used in order to improve it (e.g. microfiltration).

From the perspective of the environment, Nestlé is working on the concept of life-cycle assessment, in order to identify and address all the forms of envi-ronmental impact of bottled mineral water. Since a major part of these effects originate from the use of plastic bottles, it has invested in R&D activities aimed at reducing the plastic necessary to package and transport water. In fact, in just a few years the company has been able to cut the packaging weight per litre pro-duced by 26%. Furthermore, the plastic bottle is now 100% recyclable, it uses labels that are 30% smaller than its competitors and requires 30% less plastic than average half-litre bottles. In addition, it is more flexible, thus making it easier to crush for recycling.

Of course, another major issue concerning the environmental impact of min-eral water is transportation. On the one hand, the production of mineral water (in terms of location and of number of factories) is limited by the availability of springs managed by the company. On the other hand, the distribution of the product is generally on a national basis, which makes it necessary to move a bottle of mineral water over long distances in order to reach its final destination. In this regard, Nestlé has undertaken a number of initiatives in order to reduce the carbon footprint of transportation. First of all, it has strived to produce mineral water closer to the customer, through the use of new springs, thus reducing the average distance to be covered for the delivery of the product. Furthermore, multimodal transport solutions have been adopted, and when road transportation is used, longer trucks are employed. In order to reduce the number of deliveries, better pricing terms are offered to clients who place large orders. Finally, the migration toward less polluting technologies, as Euro 5 vehicles, has also been encouraged.

Source: www.supplychainworld.com, viewed 1 March 2016.

Logistics and physical distribution are a major area of concern for companies willing to improve their social and environmental performance. As demonstrated by the case history of Nestlé, the solutions that an organisation can adopt to achieve this result are numerous and involve a wide range of choices concerning the delivery process: from the design of the supply chain and the selection of the most environmentally sound mode of transport to 'green' packing – to mention a few.

In the remainder of this Chapter the contribution of logistics and physical distribution to social and environmental sustainability will be outlined, as well as the main technical and managerial solutions that can be adopted to improve this performance area.

6.2   SOCIAL AND ENVIRONMENTAL ASPECTS IN LOGISTICS AND PHYSICAL DISTRIBUTION

In the past few decades transportation and logistics have had a significant impact on both social and environmental sustainability. Whether they involve the transportation of humans to and from their destination or the shipping of goods and materials, transportation and logistics need to be considered as waste due to the substantial negative effects they have on the environment and on people's well-being.

On a macro-economic level, the economic impact of logistics varies significantly, mainly due to the degree of efficiency with which these activities are managed. In this respect, it is worth noting how logistics costs represent approximately 11% of the Gross Domestic Product of the United States and Europe, whereas this figure reaches 14% in Latin America (Rushton et al., 2014). If we look at national data, the variability in these costs is even more accentuated. For example, in Germany the percentage is significantly lower at 10%, but the impact of logistics costs on the GDP of India and China stands at 17 and 21%, respectively. Improvements in physical distribution management practices, such as in the infrastructures and vehicles used, therefore, produce levels of efficiency that result in lower logistics costs. This is also apparent if the trend of this indicator is analysed over time. In fact, average values stood at approximately 20% even in the more developed countries until the 1980s, a period in which more sophisticated management practices became more common, thus improving the performance of logistics processes.

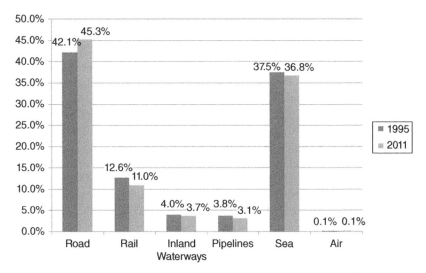

FIGURE 6.1   Transport of goods by mode in EU27, 1995–2011. *Source:* Nicodeme 2012. Reproduced with permission of European Union Road Federation.

Even if, on the whole, the efficiency of physical distribution is constantly improving, it continues to be a significant source of social and environmental risks, in particular. It must, in fact, be noted that the largest part of logistics costs is related to transportation. In Europe, the latter amounts to 40% of total physical distribution costs, whereas in the United States this figure rises to 49% due to greater distances (Rushton et al., 2014). Furthermore, the quantity of transported freight, although a function of economic cycles, has progressively increased. For instance, the total volumes transported in the European Union in the period 1995–2011 increased by 25%, maintaining the mix of transportation modes unchanged, as can be seen in Figure 6.1 (European Union Road Federation, 2013).

In recent years the logistics sector has benefitted considerably from technological innovation in vehicles, which has enabled several environmental performance areas to be improved, as demonstrated by the data on the production of the following polluting substances (EUROSTAT data, 2000–2013, EU 28 Countries):

- Emissions of nitrogen oxides (NO_x) from non-road transport: –27%.
- Emissions of nitrogen oxides (NO_x) from road transport: –44%.
- Emissions of particulate matter from non-road transport: –39%.
- Emissions of particulate matter from road transport: –45%.

These rates of change, only partially justified by the decrease in GDP in recent years, are the result of improvements in vehicle technology, which have significantly reduced consumption and polluting potential. Nevertheless, the need to monitor logistics more strictly within the context of a wider strategy of sustainability (not only corporate sustainability) emerges from the analysis of the data on the impact of transport on the total Greenhouse Gases (GHG) that, in the period 2000–2013, went from 17 to 19% (EUROSTAT data). A physical distribution management process aimed at the improvement of its environmental standards can, therefore, significantly reduce the damaging effects of atmospheric pollution on a global level (above all global warming), on a regional level (in particular, acid rain and photochemical smog) and on a local level (due to the various damaging effects of GHG on the health of local communities if high levels of such gases are reported).

The physical distribution of freight, and in particular transportation, causes other damaging effects, such as noise pollution (discussed in Chapter 5), the vibrations produced from vehicle transit, capable of causing structural damage to buildings, and traffic congestion, which in turn contributes to the worsening of the environmental performance of transportation. Furthermore, it must be noted that traffic intensity, together with the safety standards of the vehicles used, contributes to the number of traffic accidents and their victims. In reality, the trends recorded in this regard are broadly positive, due in particular to road system improvements in many countries and innovation in vehicle technology, which have increased safety levels. In the period 2000–2013, for example, there was a significant decrease in the number of people killed in road accidents in Europe, and in particular in Spain (–71%), Portugal (–66%) and Italy (–52%), whereas the lowest figure recorded was in Romania, which saw the number of victims of road traffic accidents reduced by 25% in the same period (EUROSTAT data).

Despite significant improvements, traffic congestion must continue to be monitored, and with this the need to reduce the circulation of vehicles used to transport goods, due to the fact that the number of deaths caused by road accidents in absolute terms remains high. For example, on a European level approximately 17,000 people were killed in road accidents in 2013 in the 20 countries in which this data was available (EUROSTAT data).

The numerous environmental and social effects associated with logistics highlight the need to take this performance area into consideration in the design and management of the physical distribution process, although these are traditionally driven by decisions related to cost and customer service. The main approaches and tools that can be used to do so will be illustrated in the following sections.

6.3   PHYSICAL DISTRIBUTION AND SUSTAINABILITY: A REFERENCE FRAMEWORK

Specialist literature has provided various definitions of the concept of physical distribution, with contributions that aim to highlight the different components of this process. The most well-known definitions are given below by way of example:

1. *Logistics represents the storage and flows from the final production point through to the customer or end user* (Rushton et al., 2014).

2. *Logistics is ... the management of all activities which facilitate movement and coordination of supply and demand in the creation of time and place utility* (Hesket et al., 1973).
3. *Logistics is ... the process of planning, implementing, and controlling procedures for the efficient and effective transportation and storage of goods including services, and related information from the point of origin to the point of consumption for the purpose of conforming to customer requirements* (CSCMP, 2013).
4. *Logistics is ... the process of planning, implementing and controlling the efficient, cost effective flow and storage of raw materials, in-process inventory, finished foods, and related information flow from point-of-origin to point-of-consumption for the purpose of conforming to customer requirements* (Council of Logistics Management, 1986).
5. *Logistics is the process of strategically managing the procurement, movement and storage of materials, parts and finished products (and the related information flow) through the organization and its marketing channels in such a way that current and future profitability are maximized through the cost-effective fulfilment orders* (Christopher, 2010).

These definitions highlight the main characteristics of logistics. First of all, the idea of a physical flow and an information flow as peculiar features of logistics processes are recurrent themes. Second, these definitions – although with varying levels of intensity – dwell on the performance areas that design and management of logistics are expected to guarantee, and in particular cost-effectiveness and service where the latter is understood as the ability to meet the requirements of the customer in terms of quantities, and times and places of delivery. One aspect that, on the other hand, distinguishes the various definitions concerns the scope of logistics, which ranges from the storage and transportation of finished products to all the stages along the life cycle of the product, from the supply of raw materials and components to waste management using reverse logistics processes.

In this Chapter, physical distribution will be analysed from the perspective closest to the definition proposed by Rushton et al. (2014), with a focus on the storage and transportation of finished products alone, which require the arrangement of a process for the delivery of the goods into the hands of the customer. Therefore, this Chapter will exclude reverse logistics (addressed in Chapter 7) from the scope of the physical distribution process, as well as inbound logistics and materials management, which concern the storage and flows of materials into and through the production process (addressed in Chapters 4 and 5). In view of this definition, it is therefore possible to say that the key elements of physical distribution are the following (Rushton et al., 2014):

- *Storage, warehousing and materials handling*: designing and managing this element of the physical distribution raise problems concerning, among other things, the number of warehouses, their size and location, the type of equipment to use.
- *Inventory*: it concerns decisions regarding how much should be stocked, where inventory should be held (e.g. in a central warehouse rather than in local distribution centers) and which items should be stocked.

- *Transport*: it relates to such problems as the choice of the most appropriate mode of transport, the type of delivery operations, load planning and route scheduling.
- *Packaging*: this element concerns such problems as the choice of the primary and secondary packaging, which can influence, among the others, the choice of the materials handling equipment.
- *Information and control*: this element mainly refers to the design of effective control systems, suitable for enabling a feedback and feed-forward control process.

It is evident that the number of the components of physical distribution and their complexity require a design process that ensures that the performance expected from the process in question is consistent with the configuration of the latter. The physical distribution process is designed using a complex framework, which is usually associated with the stages shown in Figure 6.2.

The physical distribution process acts as an interface between the company and the market, facilitating the identification of a series of relevant performance profiles attributable to the broader concept of 'logistic service', which is an important growth and profitability driver, especially in the sectors subject to product commoditisation (Lambert and Burduroglu, 2000). It follows that the first step of this process concerns strategic choices, which are related to the customer service level that the company seeks to ensure and refers to the following aspects in particular (Rushton et al., 2014; Frazelle, 2002):

- Speed and dependability of the delivery.
- Availability and completeness of the order.
- Order accuracy, in terms of damaged materials and returns from customers.

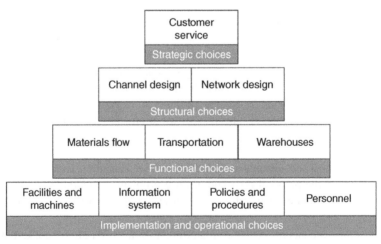

FIGURE 6.2 The design of the physical distribution process. *Source:* Copacino 1997. Reproduced with permission of Taylor & Francis.

The first component of logistic service is related to time performance, which became increasingly important starting from the 1990s, not only with regard to the new product development process, but also with reference to the management of the processes concerning the physical distribution of goods (Blackburn, 1991). The second profile is, in fact, a complement to the first, since on-time delivery requires the physical availability of a sufficient quantity of products in order to guarantee fast and complete shipments, especially in companies managed according to the make-to-stock approach. Finally, the third level of assessment is connected to the 'quality' of the delivery, in terms of physical integrity of the product and of completeness and correctness of the administrative, shipping and transportation procedures (Christopher, 2005; Frazelle, 2002).

The choices regarding the level of logistic service have considerable implications on the choices regarding the structural aspects of the physical distribution process, namely the distribution channels and the organisation of the logistic network. The latter, in particular, has significant repercussions on the level of service and on the environmental footprint of the delivery process, which will be illustrated in more detail in this section. Logistic network choices, in fact, mainly concern the number and location of warehouses and depots that goods must pass through in order to reach the customer, as well as the distinction between transit points and facilities to be used to store the products. These decisions are then implemented through functional choices, which are related to the management of warehouses, transportation and the physical flow of goods, and involve operational choices regarding the technical solutions to be used (such as the degree of automation of the warehouses and the types of vehicles used for transportation), the IT systems supporting the storage and transportation activities (in particular the Warehouse Management Systems and the Transportation Management Systems), the process management approaches typical of physical distribution (such as picking in the warehouses or the planning of milk runs) and even personnel management approaches.

There are several links between GHG emissions and the design and management of physical distribution processes. Figure 6.3 describes the cause and effect relationship between the production of CO_2 and decision-making levers, highlighting their variety and complexity.

As illustrated in Figure 6.3, CO_2 produced through logistic activities is the final result of a series of decisions, which depend on the quantity of goods produced and subsequently delivered, the distance covered to make the delivery, the size and saturation of the vehicles used and the consumption and type of fuel that they use. This set of variables, in turn, is influenced by various factors, which can be classified into endogenous and exogenous (Piecyk and McKinnon, 2010; McKinnon and Woodburn, 1996; 1993).

Factors associated with design choices concerning the physical distribution process can be considered *endogenous*. They are mainly related to the following:

- *Structural factors,* which concern in particular the organisation of the logistic network and, therefore, the number and location of depots and warehouses. Recent trends to centralise logistic networks and therefore to reduce the number

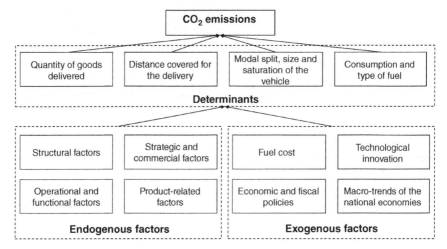

FIGURE 6.3   A framework to understand the drivers of CO_2 production in transportation. *Source:* Piecyk 2010. Reproduced with permission of Elsevier.

of transit points or storage facilities for goods before they reach the customer, on the one hand, meet the requirement to reduce inventory levels, but, on the other hand, can produce a lower level of transport efficiency, characterised by a lower percentage of vehicle saturation and the use of routes that are not always optimised. Furthermore, it must be considered that the development of e-commerce as a distribution channel is further boosting the aforesaid phenomena, since the latter involves direct home deliveries, often characterised by a lower level of transport efficiency.

- *Strategic and commercial factors,* which concern logistic service choices, related to the type and intensity of the performance that the company aims to provide to the customer. The emphasis placed on time performance in recent years, and in particular on delivery speed, leads to storage and transportation choices that have a negative impact on the environment. In order to make on-time deliveries, in fact, it is necessary to oversize supplies, so that the availability of the requested goods can be guaranteed at the time of receipt of the order and deliveries can be planned giving priority to speed, sacrificing vehicle saturation and the use of slower means of transport that have a lower environmental impact. Furthermore, whereas the provision of return logistics services for the collection of goods for recycling and reuse is an essential element for the pursuit of sustainability strategies along the product life cycle, on the other hand it creates new pressure for the transportation process, contributing to the size of its environmental footprint.

- *Operational and functional factors,* which concern logistical aspects, such as the management of the physical flows of goods, the routing of deliveries, the type of transport to be used and choices regarding the average levels of saturation of the latter. These aspects are in fact a consequence of strategic and structural choices and thus the comments made in the previous points are also applicable to them.

- *Product-related factors,* which concern in particular the unit value of the product, on the one hand, and its weight and volume, on the other hand. The relationship between these two aspects, known as *value density,* leads towards centralised logistic networks in the case of high values, or decentralised networks in the case of low values. In the former case, in fact, transportation costs (depending generally on weight and volume) would be relatively low, especially in relation to the unit value of the product. This justifies structural choices characterised by a certain inefficiency of the transport. Companies may improve product-related factors, mostly through the redesign of the product in order to reduce its size, through more efficient packaging, for example, or the use of alternative materials that weigh less. There is a clear link between these factors and the structural choices regarding logistics and the environmental footprint of the company.

Exogenous factors refer to aspects such as fuel costs, technological innovation (especially in relation to vehicle performance), economic and tax policies, trends of the global economy, the characteristics of the infrastructures of a country and, more generally, the macro-trends of the development of national economies.

6.3.1   Carbon Footprint Auditing

The starting point of any improvement initiative aimed at reducing GHG emissions is the carbon footprint auditing, which can be defined as the process of quantifying the total amount of carbon dioxide and other GHG, expressed in CO_2 equivalents, emitted directly or indirectly by an entity (McKinnon et al., 2015). Such a measurement can be carried out for a number of reasons, ranging from the necessity to comply with mandatory reporting programs set out by governmental authorities, to the possibility of participating in GHG markets, to the identification and implementation of actions aimed at improving the environmental footprint of the company, in pursuit of an environmental strategy.

In Europe the Integrated Pollution Prevention and Control (IPPC) Directive (Directive 2008/1/EC) requires that industrial activities with a high pollution potential must report emissions exceeding specified thresholds for the six GHG identified by the Kyoto Protocol, that is, carbon dioxide (CO_2), methane (CH_4), nitrous oxide (N_2O), hydrofluorocarbons (HFCs), perfluorocarbons (PFCs) and sulfur hexafluoride (SF_6) (United Nations, 1998). Such data feeds the European Pollutant Release and Transfer Register (E-PRTR), which enables analyses and comparisons among countries and sectors (EEA, 2012). Concerning the GHG market, the trading of carbon emissions is a legal way for managing an excessive production of GHG, buying the permit to overproduce from entities whose emissions are below the thresholds, thus implementing what the Kyoto Protocol calls a 'flexibility mechanism'. In this case, a condition to enter this market relies on an accurate reporting of company's carbon emissions. Finally, even when none of these conditions hold, companies might still want to quantify their carbon footprint in order to plan and implement appropriate improvement actions and to eventually gain those benefits associated with a superior environmental and social performance, as a higher ability to attract investors and to reinforce the company's competitiveness.

To properly carry out a carbon footprint audit, relevant issues must be addressed, namely (McKinnon et al., 2015):

- The overall reporting principles.
- The organisational boundaries of the system to audit.
- The operational boundaries of the system to audit.
- The measurement process.

Concerning the overall reporting principles, according to the Green House Gas Protocol Corporate Standard (WBCSD/WRI, 2004) as well as to the ISO standards relevant to this topic (ISO/TS 14067:2013, *Greenhouse Gases – Carbon Footprint of Products; Requirements and Guidelines for Quantification and Communication*, and ISO/CD 14064:1, Greenhouse Gases – *Part 1: Specification with guidance at the organization level for quantification and reporting of the greenhouse gas emissions and removals*), a company willing to measure and report its carbon footprint, either to comply with a mandatory reporting program or for a voluntary initiative, must respect the following guidelines, which lead to informative and reliable pieces of information:

- *Relevance*: it refers to the suitability of the reported GHG as a relevant input data for the decision-making processes of the company and of other external entities. This aspect is highly influenced by the selected inventory boundaries, which should be set so as to provide any user with a realistic description of the environmental footprint of the company, regardless of its legal form.
- *Completeness*: it concerns the sources of GHG that must be included in the process and the use of threshold values. In this regard, some organisations report GHG emissions when a certain degree of materiality is reached. However, since the comparison with a threshold involves a quantification of the GHG emitted, it is preferable that these be explicitly reported.
- *Coherence and consistency* of the reported data, in terms of quantification methods and unit of analysis, so as to allow comparisons over time.
- *Transparency* about the methods, the assumptions and the sources of data of the auditing process, so that an independent reader could achieve the same results by replicating the approach described in the report.
- *Accuracy* in the calculations, in order to guarantee a level of reliability as high as possible for measures of GHG based on estimates.

As far the *organisational boundaries of the system* to audit are concerned, the main problem refers to the identification of the activities that can release emissions and that the company is responsible for. If the company owns 100% of its operations, the definition of such a perimeter is rather easy since it coincides with the whole set of activities and facilities of the company. But if its structure is more complex, for example with branches and subsidiaries in foreign countries where joint ventures with local entities might be established, defining the boundaries of the system can be more controversial. In this case, either the *equity share* approach or the *control* approach can be adopted (WBCSD/WRI, 2004). In the former case, the company will be responsible for a fraction of the GHG gases emitted by an operation (e.g., a factory or any other form of facility) equal to its share of equity. In the latter case, the company will include in the boundaries of the system and will be responsible for the entire amount of emissions by all those operations over which it exerts a control. In this regard, the 'control' can be defined either from a financial or from an operational view point. The former can be observed when the company can direct the policies of the controlled unit, while the latter occurs when the company can not only direct, but also implement operating policies in the controlled unit. In cases where a single company or facility is owed by several entities, these have to apply a consistent approach to the definition of the organisational boundaries so as to avoid overlaps and double-counting.

The *operational boundaries* of the system have, then, to be defined. They concern the *scope* of the measurement process, which involves the identification of the source of direct and indirect emissions of GHG that must be considered for the reporting process. In this concern, according to the Greenhouse Gas Protocol, three possible scopes can be defined (WBCSD/WRI, 2004). Scope 1 refers exclusively to the direct emissions relative to the GHG covered by the Kyoto Protocol, which are released by sources owned or controlled by the company (e.g. generation of electricity, physical and chemical processing, transportation of goods). Scope 2 refers to the indirect emissions due to the production of the electricity bought by the company for its own use. Finally, Scope 3 covers the indirect emissions that are a consequence of the company's interaction with other entities and that are produced by sources not owned or controlled by the company itself. This may be the case for GHG emissions due to the production of purchased products and components. For companies willing to report their emissions, it is suggested to adopt at least the first two Scopes, so as to provide a detailed enough description of their environmental footprint.

The *measurement process* refers to the activity of quantifying the total amount of GHG emitted within a selected operational boundary (or Scope). In this regard, the standard approach to the calculation requires that all emissions be expressed in Carbon Dioxide Equivalents (CO_{2c}), according to conversion rates that express the Global Warming Potential (GWP) of 1 tonne of any given GHG type in terms of the equivalent amount of CO_2 that would result in the same warming effect (see Table 6.1).

For companies willing to measure the direct and indirect emissions of their activities, several cross-sector and industry-specific tools are available, suitable for

TABLE 6.1   Conversion rates of GHG into CO_{2e}

Greenhouse gas	Global warming potential (GWP) in CO_{2e}
Carbon dioxide	1
Methane	21
Nitrous oxides	310
Hydrofluorocarbons	140
Perfluorocarbons	6,500
Sulfur hexafluoride	23,900

Source: Defra (2013a).

TABLE 6.2   Conversion rates of types of fuel

Fuel Type	Units	kg CO_{2e} per Unit
Petrol	Litre	2.2144
Diesel	Litre	2.6008
Compressed natural gas (CNG)	Kilogram	2.7072
Liquid petroleum gas (LPG)	Litre	1.4929

Source: Defra (2013a).

supporting the measurement process and the deployment of the overall measure into more detailed sources of origin. This is particularly relevant when quantifying the emissions of manufacturing plants, whose activities can be articulated into a number of steps, requiring different pieces of equipment, types of transformation, each of them resulting in a bundle of GHG releases (see, for instance, http://ghgprotocol.org/calculation-tools).

If the scope of the measurement process is limited to physical distribution and, in particular, to transportation, two main approaches to the computation of the carbon footprint can be adopted: the *fuel-based* approach and the *activity-based* one (McKinnon et al., 2015). According to the former, the carbon footprint of transportation must be measured looking at the total amount of any type of fuel consumed in a given period of time, multiplied by the relative conversion rate (see Table 6.2). In order to properly implement such an approach, it is necessary to get pieces of information about the actual consumption of fuel and, in this regard, fuel receipts or financial reports about this type of expenditure can be a reliable source.

If the activity-based approach is adopted, companies must measure the carbon footprint of their distribution process starting from the activities carried out by each vehicle and from the related operating conditions (e.g. total kilometres travelled, type of goods transported, loading factors, empty running, traffic situation, vehicle category etc.). Building on these pieces of information, it is possible to compute the emissions of freight transportation through the adoption of appropriate conversion rates as those reported in the *Handbook of Emissions Factors for Road Transportation* (INFRAS, 2014) or through the use of CO_2 calculators specific to logistics, as EcoTransit (www.ecotransit.org).

6.3.2   Eliminating Transportation Waste

Once the carbon footprint of an organisation has been quantified, it is possible to set improvement targets and plan appropriate actions. The process of eliminating transportation 'waste' can be addressed through the lean approach, following the steps stated below (Wills, 2009):

- Identify all activities and processes that require transportation.
- Specify the mode of transportation and the distances covered.
- Identify solutions that can reduce the environmental impact of transportation.
- Offset the remaining negative effects of transportation.

When carrying out the first step, it must be considered that transportation can be *external* or *internal*. The former involves all those activities that occur outside the organisation, such as the shipping of goods. The latter consists of the travel required, within the company's premises, to move materials and goods from one area or process to another. Obviously, external transportation, compared to internal one, is more critical since it produces the highest impact on the environmental footprint of the company. Nevertheless, the same improvement process can be adopted for both types.

External freight transportation may be described through the identification of the items dispatched to customers or received from suppliers. To do this, all of the incoming and outgoing products and materials in the shipping and receiving areas have to be traced. For this purpose, it can be useful to review shipping and receiving logs, as well as incoming and outgoing freight bills in order to obtain a complete and accurate list of all materials flows.

The second step in the process of minimising transportation waste consists of determining the different modes of transport used (e.g. air, road, rail etc.), as well as the distance travelled through each of them. This activity can be supported by the adoption of the so-called Transportation Waste Elimination Sheet (Wills, 2009). This document, represented in Figure 6.4, shows the items received (or dispatched) by the company, the current mode of transportation and the total distance covered from the point of origin to the point of destination, thus proving a picture of the 'current state' of the external freight transportation process.

Once a detailed description of the current state has been achieved, the most challenging stage of the improvement process has to be undertaken, which refers to the

Activity: shipment of goods from the factory to the warehouse		
Current state		
Item	**Mode**	**Distance**
Item 1	Road	100 km/week
Item 2	Rail	350 km/week
Item ...	...	...

FIGURE 6.4   Transportation waste elimination sheet – example of a current state. *Source:* Willis 2009. Reproduced with permission of Taylor & Francis.

identification and adoption of solutions aimed at improving the carbon footprint, through a reduction in the total distance covered and the migration toward more environmentally sound modes of transport. Because emissions generated by physical distribution cannot be fully eliminated, companies can offset them, sponsoring projects beneficial for the environment. The most relevant improvement opportunities are reviewed in Sections 6.3.2.1–6.3.2.5.

6.3.2.1   *Local Sourcing*

In order to reduce the distance travelled to deliver goods, sourcing or producing locally are appropriate strategies (Wills, 2009). This trend is becoming popular especially in industries such as food, where customers are showing a greater and greater concern about the origin of what they buy and about the social and environmental sustainability of the production practices. Furthermore, the demand for local products is coupled with the widespread need to recover and leverage distinctive traditions and know-how of local communities, in contrast with the idea of an on-going process of standardisation of cultures, values and habits.

Widening the discussion, local sourcing and production can lead to several advantages, such as quicker and more dependable deliveries, lower inventory levels and a higher degree of interaction with local clients that enables a better understanding of their specific preferences. Furthermore, until a few years ago companies strived to engage suppliers from low-cost countries, but now the current priority is to reduce the excessive length, complexity and vulnerability that such globalisation has created in supply chains. This need is made even more urgent by the lower cost-competitiveness of some locations as China, Latin America and Eastern Europe, which are reaching parity with manufacturing costs in developed countries, if productivity, energy prices and currency conversions are taken into account.

From a marketing and logistics viewpoint local sourcing and production can determine remarkable advantages, but the technical feasibility and the economic convenience of this choice must be carefully analysed. Indeed, the availability of raw materials and production competencies must be considered, especially when specialty goods have to be obtained. This could threaten the possibility to find local good-enough sourcing solutions. Furthermore, the creation of a higher number of production facilities must also be assessed, looking at the availability of local resources (raw materials, workforce, supply base etc.) and at the implications for plant size. As a matter of fact, especially for capital-intensive operations, small manufacturing facilities would result in a poor level of production efficiency that would in turn negatively affect overall environmental sustainability, as described in Chapter 5.

6.3.2.2   *Delivery Planning and Service-Level Agreements*

A key lever to improve the carbon footprint of physical distribution consists of achieving a higher load factor, especially for road transport. In fact, it has been estimated that doubling the level of saturation from 50 to 100% of a heavy-duty vehicle, the fuel consumption of 100 tonne/km decreases from 2.1 to 1.2 litres (Rizet et al., 2012). Focusing on the carbon footprint of road transportation, available data demonstrates that in order to reduce the amount of emissions per tonne/km, the most effective strategy consists of using bigger vehicles with a high degree of saturation. As seen in Table 6.3, the quantity of

TABLE 6.3 CO_{2e} per vehicle type

Vehicle type (GVW)	kg CO_{2e} per vehicle-km	kg CO_{2e} per tonne-km
Rigid (>3.5t–7.5t)	0.59115	0.58396
Rigid (>7.5t–17t)	0.727571	0.35322
Rigid (>17t)	0.974223	0.19186
Articulated (>3.5t–33t)	0.890426	0.16159
Articulated (>33t)	0.995873	0.08452

Source: Defra, 2013b.

TABLE 6.4 CO_{2e} of articulated vehicles with (>33t) with different levels of capacity saturations

Vehicle type (GVW)	Capacity utilisation	kg CO_{2e} per vehicle-km
Articulated (>33t)	0%	0.707793
	50%	0.940113
	100%	1.172433

Source: Defra, 2013b.

CO_{2e} per tonne/km decreases as the Gross Vehicle Weight (GVW) increases. This evidence should lead to the selection of bigger vehicles whenever possible.

Furthermore, looking at the data reported in Table 6.4, it can be noted that, within the biggest vehicles class (i.e. articulated with GVW > 33t), the amount of emissions per vehicle/km does not increase proportionally with the capacity utilisation, thus demonstrating that fully saturated vehicles enjoy a better carbon footprint.

Although these solutions for freight transportation can result in better environmental performance, they have to be coupled with appropriate delivery planning strategies and service-level agreements with the clients.

As a matter of fact, numerous constraints can influence the distribution planning process and its performance (McKinnon et al., 2015; McKinnon and Ge, 2006). First of all, the customer's demand variability is a major factor influencing the ability to fully load vehicles, since suppliers' fleets are frequently dimensioned so as to cope with the peaks. Moreover, the inherent variability of the demand is artificially boosted by commercial initiatives of the clients, as promotions. Also the adoption of logics such as just-in-time among manufacturers and retailers is determining a lower degree of saturation of vehicles, due to the necessity to guarantee to the customer a high service level in terms of frequency of delivery. While on the one hand these practices result in a lower amount of stock held by the client and in the environmental benefits connected to this event (described in Chapter 5), on the other hand they bring about a sharp increase in the number of deliveries, with remarkable negative effects on the degree of saturation of the vehicles and on the carbon footprint of transportation (Arvidsson et al., 2013).

Another phenomenon that affects capacity utilisation refers to the geographical imbalance of traffic flows. The amount of freight moved from one region to another is seldom equivalent to the amount transported in the opposite direction. This determines a low saturation of the return trips and, in general, a poor performance of backhauling. This problem is made even more critical by the higher priority assigned to the outbound deliveries, which leads companies to give up backloading opportunities if these threaten quick availability of vehicles for a new outbound trip. Indeed, some slack in the transportation activities is generally created in order to deal with the unreliability of the delivery schedules, due to traffic congestion and similar problems that prevent perfect adherence to plans.

Finally, a low degree of cooperation among supply chain players as well as inadequate IT systems negatively influence the possibility to get real-time information about loading opportunities, which could lead to a better operational and environmental performance of the transportation process.

In order to address these problems, several solutions have been suggested. Using a centralised perspective and focusing on a single player of the supply chain, several algorithms have been developed and embedded into software packages suitable for supporting some decision-making processes peculiar to transportation management (Islam and Olsen, 2014). For example, the Vehicle Routing Problem with Backhauls (VRPB) aims at reducing empty trips. Similarly, the Vehicle Routing and Scheduling Problem (VRSP) attempts to efficiently assign clients to single vehicles and to route and schedule their trips. Although the benefits determined by the adoption of these types of software are numerous, it has also been contended that they cannot support the adoption of some environmentally sound practices that involve the cooperation among different players of the supply chain, because they are focused on single-company optimisation (Islam and Olsen, 2014).

Using a supply chain perspective, several solutions have been suggested, which are based, on the one hand, on the adoption of collaborative practices and, on the other, on the implementation of IT systems that boost the real-time availability of data useful for a more effective planning of the distribution activities (Arvidsson et al., 2013).

Among collaborative practices, they can be distinguished between those that promote horizontal collaboration and others focused on vertical collaboration (McKinnon et al., 2015). When the former are adopted, cooperation is pursued by competing firms (either manufacturers or shippers), which share some of their resources to achieve a higher operational and environmental performance of the delivery process. Within this typology, a consolidated practice is truck-sharing, but examples of shared logistic facilities have also been reported (Islam and Olsen, 2014). Although these solutions might be very beneficial, some obstacles are frequently observed, which can be organisational (such as the need of trust between partners) and technical (such as regulatory constraints concerning the mix of products that can be jointly transported by one vehicle).

Vertical collaboration practices concern solutions undertaken by companies that operate at different levels of the supply chain. In this regard, several practices have been developed that help companies in achieving higher visibility of demand through the systematic exchange of data and information among partners. Such practices as Continuous Replenishment Programs, Vendor Managed Inventory and Consignment Stock, in which the supplier is responsible for stock management on behalf of its client, can result in more effective production and delivery planning due to the increased predictability of demand, with remarkable positive effects on the carbon footprint of the logistic process.

Another vertical collaboration practice that has been proposed to reduce the number of trips is the Nominated Day Delivery System (NDDS). It is based on the idea that clients should adhere to a given delivery schedule, choosing ('nominating') a time window among those proposed by the carrier/supplier and placing their orders with some advance so as to enable efficient planning of the distribution activities (Hvolby and Trienekens, 2010). This practice results in a higher degree of load saturation; however, it is rarely accepted especially due to the ever-increasing diffusion of the just-in-time approach among manufacturers and retailers. To counter the negative attitude toward practices such as NDDS and stimulate a higher acceptance of waiting, their environmental soundness should be clearly pointed out by the supplier as a special value-adding element of the delivery process and better pricing conditions should be offered in order to share with the clients part of the economic benefit determined by these practices.

Finally, the implementation of updated Information & Communication Technologies (ICT) can be a major driver of improvement of the environmental performance of the delivery process. Indeed, ICT adoption supports the implementation of the aforementioned collaborative practices, enabling the real-time exchange of data among supply chain partners. Moreover, as reported previously, inside the company software packages, as Transportation Management Systems (TMS) can be leveraged to speed up and improve the planning and routing processes of the outbound logistics. Finally, updated technologies such as the Global Position System (GPS) and web-based applications can help companies in identifying real-time loading opportunities to share with supply chain partners.

6.3.2.3 Fleet Management   The selection of the most appropriate mode of transport is a critical choice from both an operational and environmental perspective. Indeed, road transportation, which is still the most adopted solution (see Figure 6.1), is characterised by a remarkable degree of volume and delivery flexibility, since the use of small vehicles as VANs can enable the shipment of minimum quantities of freight theoretically in any possible destination. However, road transportation can suffer from a unsatisfactory degree of dependability compared to other solutions, since it is exposed to the risk of traffic congestion that results in a poor delivery schedule adherence. In contrast, such modes as rail and sea transportation are more suitable for the shipment of bulk freight for long distances and enjoy better delivery dependability, although they can be slower compared to trucks (McKinnon et al., 2015). However, when the environmental perspective is also considered, it is apparent that a wide use of road transportation, which is the current standard, may result in remarkably negative effects. Table 6.5 reports the outcomes of a simulation conducted on www.ecotransit.org, in which the transportation of 100 tonnes of freight has been tested along a route in the Mediterranean coast, which can be covered alternatively by road, rail, air and see transportation.

As can be seen, although the total distance covered is substantially similar (nearly 700 km), the CO_{2e} produced by road transportation is higher than for any other

TABLE 6.5 CO_{2e} **and particulate matter with different modes of transport: an example**

	Road	Rail	Air	Sea
CO_{2e} (t)	5.158	1.080	124.992	0.497
Distance (km)	700.72	708.56	705.65	691.38

alternative, except for air. This evidence clearly highlights the necessity to shift toward greener modes, as rail and sea transport, through a wider adoption of inter-modal solutions. In order to make this shift viable, however, some enabling conditions must be met, such as relatively short loading/unloading operations in ports and rail stations, which involve relevant investments in up-to-date materials handling equipment, and the presence of third-party logistics providers capable of supporting such a shift with appropriate solutions. These aspects point out the necessity of a high commitment not only for private entities, but also for public ones.

Focusing on the single-company level, even in case of road transportation some remarkable environmental improvements can be achieved when appropriate strategies are pursued. Indeed, on the one hand, effective maintenance programs, as well as training initiatives targeted at drivers can result in a higher fuel-efficiency of traditional vehicles. On the other hand, companies can consider the use of innovative vehicles, which use alternative energy sources. In this case, several options can be considered, ranging from biofuels (as biodiesel, bioethanol and biomethane), to natural gas (as methane, liquefied petroleum gas – LPG – and compressed natural gas – CNG), to hydrogen and electric or hybrid vehicles. Although the carbon emissions produced by this type of vehicles are much lower, especially for hydrogen, electric and hybrid ones, some operational problems may arise from their adoption. In particular, refuelling stations for some types of fuel as LPG are not widely available, as well as recharging stations for electric vehicles. Furthermore, vehicle modifications have to be undertaken when LPG or CNG have to be used. Focusing on electric solutions, it must be considered that a main constraint for their use in freight transportation is that their rather short distance range, coupled with the limited availability of recharging stations, makes use of these vehicles hard to implement. Finally, even from an environmental viewpoint, this option can be less attractive than it could seem just focusing on the carbon emissions produced while running the vehicle. Indeed, if a life-cycle perspective is adopted, energy generation to recharge the batteries may dramatically affect the environment unless renewable sources are used (McKinnon et al., 2015).

6.3.2.4 Carbon Offsets These actions that companies can undertake to improve their carbon footprint cannot result in the total elimination of the CO_2 emissions. Thus, firms can compensate for them through the financial support of initiatives that are beneficial for the environment, as production of renewable energies, reforestation programs, biodiversity protection or resource conservation initiatives. Since these projects must be characterised by high standard levels and in most cases require specific competencies, they are carried out by specialised players, whose activity is validated and verified by independent third parties that certify the emissions reduction achieved through the projects. This is particularly relevant when companies purchase offset credits to comply with caps defined by national and international entities. For instance, the EU Emissions Trading System (EU ETS) has been created by the European Union in order to enforce an on-going process of GHG reduction for the most high-emitting industries (e.g. power plants, commercial airlines, energy-intensive industry sectors such as oil refineries, steel works and production of iron, aluminium, metals, cement, lime, glass, ceramics, pulp, paper, cardboard, acids and bulk organic chemicals), in accordance with the Kyoto Protocol. While taking part in the EU ETS is mandatory for the previously mentioned industries, companies engaged in other sectors can participate to this market on a voluntary basis. This system covers nearly 45% of the emissions generated by the twenty-eight EU Countries, for which remarkable improvement targets have been set, that is, −20% emissions by 2020 and −80/95% by 2050 compared to 1990 levels. The reduction of the total emissions is achieved through the creation of a 'cap-and-trade' mechanism, according to which companies can comply with the predefined limits set by the European Union through the most cost-efficient way, offsetting their emissions if necessary. EU ETS is currently the biggest market for the credits generated by emission-saving projects and accounts for nearly 75% of international carbon trading.

The rationale of carbon offsetting builds on the idea of buying carbon credits measured in metric tonnes of CO_{2e}. Each carbon credit is identified through a unique identification number, and once it is bought by a company, it is retired through third-party registries. This enables companies to claim that they have off set a given amount of their emissions, while no other organisation can buy the same credit. However, it must be considered that the amount of offset emissions are not comparable to a reduction of the GHG. Thus in the carbon footprinting process companies must, on the one hand, report the emissions generated and, on the other hand, give evidence of the amount that was compensated through the purchase of offset credits.

6.4 WAREHOUSE MANAGEMENT AND SUSTAINABILITY

The design and management of logistics infrastructures, especially warehouses and distribution centres, is an area of major concern, not only for its impact on the economics of the company and on the service level provided to the customer, but also for its effects on the environmental and social sustainability of the firm.

Breaking down the total logistics cost at the macroeconomic level, the percentage due to storage/warehousing reaches values of 23% in the United States and 32% in European Countries, thus demonstrating the economic relevance of these facilities, which are the second-most-important driver of the total logistics costs after transportation (Rushton et al., 2014). From an operational viewpoint, there is clear evidence that design and management choices concerning warehousing infrastructures

TABLE 6.6　Warehouse design and management choices

		Main Design Decisions
Warehouse design	Overall structure	Materials flow
		Location of departments
	Size and stocking capacity	Size of the warehouse and of its departments
	Layout	Aisles orientation
		Number, length and width of aisles
		Doors location
	Equipment	Level of automation
		Storage equipment selection
		Material handling equipment selection
	Operations strategy	Storage strategy selection
		Order picking method selection
Warehouse management	Receiving and shipping	Truck-dock assignment
		Order-truck assignment
		Truck dispatch schedule
	Storage	Assignment of SKUs to different departments/zones
		Assignment of pickers to zones
		Specification of storage classes
	Order Picking	Batching
		Order-batch assignment
		Picking routing and sequencing

Source: Gu 2007. Reproduced with permission of Elsevier.

(briefly reported in Table 6.6) result in remarkable effects on the performance attributes typical of such facilities, namely (Frazelle, 2002):

- *Productivity*, which measures the level of asset utilisation.
- *Quality*, thought of as the level of accuracy in order picking and shipping.
- *Cycle time*, which refers to the responsiveness of warehousing processes.

In fact, it has been observed that an improper balance between the total amount of items stocked and the capacity of the warehouse can reduce the responsiveness of the picking activities, due to the higher difficulty in finding products in the stocking locations (Denis et al., 2006), and that the use of modern technologies in picking (as voice picking) can sharply reduce the errors in order preparation (Berger and Ludwig, 2007). Thus, when designing and managing warehouses it is necessary to clearly identify the service level that the company wishes to guarantee to its customers and the degree of productivity considered consistent with the economic targets of the company.

However, it is becoming more and more evident that the design and management of warehouses must also build on the analysis of the social and environmental effects produced by these facilities. As far as social sustainability is concerned, the same studies that discuss the role of appropriate design and management choices on warehouse performance also frequently highlight the positive outcomes on employees' safety (Berger and Ludwig, 2007; Denis et al., 2006). As a matter of fact, the adoption of appropriate equipment for storage and materials handling, or the implementation of IT systems that support picking routing and sequencing, can translate into better safety conditions for the workforce, since they can reduce the unnecessary motion of the employees.

However, the major effect of warehouse design and management on sustainability comes from the environmental dimension, especially when a significant effort in terms of temperature control is required, due to the features of the products stored and/or the climatic conditions of the location of the facility (Emmett and Sood, 2010). In this regard, the design principles of Green Buildings and the criteria specific to LEED certification (Leadership in Energy and Environmental Design) should also be implemented for logistic purposes, in order to achieve a wider use of renewable energy and higher energy efficiency, through the adoption of technical solutions that increase the saturation of storage space and that reduce the amount of movements of the products inside the warehouse. While the use of renewable energy is facilitated by the availability of large roofs, where solar panels can be installed, an energy-efficient design of the buildings and its internal processes require a deeper understanding of the main drivers of energy consumption. In this regard, the main areas of energy use, which may require redesign or re-organisation, are (McKinnon et al., 2015; Emmett and Sood, 2010):

• Temperature control.
• Lighting.
• Mechanical handling equipment.

Factors that influence the energy consumption for *temperature control* are numerous, such as the external climatic conditions, the insulating power of the materials used for the construction of the building, its solar orientation and its size. It has been estimated that 1°C reduction in the warehouse temperature results in a saving of 10% of energy use (McKinnon et al., 2015). Thus, an appropriate design of such buildings is essential for a higher degree of environmental sustainability. In this regard, the most effective structural solutions are the following (McKinnon et al., 2015; Aynsley, 2011; Meller and Gue, 2009; Carbon Trust, 2002):

• Increasing the size of the warehouse; larger warehouses are more energy efficient because this solution reduces the heat loss through the external walls.
• Adopting innovative layouts, such as a U-shape or a fish-bone shape. The most frequent type of warehouse is rectangular, with a linear layout characterised by straight and parallel aisles, whose design is primarily aimed at streamlining the materials flow and speeding up order picking activities. However, in this type of layout, doors are generally located in opposite sides of the building, thus facilitating draughts and subsequent heat loss.
• Segregating departments of the warehouse with different temperature requirements and, in particular, the receiving and shipping areas where the presence of docks and doors result in draughts and heat loss.

As far as *warehouse lighting* is concerned, a strategy aimed at reducing energy use must build, on the one hand, on the correct identification of the 'lux' level (amount of light) required for the activity to be carried out and, on the other hand, on the adoption of appropriate technical and structural solutions. With regard to the first aspect, the Carbon Trust (2002) reports reference values classified on the basis of the width and height of the aisles. This is particularly relevant for aligning the artificial lighting scheme and light intensity with the achievement of appropriate working conditions, necessary for preventing errors and injuries and for boosting workforce productivity. The second aspect, which refers to the adoption of appropriate technical and structural solutions, involves careful design of the warehouse, so as to fully exploit the daylight potential, as well as the implementation of energy-efficient lighting devices. The usage of daylight depends on several factors, including the size and the positioning of the warehouse, the width of the aisles, the number of daylight hours and the weather conditions of the place in which the warehouse is located. Depending on these conditions, the building can be designed so that windows are put in the proper places, thus reducing the amount of artificial light necessary for warehouse operations. Finally, the choice of updated lighting and lamps (such as light-emitting diodes – LED), the adoption of motion sensors and automated control gears to switch lights on and off and the implementation of effective maintenance programmes (e.g. for the cleaning and the replacement of lamps) may translate into double-digit energy reduction rates.

Mechanical handling equipment is the third most relevant source of energy consumption. This concept includes both equipment driven by humans (such as forklift trucks) and fully automated equipment. Focusing on the first type, the main area of concern, from an environmental viewpoint, refers to the choice of the power unit and the type of fuel (McKinnon et al., 2015; Amjed and Harrison, 2013). The most common options are the use of an internal combustion engine – which can use either diesel, liquefied petroleum gas (LPG) or compressed natural gas (CNG) – or lead-acid electric or nickel-metal hydride batteries. In this regard, empirical evidence about the environmental friendliness of these alternatives is controversial. In fact, if the carbon footprint of the various alternatives is calculated using the entire life-cycle of the energy source as system boundaries (i.e. generation, operation and disposal), interestingly an internal combustion engine using LPG shows the lowest amount of emissions (McKinnon et al., 2015). However, it must be considered that technological innovation in this area has recently led to the development of new types of environmentally friendly fuels and engines, such as those operating with biodiesel or hybrid solutions. The adoption of these innovations can result in remarkable improvements in terms of emissions reduction. Nevertheless, this can only be fully achieved when an appropriate maintenance programme for the vehicles is implemented. As a matter of fact, it has been demonstrated that poor operating conditions, such as under-inflated tyres and misalignments, can result in a remarkable increase in energy or fuel consumption.

Fully automated pieces of equipment, such as A-frames, carousels, conveyors, sorters and automated storage and retrieval systems (AS/RS) (Baker, 2006), are generally adopted when labour costs are high, when warehousing processes are characterised by a significant degree of complexity due to the volumes and the variety of the products stored, or when these processes require remarkable speed and accuracy. In the presence of these pieces of equipment, energy efficiency is mainly achieved through effective planning of their use, which in turn requires the implementation of best practices rooted in the field of Supply Chain Management. Indeed, a higher degree of cooperation between the upstream and downstream partners along the pipeline can result, among other things, in more accurate forecasting, quicker and more dependable suppliers' lead times and better production and delivery schedule compliance. All of these improvements can lead to a reduction in the inventory level of the warehouse, which is a condition for improving storage and retrieval activities, and for more effective receiving and shipping processes, thus positively affecting the energy consumption of automated equipment (Emmett and Sood, 2010).

6.5   SUSTAINABLE PACKAGING

The role played by packaging is twofold. On the one hand, it protects the product from deterioration and damage, especially during its transportation and movement within logistic facilities, enabling it to be stored safely and efficiently. In this regard, all types of packaging (primary, secondary and tertiary) are necessary to fulfil this task. On the other hand, it contains relevant information for the customer and is frequently used as a way to convey a distinctive product image, making it more attractive in the eyes of the customer (Emmett and Sood, 2010).

However, regardless of the material it is made of, packaging is a major source of risk for the environment and is frequently considered as one of the most relevant areas of improvement for achieving a green supply chain. In fact, along its life-cycle it involves the use of materials – paper, board, glass, plastic, metal and other production inputs (whose environmental effects have been described in Chapter 5) – and requires transportation in order to be delivered to the premises of the customer. Furthermore, during its use it can negatively affect the carbon footprint of the product if its shape and size determine a low value density, thus leading to a subsequent decrease in freight transportation efficiency. Finally, packaging is often land-filled, causing environmental degradation when it is made with non-biodegradable materials. Therefore, if a life-cycle approach is used to assess environmental impact, the packaging of a product frequently has a greater effect on the environment than the product itself, as often is the case in the food industry (Verghese et al., 2010; Lee and Xu, 2005).

These reasons are causing customers to increasingly take the features of a product's packaging into consideration, which is resulting in strong pressure on companies to take appropriate action. In this regard, the following levers seem to be the most promising for achieving 'green packaging' (Emmett and Sood, 2010):

- *Reduce*: this option aims at reducing the volume and the weight of packaging, as well as the amount of materials that it is made of. This lever, which builds on the Design for Environment approach (see Chapter 3), can have remarkable positive effects, because it can result, among other things, in a more favourable value density of the product. In this regard, several experiences have been reported in the fast-moving consumer goods industry (Lee and Xu, 2005). However, it must be considered that this solution can also involve some relevant changes in the appearance and size of the packaging, thus threatening its ability to attract customers' attention. Therefore, improvement initiatives based on the 'reduce' principle must be backed by marketing research on customers' preferences as far as packaging functions are concerned (Svanes et al., 2010).

- *Reuse*: this is based on the full responsibility of the producer for taking back the packaging of the delivered product, establishing a closed-loop supply chain. This is frequent in business-to-business relationships, in particular when industrial equipment is delivered, and can be observed also in the delivery of products, such as furniture and white goods, to the premises of the final consumer. The way in which companies use this lever is influenced by the take-back legislation concerning packaging. In Europe, it is based on EU Directive 94/62/EC of 20 December 1994 on *Packaging and Packaging Waste* (eventually amended to update areas of applications and objectives), which provides measures aimed at limiting the production of packaging waste and promoting recycling, re-use and other forms of waste recovery. Although the scope of this directive is broader, it specifically mentions the re-use of packaging as an objective that EU Countries must pursue. While the re-use of primary packaging can pose a higher degree of difficulty, in particular in relation to the requirement to guarantee compliance with appropriate hygienic conditions, secondary and tertiary packaging is an area that represents great potential for improvement. Indeed, companies that switch to reusable packaging (e.g. pallets, hand-held containers, bulk containers and other transport packaging items, generally made of plastic, wood, steel or other durable material and specifically designed for multiple trips and extended life) experience a number of advantages. On the one hand, it can reduce waste management costs, since the amount of packaging materials that is disposed of or that ends up in landfills is sharply reduced. On the other hand, a higher product protection is achieved, as well as better ergonomics and improved worker safety, due to the redesign of such packaging items, which is often carried out in order to enable the use of new and durable materials.

- *Recycle*: this involves the collection of packaging waste and its physical and chemical treatment, aimed at recovering the materials it is made of or producing energy through its incineration. Legislation also plays a major role in this regard, in setting specific targets concerning the reduction of the content of hazardous substances and materials in the packaging and its components, the amount of packaging waste that must be recycled or incinerated, and the use of marking and identification systems, which must clearly indicate the nature of the materials used in order to facilitate their identification and classification. Recycling is often preferred to the re-use option. However, it is still controversial whether this choice is preferable from an economic and environmental viewpoint, given the fact that the cost of collecting, cleaning and treating mixed and contaminated packaging can be high.

- *Reform*: this builds on the idea of finding alternative materials or solutions that can perform the same functions as traditional packaging, but with a lower polluting potential. Compostable or biodegradable packaging is now obtained using agricultural polymers that come from corn, sugar beets or other natural sources. The benefits of such innovations lie in the fact that biodegradable materials, once land-filled, break down into natural elements in a period generally shorter than one year after disposal. Corrugated cardboard, corn starch items, bubble wrap and even some types of plastic are examples of this. Compostable materials go one step forward by providing land with nutrients at the end of their biodegradation process. However, these materials are generally difficult to mould and have poorer physico-chemical properties compared to synthetic polymers such as PET and PVC (Peelman et al., 2013).

7

REVERSE LOGISTICS MANAGEMENT AND CLOSED-LOOP SUPPLY CHAIN

7.1 INTRODUCTION

'*Renault's plant in Choisy-le-Roy, near Paris, remanufactures automotive engines, transmissions, injection pumps, and other components for resale. The plant's remanufacturing operations use 80% less energy and almost 90% less water (as well as generate about 70% less oil and detergent waste) than comparable new production does. And the plant delivers higher operations margins than Renault as a whole can boast.*

More broadly, the company redesigns certain components to make them easier to disassemble and use again. It also targets components for closed-loop reuse, essentially converting materials and components from worn-out vehicles into inputs for new ones. To support these efforts, Renault formed joint ventures with steel recyclers and a waste-management company to bring end-of-use expertise into product design. Together, these moves help Renault to save money by maintaining tighter control of its raw materials throughout its vehicles' life cycles – or use cycles. Renault also works with suppliers to identify 'circular benefits' that distribute value across its supply chain. For examples, the company helped its provider of cutting fluids (a coolant and lubricant used in machining) to shift from a sales- to performance-based model. By changing the relationship nature and terms, Renault motivated suppliers to redesign the fluid and surrounding processes for greater efficiency. The result was a 90% reduction in the volume of waste discharge. This new arrangement benefits both companies:

Sustainable Operations and Supply Chain Management, First Edition. Valeria Belvedere and Alberto Grando.
© 2017 John Wiley & Sons Ltd. Published 2017 by John Wiley & Sons Ltd.

the supplier is moving up the value chain so that it can be more profitable, while Renault's total cost of ownership for cutting fluids fell by about 20%' (Nguyen et al., 2014).

Once upon a time, fossil fuels were cheap, and raw materials were abundant. In those days of the 'linear economy', raw materials were extracted to make products, which were used and then simply thrown away. Today, Renault is helping change all that by moving towards the 'circular economy'. Indeed, Renault is turning its circular economy approach into a competitive advantage.

Basically, the circular economy is the ultimate recycling programme, where ideally nothing goes to waste. For the new wave of economists and business analysts, it's a new growth model that allows two previously incompatible factors to coexist: the stakes of economic growth and environmental challenges. It's about dealing with issues such as dwindling raw materials and volatile price fluctuations, without making the wrong compromises.

In the circular economy, we think of waste products as a resource. We dismantle old unusable vehicles, to transform parts and materials so they can be used again (and again) to make new products.

Nothing goes to waste in a natural cycle. Everything is reused, composted or digested. Likewise, a manufactured product like a car can be made at a minimum cost in energy terms by integrating the car itself into the ongoing production process. Instead of planning for disposal at the end of the product's life, we plan to reuse, repair or re-manufacture. The last generation and next generation of cars become part of the same circular production process.

Renault is going further than ever before to reduce its environmental impact. Beyond drastically cutting the carbon footprint of each vehicle produced, Renault is looking at the whole life of the vehicle. Already, you can drive a Renault Espace that is 90% recyclable. In fact if you consider any vehicle in the Renault lineup today, you will find it is made from 30% recycled materials, a figure set to rise to 33% by the end of 2016.

Yet the circular economy requires us to go even further. So Renault is leading the way, for example, in repairing and reusing products. Ellen MacArthur saw this in action herself at Renault factory in Choisy-le-Roi, France. Here, parts from old cars are removed and made useful again. As Ellen MacArthur writes: 'When a re-manufactured gearbox leaves Choisy, it contains an average of 75% pre-used but tested parts. When an engine leaves Choisy, it contains 38% pre-used tested parts.'

In a similar vein, Renault is investing in car recycling with its subsidiary INDRA, which dismantles 'end-of-life vehicles', using them as a resource for spare parts, and the further recycling of components and materials.

Sources: Nguyen et al., 2014, pp. 48–50; Group Renault web site, http://group.renault.com/en/news/blog-renault/circular-economy-recycle-renault/, viewed 24 August 2015.

The example in the introduction summarises the approach developed at one of the factories of the Renault Group oriented toward all possible recovery options – reuse, remanufacturing and recycling – that enable sustainability and profitability goals to be pursued. In this Chapter, we will describe how to develop systems that extract value from end-of-life products and how to effectively reintroduce them into the market, according to Circular Economy logics. In the first part of the Chapter, distinctions are made between the concepts of reverse flows, reverse logistics and reverse supply chain, drawing from specialist scientific literature on the subject. Subsequently, several examples are given of how different methods are used to design appropriate Closed-Loop Supply Chain systems in order to integrate forward and backward flows and to manage Sustainable Supply Chains. In the second part of the Chapter, the characteristics and management methods of these systems are studied in more depth, from the perspective, defined in literature, of the Why, Who, What and How. Finally, the Chapter closes by analysing the hierarchy of possible recovery options in terms of the generation of value, illustrating their main characteristics and highlighting the best methods to efficiently manage the time-value depreciation and the obsolescence of the observed products.

7.2   REVERSE FLOWS AND SUSTAINABILITY

It has already been highlighted several times that Sustainability can be defined as the set of practices and behaviour that make it possible for the needs of the present to be met without compromising the ability of future generations to meet theirs. Furthermore, as it has been seen, the management of a company's logistics flows can be observed in its upstream flows, responsible for providing the input resources, and its downstream flows, responsible for distributing the output products (Sanders, 2012). From a sustainability point of view, as far as the first component is concerned, the selection and use of scarce resources and the management of socially correct relations with the providers of global sourcing politics are the main concerns. With regard to downstream flows on the other hand, the subjects of pollution risks and transportation policies and their connected environmental impact are more important.

As already stated, the design and running of management systems oriented at sustainability correspond with four sets of objectives (De Brito and Dekker, 2010): compliance with regulatory and legislative obligations; the choice to comply with voluntary certifications and regulations; ethical and values-based incentives linked to respect for the environment and attention to the creation of social capital; and last, but not least, the possibility of increasing the company's competitive potential by reducing costs, waste and environmental impact, on the one hand, and improving its sales, margins and reputation, on the other hand.

In Chapter 2 we defined Supply Chain Management (Cooper et al., 1997; Christopher, 1998; Mentzer et al., 2001; Mentzer, 2004; Lambert et al., 2006; Sanders, 2012). According to these definitions, the flow of materials, semi-finished goods and finished products – operating typically as a one-way flow – goes from up- to downstream, starting from the source of supply and going through a series of transformation, transportation and storage operations until it reaches the point nearest the consumer. The subject we are examining in this Chapter, on the other hand, refers to the design and management of a reverse flow that, although moving in an opposite direction from the point of view of development – that is, from down- to upstream – pursues the same goals of creating value, as well as, from our perspective, reducing environmental and social impact.

In the same way that some authors make a distinction between Logistics Management and Supply Chain Management, where – as highlighted before (see Chapter 2) – the former is a subset of the latter (Cooper et al., 1997), in the literature there are also different interpretations of the elements that distinguish Reverse Logistics Management, Reverse Supply Chain Management, Closed-Loop Supply Chain Management and even Green Supply Chain Management. Some share similar approaches, others highlight their differentiating elements (De Brito and Dekker, 2010; Dekker et al., 2010; Srivastava, 2007; Prahinski and Kocabasoglu, 2006; Guide and van Wassenhove, 2002; Rogers et al., 2002; Tibben-Lembke, 2002; Rogers and Tibben-Lembke, 2001; Vachon et al., 2001; Dekker et al., 1998; Stock, 1998; Pohlen and Farris, 1992). As stated, 'The terms reverse logistics, green logistics, reverse supply chain, and closed-loop supply chains are often used interchangeably to deal with the reverse flows and products' (Skjott-Larsen et al., 2007, p. 292).

It is not the intention of this Chapter to go into the details of this debate, but it is worth stating some of the most well-known definitions in the literature, so that the considerations that follow are placed correctly.

Several common traits can be identified from among the many definitions coined by specialist literature, some of which are stated next. Reverse Logistics Management is, in fact, defined as:

- *... a broad term referring to the logistics management and disposing of hazardous or non-hazardous waste from packaging and products. It includes reverse distribution ... which causes goods and information to flow in the opposite direction of normal logistics activities* (Kopicki et al., 1993, p. 323).
- *The process whereby companies can become more environmentally efficient through recycling, reusing, and reducing the amount of materials used* (Carter and Ellram, 1998, p. 85).
- *The process of planning, implementing and controlling the efficient, cost effective flows of raw materials, in-process inventory, finished goods and related information from the point of consumption to the point of origin for the purpose of recapturing or creating value or proper disposal* (Rogers and Tibben-Lembke, 1999, p. 2).
- *... all activity associated with a product/service after the point of sale, the ultimate goal to optimise or make more efficient aftermarket activity, thus saving money and environmental resources* (Reverse Logistics Association, 2002).

Other Authors define Reverse Supply Chain Management as:

- *It's the series of activities required to retrieve a used product from a customer and either dispose of it or reuse it* (Guide and van Wassenhove, 2002, p. 25);

- *The effective and efficient management of the series of activities required to retrieve a product from a customer and either dispose it or recover value* (Prahinski and Kocabasoglu, 2006, p. 519).

As reflected in these definitions, there are several distinguishing elements that, irrespective of the defining distinction between Reverse Logistics and Reverse Supply Chain, can be summarised as follows:

- The physical flow moves from customer to vendor, in an opposite direction to the traditional physical flow and involves a series of specialised players, responsible for the management of the different phases that move from the downstream to the upstream markets.
- The fundamental objective lies in the recapture, and if possible creation, of differential value from the management of this reverse flow, either through reprocessing operations, or through the disposal of direct and indirect materials.
- The process must be managed along the entire supply chain while attempting to optimise overall costs efficiently and must also take its external effects into consideration.
- The possibility of creating value by exercising the most appropriate recovery options is linked to the most complex choices of Supply Chain Management, namely product design and the underlying purchase, production and distribution processes, one of which we have defined as Reverse Logistics.

7.3   REVERSE LOGISTICS AND CLOSED-LOOP SUPPLY CHAIN: NOT ONLY A SEMANTIC DIFFERENCE

In order to have a better understanding of the distinction in the concepts a discussion will follow, which is not only semantic; it is worth recalling the definition proposed by some authors which, although using the term 'Reverse Logistics', clearly makes a distinction between the operating environments associated with a more stringent or broader vision of the subject. Stock argued that

> *the term often used to refer to the role of logistics in recycling, waste disposal, and management of hazardous materials; a broader perspective includes all issues relating to logistics activities to be carried out in source reduction, recycling, substitution, reuse of materials and disposal* (1992, p. 20).

Kopicki et al. asserted that

> *Viewed narrowly, it can be thought of as the reverse distribution among channel members. A more holistic view of reverse logistics includes the reduction of materials in the forward system in such a way that fewer materials flow back, reuse of materials is possible and recycling is facilitated* (1993, p. 323).

The distinction between a narrower and a broader meaning is therefore linked to the perspective adopted in the analysis. In fact, the concept is clearly highlighted by

Srivastava: 'Similar to the concept of supply-chain management, the boundary of green supply chain management is dependent on the goal of the investigator' (2007, p. 54).

With the aim of including the previously mentioned elements and integrating both forward and backward flows, a new concept has been developed in many supply chains and in many sectors: the Closed-Loop Supply Chain. For our purposes, the distinction between Reverse Logistics Management (or Reverse Supply Chain Management) and Closed Loop Supply Chain Management refers to the strategic design intentions that lead to the design of reverse flows and the last targeting of the designed supply chain architecture.

In our perspective, it therefore would be consistent, as was the case with the definition and meaning of Supply Chain Management, to adopt the concept of Closed Loop Supply Chain Management as a representation of the set of choices that enable the complete flow of materials and products to be managed in line with sustainability goals. On the other hand, the term 'Reverse Logistics' will be identified as its subprocess, dedicated to the phases of product transportation to facilities for inspection, sorting and disposition (Guide and van Wassenhove, 2002).

Regarding the strategic design intentions that lead to the implementation of reverse flows, in line with the distinctions made before, we will define Reverse Logistics as the process that regulates the backward flow closely linked to the management choices regarding transportation, storage and operations in the strict sense, which are aimed at the exercising of recovery options, regardless of whether the product or forward logistics have been created, designed and managed for these purposes. On the other hand, we will define Closed-Loop Supply Chain as the process that deliberately pursues value-creation goals, starting from corporate strategic choices and the design of products, services and the associated processes, which incorporate this goal from the beginning[1]. From our perspective, the distinction between Reverse Logistics and Closed Loop Supply Chain Management leads one to believe that the former plays an instrumental and ancillary role in the pursuit of the objectives of the latter. The integration of the Closed Loop Supply Chain Management flows pursues the complex goals of creating value, while also exploiting Reverse Logistics choices. In this sense, Closed Loop Supply Chain Management concerns 'The design, control and operations of a system to maximise value creation over the entire life cycle of a product with dynamic recovery of value from different types and volumes of returns over time' (Guide and van Wassenhove, 2009, p. 10). However, reverse flows can be designed to manage product returns not necessarily linked to the subject of sustainability, but also to other possible objectives, as will be seen later. 'Product returns may occur for a variety of reasons over the product life cycle' (Guide and van Wassenhove, 2009, p. 11).

In reference to the topic being dealt with in this book – sustainability – the managerial requirement to manage supply chain flows according to sustainability principles

---

[1] In this regard, even if restricted to the environmental perspective, the interpretation given of Green Supply Chain Management 'defined as the integrating [of] environmental thinking into supply-chain management, including product design, material sourcing and selection, manufacturing processes, delivery of the final product to the consumers as well as end-of-life management of the product after its useful life' appears to be consistent (Srivastava, 2007, pp. 54–55).

appropriately is substantiated in the progressive integration of both forward and backward flows. The Closed Loop Supply Chain 'indicates a supply chain where there is a combination of forward and reverse flows, such that these two types of flows may impact each other, and may thus require some level of coordination' (Souza, 2012, p. 5).

As already mentioned, the need to manage these flows can be the result of the imposition, on the part of regulators, of a choice motivated by the possibility of generating profits along the supply chain or a values-based decision imposed by respect for the environment and social awareness.

7.4   CLOSED-LOOP SUPPLY CHAIN MANAGEMENT: INTEGRATING FORWARD AND BACKWARD FLOWS

Although they are used at times by different players, the two flows – forward logistics and backward logistics – included in Closed-Loop Supply Chain choices form part of a single loop, as illustrated in Figure 7.1. A factor that distinguishes the features of the two flows is the fact that whereas forward logistics is generally a one-to-many flow, since a greater number of delivery points are nourished from one or a few nodes, reverse logistics can be compared to a many-to-one flow, since it is based on a collection from several withdrawal points in order to concentrate products and materials in one or a few points dedicated to the subsequent sorting and treatment processes.

As a result of these definitions, attention is once again drawn to the integrated management of the two opposite flows: forward flow and backward flow (Tibben-Lembke and Rogers, 2002).

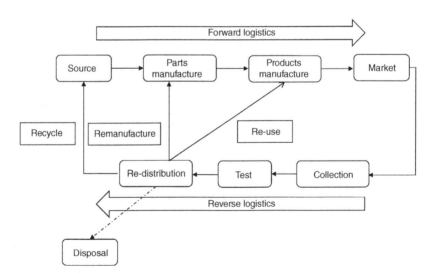

FIGURE 7.1   Forward and reverse logistics systems to exploit recovery options. *Source:* Rahman 2012. Reproduced with permission of John Wiley & Sons.

Although comparable in logistical terms, in terms of uncertainty and complexity, there are fundamental differences between the management of the forward flow, which makes the product available to the consumer, and the management of the reverse flow, which aims to recover the residual value of the product at the end of its life cycle. Indeed, reverse flows are characterised by (Grant et al., 2013, p. 19):

- Uncertainty on qualitative, quantitative characteristics and timing of the reverse flows. In fact reverse flows show higher levels of uncertainty than forward flows with reference to:
  ○ Quality and conditions of the product.
  ○ Quantity, resulting in a lower forecast reliability.
  ○ Timing of the backward flows, strongly influenced by the final consumer, as a starting point of the process.
- Uncertainty on consumer behaviour regarding the willingness of the final consumer to:
  ○ Return rather than waste the product.
  ○ Buy recovered/remanufactured products rather than new ones.
  ○ Value and pay a price for a recovered or remanufactured product.
- Complexity concerning the features of the product and of the facilities in charge of its treatment, with reference to:
  ○ The number, location and accessibility of collection points.
  ○ The conditions of the product and the related information linked to the willingness of the consumer to cooperate in the recovery process.
  ○ The cost-effectiveness of the recovery process, highly influenced by the inspection and sorting stages, which are in general labour intensive.

With regard to these elements of complexity and uncertainty, the possibility of designing and managing suitable sustainable supply chains seems to be increasingly rewarding and is connected to a series of variables described in the following paragraph.

7.5 SUSTAINABLE SUPPLY CHAINS: WHY, WHO, WHAT AND HOW?

In order to fully understand the relevance and scope of the subjects related to Reverse Logistics, it is worth introducing different investigation perspectives that can be summed up in the fundamental questions – Why, Who, What and How? – described by De Brito and Dekker (2010).

- *Why* refers to two different perspectives: the *driving forces* – defined as Why – drivers – underlying the choices of the parties that implement reverse flow processes (receivers) and the *return reasons* – defined as Why-reasons – connected to the reasons that motivate different players to act as senders.

- *Who* refers to the players involved in the different activities that can make up a reverse flow chain and their role in the process that ranges from the collection of the products, materials and components to be recovered to their selection and directing towards the appropriate exploitation methods.

- *What* has to do with the features of the products, materials and packaging involved in the return operations, manufactured either in order to reach cost-effectiveness objectives or to comply with legal obligations or, as it has been stated several times, to meet ethical aspirations.

- *How* mainly concerns the methods that make it possible to extract value from the aforesaid processes, which will be analysed below in terms of recovery options.

7.5.1   Why? Drivers and Reasons in Sustainable Supply Chains

As far as the first question – *Why?*– is concerned, and in particular from the perspective of Why-drivers, it has already been highlighted several times that the driving forces that lead to the implementation of these processes refer to:

- The possibility of achieving economic, strategic, reputational and relational advantages.
- Legal obligations and compliance with voluntary certifications.
- Ethical choices inspired by socially-responsible behaviour.

These aspects have already been analysed in Chapter 1. With regard to the Why-reasons on the other hand, namely the reasons underlying the need to manage a reverse flow appropriately, it is necessary to make a distinction between those prompted by business demands or competitiveness in a more general sense and those more closely linked to the subjects dealt with in this book. Sometimes these are generically called return flows and can be summarised in the following five points (Dale et al., 2002):

1. *Consumer return.* This generally has to do with the broader category of returns, due to defects discovered by customers, requests for replacement under warranty, repairs and end-of-use or end-of-life returns and so on. The arrival of e-commerce has significantly increased this type of returns in business to consumers (B2C) environments, due to the clauses in force regarding rights to return goods in almost all countries.

2. *Marketing or distribution return.* In this case the returns are imposed by the Marketing and Sales Departments of a company for various reasons, such as the reallocation of the product between different nodes along the distribution network through compensatory measures, to need to meet

slowdowns in demand or to withdraw products at the end of season or, in the case of obsolescence, to 'clean the channel' (end-of-life returns), withdrawing articles being phased out, in correspondence with the launch of substitute products.

3. *Asset return.* This is the case of companies in which an asset is recaptured and repositioned in order to reuse it in a different way (end-of-use returns). This return, typical of business to business (B2B) environments and hardware-leasing businesses, may refer to industrial equipment, quarry machinery, reusable containers, racks that are collected to be fed back and re-entered into the distribution cycle, as in the case for products like CDs, DVDs, food and beverage and over-the-counter products and so on.

4. *Product or manufacturing recall.* This decision is made in special circumstances, such as, for example, safety issues for the user or the case of serious quality problems (warranty returns), or due to restrictions connected to the use of materials or components imposed by regulatory bodies. Recalls may refer not only to products, but also to materials and components that have manifested quality problems that need reworking, or the need to re-enter sub-products or surplus materials and so on into the production cycle. If these phenomena arise during the production phases, they are also called manufacturing returns (De Brito and Dekker, 2010).

5. *Environmental return.* This last type refers to returns connected either to regulatory compliance requirements, such as the case of the WEEE regulations – Waste Electrical and Electronic Equipment (Directive 2002/96/EC), which contain measures aimed at the prevention of the disposal of electrical and electronic equipment and their reuse, recycling and other forms of recovery, or the regulations that impose waste packaging recovery activities on the seller, or can also refer to returns connected to the possibility of recovering products, components and materials based on the value associated to the different recovery options.

In view of the focus of this book, we will dwell mainly on the last point listed above, analysing the main features of the objects involved in these processes (What), the players and systems in reverse flow management (Who), and finally the recovery options that a company may exercise (How). Once again, we will embrace a broad perspective in an attempt to focus our attention on the convergence between sustainability, environmental orientation and supply chain management, with the meanings adopted in this paper (Linton et al., 2007).

7.5.2 Who? Main Players in Sustainable Supply Chains

The term *Who* refers to the players involved in the process and their different responsibilities in the management of the flows along a supply chain (Fuller and Allen, 1995).

The structure of the most complex process aimed at the management of logistics flows can be designed according to two methods (Rahman, 2012; Prahinski and Kocabasoglu, 2006; Guide et al., 2003; Fleischmann et al., 1997; Kopicki et al. 1993):

1. *Open-loop network (or systems)*, in which the forward flows unfold through several logistics nodes and the reverse flows are managed by other players (collectors) that assign them to secondary markets, after having managed possible recovery options. In this case, the recovered materials are allocated to markets other than those that originally generated them, such as in the case of waste from polyethylene bottles, assigned to the production of sportswear articles made of pile, or food production waste used for the production of fodder for animals or fertilisers and so on.

2. *Closed-loop network (or systems)*, in which the origin and destination of the flows coincide, and thus the flows move within the system. In this case, products and packaging often return to their original producers. This is an option adopted in chemical or electrical components companies, or in logistics structures involved in the reuse of pallets and returnable containers (Rahman, 2012).

The two flows, managed through a series of B2B exchanges until the final customer is reached, are shown in Figure 7.2.

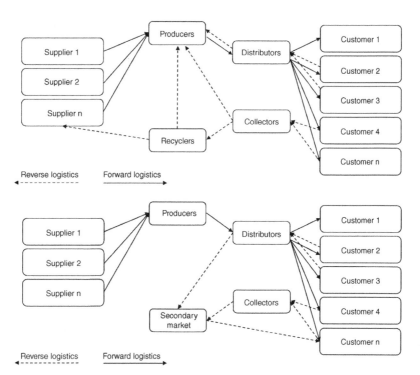

FIGURE 7.2   Closed-loop and open-loop networks. *Source:* Rahman 2012. Reproduced with permission of John Wiley & Sons.

7.5.3   What? Products, Materials and Packaging in Sustainable Supply Chains

The connection between the Why-reasons, described previously, the What, namely the features and types of objects involved in these processes, and the profile of the Who, namely the players involved in the reverse flow process, can be summarised by analysing the variety of activities and items involved in the reverse flow crossing two viewpoints: the viewpoint of the objects – What? – that is, distinguishing between products and packaging, and the viewpoint of the sources of these flows – Who? – that is, distinguishing between players in the supply chain, such as retailers, distribution centres and end users. As illustrated in Figure 7.3, the different types of returns can be linked to commercial requirements or requirements more closely connected to sustainability issues – Why-reasons, as already illustrated before.

If we focus our attention on the reasons connected to the environmental sustainability, marked in bold font in Figure 7.3, it is possible to highlight the characteristics of a product, components or packaging – *What?* – that can lead to different recovery options. These are related to (De Brito and Dekker, 2010, p. 17):

- Composition.
- Deterioration.
- Use pattern.

Composition means the number and variety of components and materials used in the manufacturing of the product involved in the process and their characteristics. These attributes are linked to the choices of the breadth and depth of the product base and the use of materials that are heterogeneous. Furthermore, as already illustrated with the reference to Design for the Environment (see Chapter 3), composition refers to the intrinsic characteristics of the materials used, the utilisation of multi-material

		Who	
		Supply Chain partners	**End users**
What	**Products**	Stock Balancing returns Marketing returns End of life/season Transit damage	Defective/unwanted Products Warranty returns Recalls **Environmental disposal issues**
	Packaging	Resuable totes Multi-trip packaging **Disposal requirements**	**Reuse Recycling Disposal restrictions**

FIGURE 7.3   Characterisation of items in reverse flow by Type and Origin. *Source:* Rogers 2011. Reproduced with permission of John Wiley & Sons.

components or 'monstrous hybrids' composed of hazardous and non-polluting components. These aspects significantly influence the costs and time linked to laborious and often uneconomical or impossible disassembly and sorting processes of the materials used and, consequently, affect the feasibility of the different recovery options. In order to facilitate the use of recovery options, it is in fact preferable to have components that have been designed according to the principles of modularity, namely in which there is a one-to-one correspondence between the component and the function carried out and for which the interfaces between components are coupled in such a way that if any changes are made to the design it is always possible to replace obsolete components with new ones. Furthermore, it is necessary to avoid the combined use of biological and technical materials, which are difficult to recycle, and to encourage methods of design for disassembly.

A second aspect that conditions the possibility of reusing a product or its components in order to recover its residual value concerns the characteristics of its *Deterioration*, namely an appreciation of its residual functional capacity. The recovery potential of a product or its parts can be influenced by multiple factors, several linked to usage phenomena or cases of technological obsolescence, others to aspects of economic obsolescence or the unprofitability in the trade-off between its replacement with a new product and its re-entry on the market. The former case is typically linked to intrinsic deterioration, namely the usage deriving from prolonged use over time and can manifest itself as homogeneous usage, that is, usage connected to the general ageing of a product, or non-homogeneous usage, that is, usage linked in particular to several of the parts of a product that are more exposed to deterioration.

The third factor that can influence the effectiveness and efficiency of reverse flow processes is the *Use Pattern*, understood as the location, intensity and duration of use:

- *Location of use:* as already mentioned, one of the characteristics of reverse flows lies in the fact that it is a many-to-one flow, thus its degree of efficiency is linked to the location and dispersion of the users of a product and its collection points. In this regard it appears obvious how the nature of the user – individually or collectively – can influence the effective location of the collection points and the effort required from the user to implement the process. Take, for example, the different impact of plastic packaging in recovery and recycling processes, in terms of volume and associated costs, if the user is an individual, no matter how sensitive he/she is to environmental problems, or a company or a supermarket capable of generating enormous volumes of product to be directed towards the processes described herein in a short period of time.

- *Intensity of use:* a further factor is the intensity of use that influences the possibility of reselling a product as-is in the secondary market, such as a book, a car or industrial equipment, or reusing a component as a spare part or in remanufacturing processes following recovery.

- *Duration of use:* finally, duration is generally directly proportional to its intensity, even if it can be examined independently. In fact, there are products that can be used for a long period of time, but with low intensity (and consequently low use). This is the case of some components, such as starters or water pumps in the auto parts industry, or sophisticated equipment and tools for occasional use, or products such as boats or caravans (long duration and low intensity of use), for which, in fact, there are secondary reselling markets or demolition yards dedicated to the disassembly and recovery of all useful parts or components.

7.5.4   How? Recovery Options in Sustainable Supply Chains

Finally, as already stated, the *How* perspective refers to the phases along which the reverse flow develops, as well as the choice of the most appropriate recovery options that the company can pursue. In view of the relevance of the subject for this book and the need for more in-depth study, this will be dealt with in greater detail in the following Section.

The management of a reverse flow involves a series of steps that can be configured differently, but that generally refer to the following phases (Rogers and Tibben-Lembke, 1998; De Brito and Dekker, 2010):

- *Gatekeeping*, in which the decisions regarding the products to be guided to the reverse logistics processes are made.
- *Collection*, in which the identified products are collected and grouped, transferring them to the point of recovery.
- *Inspection or testing*, in which the conditions of the materials and products are assessed, and possible functional and diagnostic tests are performed.
- *Sortation or selection*, in which products are separated per type of goods and per recovery option allocation.
- *Disposition*, in which the products are sent to the specific destinations.
- *Recovery*, in which the recovery of residual value and the assessment of the best available option are specified.

The reverse flow processes may involve products and their components, as well as packaging (Fleischmann et al., 1997), and have rather different effects on the different sectors and organisations. In some sectors, there may be the return of new or almost new products, such as books, videos, electrical appliances and computers, which are redirected to sales channels on secondary markets or in emerging countries. In other sectors, such as machinery, engines and complex pieces of equipment, the products are disassembled, and the components that still work properly are reconditioned and reintroduced to the market as spare parts for warranty claims at lower costs than components originating from OEM – Original Equipment Manufacturers – sources. In other cases, the returns are treated as scrap or recycling, after the products have been destroyed, as is the case of waste paper, metals or plastic packaging. The use of product returns or the salvage of parts and materials from end-of-life products is also a management lever used to significantly reduce the level of waste of new components, which is necessary in order to guarantee service to the markets and to implement efficient build-to-order management processes. If in the past, the main motivation connected to the appropriate design and management of the Closed Loop Supply Chain was mainly linked to economic objectives and overall system efficiency, in recent years, either due to the assertion of more stringent regulations or an increased awareness of companies and stakeholders, the topic has been enriched with implications linked to the sustainability of company choices and the need to limit their environmental impact. One only needs to think of the increase in the costs connected to the growing scarcity of areas that can be used for landfills, the diffusion of regulations that prevent the dumping of many contaminating products in landfills, the pressure and the concerns of public opinion regarding environmental risks, the possibility of reaching additional profit margins by exploiting appropriate recovery options and reducing the consumption of materials, components and packaging, or the limiting of the energy and manufacturing costs linked to the increasingly reduced useful life of products.

The methods used to implement reverse flows differ from and depend on the possibility of reselling or reusing the product or the packaging 'as-is' within the supply chain or in secondary markets (Tibben-Lembke, 2004) or, on the other hand, the need for the product or packaging to be reconditioned, remanufactured or refurbished by the original producer or by specialised third-party operators, or even for lower-value operations to be implemented, such as recycling or disposal.

In general, the aim of extracting value from the reverse flow processes is based on the assessment of the possible alternative actions (Rogers and Tibben-Lembke, 1998). The possibility of recovering or creating value from the appropriate management of a reverse flow is therefore linked to the recovery options that a company or a system of companies can exercise during the different phases of the reverse logistics flow.

Products
- Return to supplier.
- Resell.
- Sell via outlet.
- Salvage.
- Reconditioning.
- Refurbish.
- Remanufacture.
- Reclaim materials.
- Recycle.
- Landfill.

Packaging
- Reuse.
- Refurbish.
- Reclaim materials.
- Recycle.
- Salvage.

Several authors have made a distinction between the possible exploitation options of products, materials and packaging along the reverse flow, distinguishing between options that involve product reconditioning and upgrade, such as repackaging, repair, refurbishing and remanufacturing, where the effort to upgrade the product increases progressively from the first to the last option, to others like cannibalisation and recycling, in which parts and/or materials are recovered, but not the product (Thierry et al., 1995). These options in any case depend on the nature of the object of recovery and the inexpensiveness of the underlying operations. For example, in the case of packaging there may be primary or secondary packaging, 'to be lost', which in this case can be compared to the flow of materials for recycling, or packaging 'to be returned', on the other hand, and in this case the packaging re-enters the cycle after several inspections of its wholeness, cleaning and so forth.

Figure 7.4 briefly illustrates the position of the different recovery options along a hypothetical supply chain.

A key point of the process that was illustrated at the beginning of this Chapter in Figure 7.1, which discusses the case of a Closed-Loop Supply Chain, lies in the test (or sortation) phase of the recovered material. The aforesaid phase, which can obviously be found at various stages along the reverse flow, plays a crucial role, as it is responsible for defining the best value-recovery option to be exercised for each analysed product, component or material. As will be illustrated later, the different recovery options can create different levels of value, from high-value options, such as, for example, the option of reusing reconditioned products or components, to options with substantially zero value, if not negative value, such as the option of disposal without energy recovery.

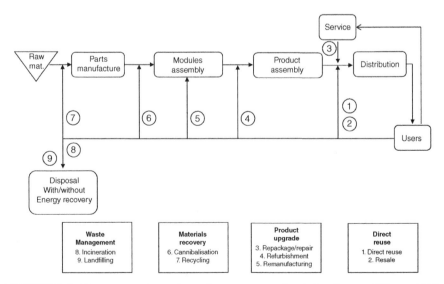

FIGURE 7.4 Recovery options along the reverse supply chain. *Source:* Thierry 1995. Reproduced with permission of California Management Review.

The possible recovery options can be summarised in the following five categories:

1. Resale (as-is) and reuse.
2. Remanufacturing, refurbishment or repair.
3. Parts harvesting, cannibalisation and recycling.
4. Disposal with energy recovery.
5. Disposal without energy recovery or land filling.

In fact, two further options can be added to these recovery options, but they cannot, however, be dealt with together with those stated before, as they do not belong to the family of recovery options, but rather to the design choices of the product, which have already been analysed in Chapter 3, and the maturity of the sensitivity of the markets towards more conscious consumption. In particular:

- The first, known as Resource Reduction, originates from the possibility of designing products and systems capable of reducing the use of the resources used in industrial and logistics processes; this is defined as the 'minimisation of materials used in products and minimisation of waste and energy achieved through the design of more environmentally efficient products' (Carter and Ellram, 1998, p. 91).
- The second, which is beyond the scope of this book, falls within the set of actions aimed at influencing the market in the direction of more responsible consumption. The latter has to do with the regulations and information implemented by institutions and companies in order to influence the purchasing and consumption behaviour of the final client. Several recent contributions are addressing the issues related to the consumer's intention to purchase green products (Johnstone and Tang, 2014).

7.6 VALUE CREATION THROUGH RECOVERY OPTIONS

As pointed out by Blackburn et al. (2004) 'returns and their reverse supply chains represent an opportunity to create a value stream, not an automatic financial loss' (p. 7). The main recovery options are described next with the goal of illustrating the area in which they are implemented and the value potentially associated with these:

1. *Resale and Reuse.* This concerns two different options, but for our purposes they can be dealt with together. In both cases, this option involves the possibility of reusing (and possibly reselling) products and components for the same purpose for which they were originally designed and produced. The first, Resale, can be exercised in different ways, through forms of selling via outlets and/or discounts, which is typical of products originating from retail chains and caused by returns due to overstocks or, if a secondary market exists, through the sale of used products or components as-is, without any particular

reconditioning (Souza, 2012). The first case, also known as 'sell-as-new' is typical in the clothing and furnishing sectors, etc. The second is the case of the sale of used products, such as cars, books, DVDs, laptops or any other product that can find a buyer, and is prevalent in B2C markets, although examples can also be found in B2B markets, such as industrial machinery, earth-moving equipment and so on. As this does not involve resale in the strict sense, the returns linked to non-profit organisations that manage the processes aimed at donating the product to charitable organisations also form part of this category (Reyes and Meade, 2006).

2. The second option – *Reuse* – refers to components or packaging, as well as finished products; it often involves reconditioning and is more frequently found in B2B exchanges. For several articles, such as packaging, pallets, containers, pads and cog wheels, products can be reused after simple inspection and cleaning. Since this option is often used for low-value products, it is profitable in the cases where inspection, cleaning and possible reconditioning are simple and inexpensive. In other cases, typically involving more complex products, it is necessary to perform tests, reconditioning and/or light repairs (with the possible replacement of small used components). This is the case, for example, in the option offered by car manufacturer to buy cars with either a new or a guaranteed reconditioned GPS navigation device. If, on the other hand, a careful inspection of the individual components is imposed after the produced is disassembled, depending on the value that could be recovered and the comparison of the cost with the complexity of a new regeneration, the options of remanufacturing, part harvesting or finally recycling can be exercised, as illustrated in Figure 7.5.

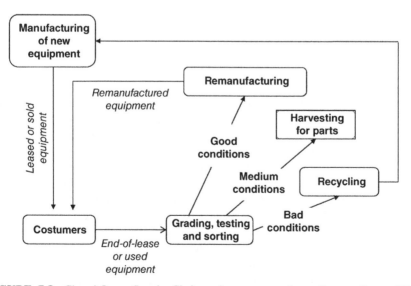

FIGURE 7.5 Closed–Loop Supply Chain and recovery options. *Source:* Souza 2012. Reproduced with permission of Business Expert Press.

- *Remanufacturing.* The remanufacturing option, also known as refurbishing, repairing, rebuilding, restoring or reconditioning depending on the sector in question, is performed through the disassembly of the product into its components in order to extract its potential residual value. As this option involves potentially complex and costly transactions, it is justified in the case of products whose recovery potential is associated with an increase in value. 'Remanufacturing is the process of restoring a used product to a common aesthetic and operating standard' (Souza, p. 90). The goal of remanufacturing is therefore to return the product to the same state as the new product in terms of functional and aesthetic performance. This option is often adopted for products like computers, printers, photocopiers, industrial machinery, car engines and so on. At times the replacement of original components with more recent components makes the quality of the remanufactured product higher than the original (Rahman, 2012). Remanufacturing involves a series of recovery processes, which can also be extremely complex and composed of multiple operations. As a very brief summary, it is necessary to disassemble, clean and inspect all of the parts of a product in order to assess its state and if necessary, replace them with other new or reconditioned (reworked) parts and finally reassemble the product and retest its functions. These processes are facilitated if the product has already been designed according to modularity, design for disassemble and design for re-manufacturing principles. However, it is not always profitable for an OEM company to design products and manage processes aimed at remanufacturing. This is for the following reasons, among others (Souza, 2012, p. 69):
  - Technological obsolescence: in environments where technological evolution is very rapid or in the cases where new product generations consume considerably less energy than previous ones or the products are manufactured using innovative materials. In all these cases consumers favour products that incorporate new materials and updated and more efficient technology, and therefore remanufacturing is not profitable; nevertheless, in fast-moving sector remanufacturing is made easier by the fact that customers generally return products when they are still in good conditions.
  - Fashion products: fashion goods and products with short life cycles are not suited to remanufacturing, as they do not have many possibilities of re-entering the markets. In the same way, several aesthetic components that characterise the external appearance of an overall product offer reduced possibilities of remanufacturing, unless as spare parts. The producer is generally driven to develop remanufacturing processes for non-visible components and therefore those that are less exposed to the evolution of the tastes of the consumer. For example, the mechanical components of a car or a motorcycle are more prone to remanufacturing, compared to the bodywork, seats or internal parts, which are generally recycled.
- *Part Harvesting and Recycling.* Whereas the remanufacturing option generates a high value-added recovery, aiming at recovering the intrinsic functional value of complex products, groups or components, Parts Harvesting or Cannibalisation and Recycling are generally associated with a more limited value, as the choice

of components or materials recovery is narrow. In this case, the options are also theoretically different, but they can be dealt with together as they are often practised by the same economic actors. In general, the underlying process takes the form of the collection, disassembly, and separation of materials and components into similar types. In certain circumstances – Parts Harvesting or Cannibalisation – several components that are disassembled, duly separated and treated, can be effectively reused as after-sale replacements or spare parts under warranty. These can be reconditioned, such as in the case, for example, of mechanical parts subject to modest usage processes or functioning electronic parts. Otherwise, Recycling is the only option, such as in the case of ferrous materials, alloys, plastic materials, wood, paper, glass and so on. The Recycling option is associated more frequently with materials with a very limited residual value, due to either compromised quality conditions or the economic obsolescence that makes its reuse improbable. These materials can be reused either in the same industry, such as scrap iron for steel production or paper scrap for the paper industry, or in different supply chains that use these materials as raw materials or components for further manufacturing, such as plastic bottles for the production of textiles or aluminium tin cans for the production of manufactured products. Often the intrinsic residual value of several waste materials is underestimated, but, thanks to appropriate differentiated waste collection and dedicated industrial processes, economic value can be generated by manufacturing products made from waste materials, without considering the benefits linked to lower environmental impact.

In this regard, please refer to Box 7.1.

BOX 7.1   NOTHING IS CREATED AND NOTHING IS DESTROYED, BUT EVERYTHING IS TRANSFORMED

Examples of the exploitation of recycled materials
Steel
- 1 frying pan can be made from 13 tins of peeled tomatoes
- In 19,000 pots of jam there is enough steel to make 1 car

Plastic
- 1 fleece jacket can be made from 27 bottles
- 67 bottles produce enough padding to fill a quilt for a double bed

Aluminium
- 1 bicycle is made of 800 tins
- 640 tins produce enough aluminium to make 1 rim of a car wheel

Wood
- 1 small box of wood can make a clothes hanger
- 1 desk can be made from 4 pallets

The increasing attention being paid by the regulator to recycling is aimed at making recycling easier. The success and cost-effectiveness of this process are in fact linked to the quality of the materials collected, the result of careful separation and the existence of a market willing to use them. In some cases the recovered materials are directed to a range of subsequent 'cascaded' uses, or are used across value streams and in industries. This is the case, for example, of clothes that cannot be reintroduced to a secondary market and that are used to generate new products and used as materials for other products, like rags for cleaning, fabric for overalls or fibre for insulation in the automobile or building sectors.

- *Disposal with energy recovery.* This is a residual option, in which there is, however, the possibility of recovering a fraction of value through waste-to-energy and combustion (incineration) processes or the co-production of energy through biomass gases. This is the case, for example, in the cement production plant of the Italcementi Group located in Calusco, Italy, which, under an agreement made with the local council, uses an alternative fuel to partially replace fossil fuels, deriving from the recycling of selected municipal solid waste that otherwise could not be recycled in order to feed the furnaces used in the production process of clinker slabs. This innovation enables savings to be made in relation to the use of fossil fuels, reduces the environmental impact linked to CO_2 emissions and makes a social contribution to the region, in perfect harmony with the principles of the Triple Bottom Line. This option is justified either by the inability to recover the waste material or by the low value associated with it, such as the case of chipboard or woodchips, combustible oils that cannot be regenerated, the case of incineration, material deriving from the collection of wet waste or originating from the production of fruit and vegetables or agro-food and the case of the gas production from biomass.
- *Disposal without Energy Recovery or Landfilling.* When it is impossible to exploit any of the recovery options analysed previously, the extreme option is Disposal without Energy Recovery or Landfilling. In this case the only value created consists in the minimisation of environmental impact.

Regarding disposal options, one only needs to think that

current global MSW (Municipal Solid Waste) generation levels are approximately 1.3 billion tonnes per year, and are expected to increase to approximately 2.2 billion tonnes per year by 2025. This represents a significant increase in per capita waste generation rates, from 1.2 to 1.42 kg per person per day in the next fifteen years. However, global averages are broad estimates only as rates vary considerably by region, country, city, and even within cities (WB, 2012, p. 24).

It is possible to identify a hierarchy between the recovery options, in terms of potential value created, and the level of eco-efficiency. As illustrated in Figure 7.6, the option of Resource Reduction is at the top of the pyramid of value creation, whereas the option of Disposal without Energy Recovery is found at its base.

It is clear to see how the possibility of exploiting the options with higher added value as much as possible is closely linked to the design and manufacturing methods of products and components. As explained in detail in Chapter 3, in fact, the use of

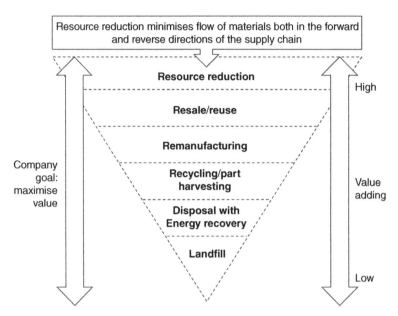

FIGURE 7.6 Recovery options and value creation. *Source:* adapted from Carter and Ellram, 1998; Stock, 1992; Kopicki et al., 1993.

Design for the Environment, Design for Remanufacturing or Design for Disassembling techniques can have a considerable impact on the efficiency and effectiveness of remanufacturing or recycling practices, such as, for example, several projects introduced by the automobile industry to facilitate the disassembly and reuse of materials, by reducing the number of parts, abandoning chemical bonds and screws and rationalising the materials and snap-fitting components.

Clearly, managing time is key to leveraging the opportunity of creating value through recovery options, as claimed by Blackburn et al. (2004, p. 6) 'the longer it takes to retrieve a returned product the lower the likelihood of economically viable reuse options.' It is widely believed that a product recovered through a reverse supply chain loses approximately 50% of its value on average, mostly due to the downgrading of a product sold as remanufactured, but also due to the effects produced as time goes by, defined as time value depreciation or Marginal Value of Time for Return. This loss in value differs considerably in different sectors: for example a PC or laptop is estimated to lose 1% of its value per week (Blackburn et al., 2004, p. 10).

To maximise value recovery options, companies and their supply chain partners must design closed-loop systems capable of properly managing the trade-off between speed, linked to the time value depreciation issue, and low cost, related to the need to minimise the remanufacturing cost to retain the marketability of downgraded product.

According to the approach proposed by Blackburn et al. (2004), different types of Closed-Loop Supply Chains can be designed, in which the backward flow is managed taking the level of time value depreciation into consideration:

1. For products with a low time value depreciation, such as machine tools, preference is given to Centralised Efficient (Cost-Effective) Return Systems,

in which – since the objective is to minimise the overall process cost, to the detriment of its speed – the inspection, sortation and disposition phases are centralised in a central facility. This makes it possible to obtain economies of scale during this phase, after which, once evaluated, the product is directed to the most appropriate recovery option; the exploitation option is postponed downstream of the product condition evaluation. In this case the retailer and the reseller play no part in the product evaluation process and therefore ought not to sustain any costs related to the acquisition of testing and sorting competences. Furthermore, this system guarantees economies of scale in the transportation of multiple products sent to the central testing facility and from there to multiple locations according to the different recovery options.

2. For products with a high time value depreciation, such as PCs and laptops, Decentralised Responsive (Time Effective) Return Systems are suggested, in which the speed objective in the management of the diagnosis process of the functionality and obsolescence of the product prevails, to the detriment of the overall cost of the process. In this case, the testing, sortation and disposition phases are managed directly by retailers and resellers, in a process defined as *preponement*. In this phase, for example, products characterised by low intensity or duration of use can be immediately restocked and reintroduced to the sales process; others, on the other hand, are re-sent to a central testing and repairing facility for a more detailed analysis or to then be allocated to the different recovery options. The need to contrast the reduction in value linked to

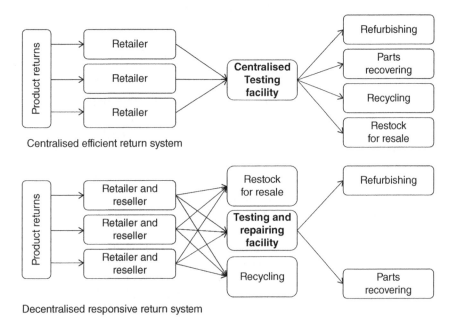

Centralised efficient return system

Decentralised responsive return system

FIGURE 7.7 Efficient and Responsive Return Systems. *Source:* Blackburn 2004. Reproduced with permission of California Management Review.

the passage of time prevails over the opportunity of obtaining economies of scale during the process phase and in transportation.

The two options are summarised in Figure 7.7.

Returning to the more general subject of this book, Closed-Loop Supply Chain systems must be considered to be useful tools in the appropriate management of physical and information flows, within more extensive strategic visions and management logics, based on cradle-to-cradle principles and the concept of the Circular Economy (see Chapter 3).

8

MEASURING SUSTAINABILITY

8.1 INTRODUCTION

Syngenta is a leading agricultural company based in Switzerland, which in 2014 employed 29,340 people at world-wide level and reported a turnover of $15.1 billion. It is specialised in the following product types:

- *crop protection and seedcare products, to support and protect the growth of the plant throughout its entire life, from the development of the root to the later stages, so as to obtain more healthy plants and prevent any yield loss.*
- *seeds: they concern several types of crops, such as rice, sugar cane, corn, soybean, sunflower, oilseed rape, as well as vegetables and flowers.*
- *lawn and garden, which refer to the plant protection products targeted to consumers and professional growers, as ornamental growers and golf course managers.*

Quoting Syngenta's website,

> *Syngenta's products and offers can help address one of the planet's most challenging dilemmas: how to grow more crops using fewer resources. Our ambition is to bring greater food security in an environmentally sustainable way to an increasingly populous world by creating a worldwide step-change in farm productivity. Our ambition encompasses the 8 million large farms worldwide with over 100 hectares as well as the 450 million small farms with 2 hectares or less.*

As explicitly claimed in the company's website, the concern of Syngenta toward sustainability is twofold: on the one hand, it is of major importance for this company to offer a valid support to the improvement of farm productivity, which in turn results

Sustainable Operations and Supply Chain Management, First Edition. Valeria Belvedere and Alberto Grando.
© 2017 John Wiley & Sons Ltd. Published 2017 by John Wiley & Sons Ltd.

in the possibility to feed as many people as possible. On the other hand, Syngenta is concerned with the sustainable production of its own items, which requires the adoption of appropriate tools and initiatives to guarantee that the supply and transformation activities are carried in accordance with this principle.

In a company present in 90 countries and endowed with 111 production and supply sites and 141 R&D ones, the dissemination of this culture and its implementation through appropriate actions require the identification of specific areas to be addressed. Looking at the Annual Review 2014, it can be seen that a specific section is devoted to 'Sustainable Operations', which helps identify the performance areas over which Syngenta focuses its improvement efforts, as well as the indicators adopted. They can be summed up as follows:

- *Social sustainability performance: this performance profile refers to work and product safety and to the support offered to local communities. The former is addressed in the Annual Review through the provision of ad hoc synthetic indicators (recordable incidents per 200,000 hours, equal to 0.37 in 2014, and recordable occupational illness per 200,000 hours, equal to 0.04 in 2014) and the description of the main prevention programmes conducted in 2014 to improve work safety. These indicators are deployed into more detailed ones, which take into account the geographic distribution of the phenomena, as well as the type of illness. Furthermore, safety is also concerned with the product, which can be a source of risk for the user due to the problem of counterfeiting. The report, thus, also provides information about the initiatives undertaken by the company to cope with this phenomenon. The support to local communities is measured in terms of 'economic value shared' ($14,982 in 2014), which expresses the economic benefit brought by Syngenta through its operations to the local communities that host its premises, in the form of taxes, wages, value of products and services sourced locally etc. Also this indicator is deployed in terms of the subjects that receive an economic benefit from the presence of the company in a given area (e.g. employees, suppliers, government etc.). On top of this, the report provides information about other 'social' activities undertaken by the company, such as training programmes, not only for company's employees.*
- *Environmental sustainability performance: the most critical environmental impact of Syngenta's operations concerns hazardous materials, wastewater, energy and water consumption. Such performance is measured both in absolute and intensity-based terms. In this regard, the Annual Review provides both synthetic and deployed indicators. For instance, concerning energy, the total amount of Joules consumed is reported, as well as MJ/$ sales, which refers to energy intensity, equal to 0.66 in 2014 and deployed in terms of types of energy. Similar pieces of information are reported for the CO_{2e} (deployed for source and typology of greenhouse gas), water usage (deployed in terms of type of usage and origin), industrial wastewater (deployed for type of chemical features), waste (deployed in terms of the hazardousness and type of treatment).*

Source: Syngenta website, viewed 30 November 2015; Syngenta's Annual Review 2014, available at www.syngenta.com, viewed 30 November 2015.

As can be seen in the case of Syngenta, the measurement of sustainability involves relevant issues to be addressed. First of all, it is necessary to identify the performance profiles against which to assess the company. Then, appropriate indicators must be designed, able to capture the whole phenomenon and then to deploy it into its main determinants, so as to drive appropriate improvement actions. Such a design process of the performance measurement system exposes the company to several risks, mainly concerning the possibility of neglecting relevant profiles and of adopting an excessive number of indicators, which provide a misleading view of the phenomenon under analysis.

In this chapter, we will address the problem of how to measure the sustainability of a production and logistic process. We will move from a brief analysis of the contributions concerning the measurement of sustainability at a macroeconomic level, since these are relevant antecedents of the main proposals made for companies in this regard. Then, we will focus on the design of functional measurement systems and, finally, a brief overview of the main reference models will presented.

8.2   MEASURING SUSTAINABILITY IN MANUFACTURING COMPANIES

Measuring the performance of production and logistics processes means establishing the objectives that business operations ought to pursue, the indicators that can be used to quantify the targets to be reached and, finally, how to carry out a systematic process for analysing and interpreting the achieved results. As explained in Chapter 2, in the last twenty years a general consensus has been reached on the fact that the performance profiles peculiar to business operations consist of time, cost, quality and flexibility. Many indicators, used to quantify their various attributes, have been identified for each of these profiles. The wide variety of key performance indicators (KPIs) that are potentially available has subsequently led to the need to make a selection thereof, in order to help business management to focus its attention and its improvement efforts on a few important areas of performance. This has caused a growing interest in the design of measurement systems suitable for guiding actions through 'dashboards' that are capable of coordinating choices made on a functional level with the long-term objectives of the company.

This has determined the proliferation of various reference frameworks for the design of measurement systems – primarily the balanced scorecard (Kaplan and Norton, 1992).

The key assumption of these models, which have been popular since the 1990s, is the fact that the long-term success of the company is measured taking its economic and financial results into consideration, and consequently the contribution of each company function consists of supporting the strategies implemented to pursue these objectives. With this in mind, optimising time, cost, quality and flexibility performance is useful to the extent that it enables the economic results of the company to be increased and sustained.

Nevertheless, during recent years this approach has been called into question. The company is no longer viewed only as a vehicle for economic progress in the strict sense, but also as a promoter of the development of the community and the ability of individuals to increase and make the most of their potential abilities and skills (Nussbaum, 2011; Sen, 1992; 1999). This new perspective creates further challenges in the measurement of the performance of the production and logistics process, as it requires the role that it is called upon to play in 'sustainable' companies to be taken into consideration. Measuring the performance of operations from the 'sustainability' perspective, therefore, implies a vision of the company that seeks to respond to these demands.

This chapter deals with the topic of sustainability measurement, first from a macro-economic perspective and, then, by taking a closer look at the subject on a company level.

8.3   SUSTAINABLE DEVELOPMENT MEASUREMENT

8.3.1   The Measurement of GDP: Limits

The increasing interest in the subject of social and environmental sustainability, as well as the serious and on-going economic crisis that has hit many countries in recent years, have led to the challenging of the most established models for quantifying the well-being created by national economic systems, based essentially on the estimate of Gross Domestic Product (GDP).

The assessment of the well-being of a nation on the grounds of its GDP is based on the assumption that the countries capable of 'producing' economic value are also environments that are more favourable to the development of individuals and the improvement of their quality of life. This approach has been widely criticised since the 1960s, because it regarded economic growth as the single indicator of progress, the well-being of society and, ultimately, the happiness of the individual (Blanchflower and Oswald 2004; Easterlin, 1974; 1995; 2001). In 1968, in a famous speech at the University of Kansas, Bob Kennedy claimed that no country could pursue the accumulation of material goods as its one and only purpose or measure its success without using indicators that take the health of its citizens, their cultural level, the quality of their existence or the environment in which they live into consideration. In short, the re-discovery of an ethical dimension was already being sought back then, not only in the identification of the objectives that the company and its government bodies ought to set, but also the measurement tools aimed at quantifying the achieved results. From this perspective, the GDP presents a series of limits, which compromise its ability to be a truly useful tool for the quantification of the well-being of the community. Several distortions in the GDP, in fact, emerge, when the following aspects are taken into consideration (Stiglitz et al., 2010):

- *Assessment of public services*: if a product/service does not have a market price, it is conventionally valued by taking the resources used to produce/deliver it into consideration, as is the case for many public services. For example, if the contribution that sectors such as public health make to the GDP is quantified, the total expenditure incurred on a national level is assessed, but this does not always express the degree of productivity of the system and, therefore, its contribution to the well-being of the community. In this regard, it can be considered that the United States are among the countries with the highest healthcare costs, which according to the OECD statistics in 2012 was 16.4% of its GDP, while in Italy it was 8.8% in the same year (OECD data). Nevertheless, several of the key performance indicators in this sector in the United States are clearly lower than those of other countries that are just as developed – especially life expectancy at birth, which in 2012 for a US new-born was equal to 78.8 years, compared to 82.3 years for an Italian one. Similar problems emerge when the growth of the economy is supported by public spending, which sometimes is allocated to the pursuit of expansionary policies and not to actually improve specific areas.

- *Improvement of product quality*: many products are significantly improved over time, guaranteeing standards of quality and features that are clearly higher than they were in the past, such as consumer electronics, for example. At the same time, especially due to technological innovation and the increasing efficiency of production systems, the costs of these goods are reduced, thus producing almost paradoxical effects in national accounting, which tends to underestimate the contribution made by these sectors to the economic development of the country.

- *Increase in GDP as a result of inefficiencies of the system*: it may be the case that the higher expenditure of companies or individuals (and therefore their contribution to GDP) is linked to the need to cope with various forms of inefficiencies that can be observed in some countries. For example, an outdated and unreliable railway network leads to a wider use of private means of transport, with consequent higher transport costs, longer travel times and a higher frequency of accidents.

- *Stock vs flows*: GDP is a measurement of flow, not stock. This means that if economic well-being is to be measured using GDP, only what has been produced during the year is taken into consideration, whereas any stocks accumulated over time will be ignored. This is obviously a limit, given that – especially from a family perspective – saving is an essential component of financial soundness and material well-being.

- *Transactions as value drivers*: the GDP of a nation grows depending on the number and value of business transactions. It can, however, be easily verified that not all of them lead to an improvement in the well-being of the community or the individual. For example, eating a meal prepared at home contributes less to the growth in the GDP than buying a hamburger at a fast-food outlet. It is rather evident, however, that in terms of physical well-being, the first option is preferable to the second one.

These considerations in fact lead to the formulation of two categories of challenges. The first concerns the improvement of the techniques for measuring the economic development of a country. The second category concerns the quantification of aspects of well-being that go beyond the GDP measurement and take the quality of life of individuals into consideration.

With regard to the first aspect, many contributions have been made that, although they do not lead to a final resolution of the issues stated above, provide methodological guidelines for renewing national accounting systems (Fleurbaey and Gaulier, 2007; Talberth et al., 2006; Cobb and Cobb, 1994; Zolotas, 1981; Nordhaus and Tobin, 1973). Among these the work of Stiglitz, Sen and Fitoussi stands out, who, on the initiative of the Presidency of the French Republic, set up the Commission on the Measurement of Economic Performance and Social Progress in 2008. This body, which saw the contribution of many other economists and social science specialists, led to the drawing up of a report (that can be found on the website www.stiglitz-sen-fitoussi.fr/en/index.htm) containing twelve 'recommendations' for guaranteeing a way of measuring economic development that overcomes the problems pointed out previously (Stiglitz et al., 2010).

The second aspect, namely, the measurement of well-being, was dealt with through the proposal of several indicators capable of expressing the dimensions of the quality of life that are not strictly linked to material well-being. Attention is also to be drawn to the many proposals in this field, especially from international bodies, among which the Genuine Savings Indicator and the Ecological Footprint. The first model, put forward by the World Bank, focuses on the allocation of the natural, human and capital resources of each country, with the objective of understanding how these evolve over time. This indicator measures the impact of a series of phenomena ignored in the traditional systems of national accounting, such as the damage resulting from CO_2 emissions (Bolt et al., 2002), to be assessed in economic terms. The second measurement system, proposed by Wackernagel and Rees (1995), is based on the idea of calculating the number of hectares of land required to sustain current standards of living in various countries around the world. In this calculation, a gap in resources could emerge, to the extent that the stock of hectares actually available (measured in 'global hectares') would be lower than the number required for continuing to maintain a certain global production, consumption and disposal flow (so-called 'bio-capacity'). As can be seen in Figure 8.1, this is what has already been happening since the end of the 1970s.

Nevertheless, the most well-known indicator of well-being, without doubt, is the Human Development Index.

8.3.2 Human Development Index

The quantification of the overall well-being of a community involves an assessment on the aspects that create value for the individual. In this regard, a new model, known as the 'human development approach' or 'capability approach', is now replacing the principle that regards economic wealth as the main, if not exclusive, measurement of well-being. This new model assesses the progress of a country based on the opportunities that are made available to each individual (Nussbaum, 2011; Sen, 1992; 1999).

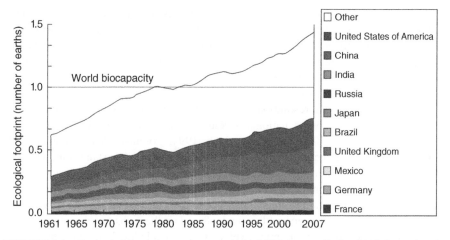

FIGURE 8.1   Ecological footprint per country: 1961–2007. *Source:* Ewing 2010. Reproduced with permission of Global Footprint Network.

From this perspective, asking the question if and to what extent an economic system contributes to personal well-being also involves asking about the 'means' available to citizens, so that they can make the most out of their capabilities. Economic development, therefore, is not the 'end' but the 'means' through which individuals develop their capabilities. These capabilities must be regarded as the 'substantial freedom' to choose and to act, and they do not depend solely on the innate abilities of the individual, but also on a set of conditions that refer to the background, politics, the economy and society. 'Poverty', therefore, is to be understood as a 'lack of opportunity', which does not depend on income alone, but, like income, may vary significantly from one community to another.

This new approach has been adopted by many institutions, such as the World Bank and the United Nations Development Program (UNDP). The UNDP, in particular, has been publishing the Human Development Reports since 1990, which measure and compare the degree of progress of countries annually using a system of indicators that reflects the thinking of Sen (1992; 1999). These reports are based on the calculation of the Human Development Index (HDI), which is currently the most widely used measurement for expressing the results achieved by various national economies in three different areas:

1. *Physical well-being*, in terms of life expectancy.
2. *Degree of education*, measured as the average degree of literacy and schooling (actually recorded among adults, or expected for newborns).
3. *Decent standard of living*, expressed as the Gross National Income per capita, assuming purchasing power parity (in US dollars).

Each of these assessment profiles is quantified by an indicator that expresses the position of each country compared to the best performer. In general terms, the formula used for each of the requested aspects is as follows:

$$I = \frac{\text{actual value} - \text{minimum value}}{\text{maximum value} - \text{minimum value}}$$

The calculation of these indicators, the values of which vary from 0 to 1, requires the identification of the minimum and maximum values of each assessment profile. For the Life Expectancy Index (I_{life}) the minimum value, equal to 20 years, comes from a long-term analysis conducted globally. As for the Education Index ($I_{education}$), it is assumed that a community can exist with a complete absence of schooling, therefore, the minimum value is 0 years. Finally, with regard to the Gross National Income Index per capita (I_{income}) the minimum stands at US$100, which is the lowest income per capita recorded using an international comparison system over the period from 1980 to 2010. The maximum values come from annual recordings and consequently are subject to more frequent modifications. See Table 8.1 in this regard. From a methodological point of view, it must be noted that the Education Index is derived from the average of two sub-indicators, related to the average schooling of adults and the expected schooling for newborns, respectively.

The Human Development Index (HDI) is obtained from the geometric average of the previous three indices, using the following formula:

$$HDI = \sqrt[3]{I_{life} \times I_{education} \times I_{income}}$$

The methodological choice of the geometric average stems from the need to avoid the compensatory effects implied in the use of the arithmetic average, such as the situation illustrated in Table 8.2.

Let's assume that in period t the country has recorded a value of 0.70 for each of the three determinants of the HDI. In this case, the geometric average and the simple average produce perfectly identical results. Nevertheless, if it is assumed that in the subsequent period $(t + 1)$ the I_{income} of the same country increased to 0.90, its $I_{education}$ decreased to 0.50 and its I_{life} value remained at 0.70, the choice of calculation method for the HDI would produce a different intertemporal assessment of the national performance. In fact, the use of the simple average ensures that the deterioration of the $I_{education}$ value is perfectly compensated by the equal improvement in the I_{income}. This would lead one to believe that nothing has changed compared to the previous period. However, the improvement in one of the assessment profiles was obtained to the detriment of another, and this cannot be considered acceptable due to the basic

TABLE 8.1 Minimum and maximum values for the calculation of the HDI

Indicator	Observed maximum	Minimum
Life expectancy (years)	83.6 (Japan, 2012)	20.0
Mean years of schooling	13.3 (United States, 2010)	0
Expected years of schooling	18.0 (capped at)	0
Combined education index	0.971 (New Zealand, 2010)	0
GNI per capita (PPP US$)	87,478 (Qatar, 2012)	100.0

Source: Human Development Report, United Nations.

TABLE 8.2   The calculation of the HDI

	I_{life}	$I_{education}$	I_{income}	Geometric average	Simple average
Period t	0.70	0.70	0.70	0.70	0.70
Period t + 1	0.70	0.50	0.90	0.68	0.70

philosophy that underlies this approach, which is also inspired by a principle of fairness. To get around this methodological problem, it is therefore considered more correct to use the geometric average, which, in the case described in Table 8.2, leads to the highlighting of the deterioration in the overall performance of the country being assessed from period *t* to period *t + 1*.

8.4   SUSTAINABILITY MEASUREMENT IN COMPANIES

8.4.1   Relevant Profiles

In a company environment, the measurement of sustainability is based on the Triple Bottom Line Model (Elkington, 1997), according to which companies must jointly pursue economic, social and environmental objectives. This trend is also reflected in the indications explicitly provided in this regard by Agenda 21, the document drawn up following the United Nations Conference on Environment and Development held in Rio de Janeiro in 1992. Chapter 40 of this document emphasises the need to support the decision-making processes of institutions and private organisations through appropriate indicators capable of measuring their development, understood in its various forms. In the wake of this trend, the United Nations Commission on Sustainable Development drew up a document specifically dedicated to the subject of sustainability measurement. The most recent version of this document puts forward a limited set of fifty indicators, each with explanations on their methods of calculation (United Nations, 2007). This has influenced the way in which private organisations approach the subject of sustainability measurement.

In a company environment, sustainability reporting is now an established practice and is widely used, especially in larger companies, with values of 76% in America, 73% in Europe and 71% in Asia (KPMG, 2013). Furthermore, the variability of these rates among different sectors is constantly being reduced, with the percentage of companies involved in sustainability reporting never falling below 50% (KPMG, 2013). Although the sustainability reports drawn up by companies are not completely consistent in the type of indicators computed, they draw on the threefold structure already illustrated, which leads to combining the measurements of the environmental and social sustainability of the activities of the company with its economic and financial results.

Focussing on the performance indicators that companies can use to quantify their results in the environmental and social field, it is worth remembering that the goal of performance measurement consists, first of all, of supporting management in the strategic planning process and, then, enabling the monitoring and final assessment of results (Gauthier, 2005). If objectives have not been reached, the system of indicators needs to highlight the causes of the problem and lead management towards the most appropriate improvement measures.

With reference to environmental sustainability, it is common practice to use indicators that are aimed at quantifying specific performance areas, and also checklists related to the initiatives undertaken to protect the environment. This can be observed in Table 8.3, which identifies sub-groups within these two categories,

TABLE 8.3   Environmental Sustainability Assessment Profiles

Categories	Subcategories	Measurable or verifiable elements (examples)
Environmental protection practices	Pollution control	'End-of-pipe' measures
		Compensation measures
	Prevention of pollution	Modifications to the product
		Modifications to the process
		% suppliers without EHS violations
		% suppliers participating in raw materials or packaging LCA
		% distributors supporting/implementing take-back policies
	Environmental Management System (EMS)	Definition of environmental policy
		Planning of environmental objectives
		Assignment of responsibilities
		Assessment of activities undertaken
Environmental Performance	Consumption of resources	Total consumption of fresh water
		Total volume of water recycled and reused
		Total consumption of raw materials per type
		Percentage of recycled materials
		Total energy use (in kWh) over the life cycle of the product
		Total energy use (in kWh) for transportation
		Total vehicles km travelled
		No. of initiatives to exploit renewable energy sources and improve energy yield
		Total surface land held, rented or managed for activities of production or extraction
		Number of endangered species in areas affected by the company's activities
		Percentage mass of products sold that can be recovered and reused at end of life and percentage that is actually recovered
	Production of pollution	Greenhouse gas emissions in equivalent tonnes of CO_2
		Significant emissions into the water per type
		Significant accidental linkage of chemical products, oil and fuels (number and total volume)
		Total quantity of waste per type and destination
		Penalties for non-respect of environmental law

Source: adapted from Morana, 2013; Dou and Sarkis, 2010 and Veleva and Ellenbecker, 2001.

which can be used to decide whether to use quantitative indicators (e.g. the consumption of energy) or systems to check the existence of conditions for improvement (namely, checklists related to the activities included in the Environmental Management System – EMS, such as the identification of improvement goals, the assignment of responsibilities etc.). Environmental sustainability profiles play a particularly important role in industrial companies, since there is a clear risk that industrial plants may generate a negative impact on the external environment (Sarkis, 2001). In contrast, the type of environmental impact produced and the actual danger posed can vary, depending on the activity carried out, ranging from particularly critical situations, like the production of chemicals or iron and steel, to other less problematic aspects, such as mechanical assembly or the production of garments. It follows that the mix of indicators to monitor, especially those related to the production of pollution in the strict sense, must be gauged depending on the nature of the production process.

As far as the measurement of social sustainability is concerned, it must be noted that company activities have an influence on the well-being of parties both within and outside the organisation (Gauthier, 2005). Therefore, as stated in Table 8.4, a

TABLE 8.4 Social Sustainability Assessment Profiles

Categories	Subcategories	Measurable or verifiable elements (examples)
Social sustainability profiles within the company	Practices related to personnel management	Compliance with regulations on the protection of child labour, gender discrimination, safety etc.
		Use of job flexibility forms
		Performance bonuses
		No. of training activities
		No. of skills development projects
	Practices for safety at work	No. of workplace injuries
		No. of injuries per type and origin (task)
		Lost workdays for injuries and illness
		No. of days of health-and-safety training
		No. and type of injuries prevention procedures
Social sustainability profiles outside the company	Projects for local communities	No. of training support projects for local workforce
		No. of housing projects
		Infrastructure improvement projects
		No. of projects to support local schools
		No. of projects to support local hospitals
		Amount of donations and sponsoring
		% products consumed locally
	Projects related to other stakeholders	No. of supplier training projects
		% suppliers from local area
		% products consumed locally
		No. of customer training projects

Source: adapted from Morana, 2013; Dou and Sarkis, 2010 and Veleva and Ellenbecker, 2001.

distinction must be made between these two different categories, which in turn may be further deployed in order to identify more specific assessment profiles. Also in this case, several aspects can be quantified numerically while others are elements that are verifiable only through checklists, which enable the company to determine the existence of the essential conditions for the achievement of an overall satisfying performance. With reference to social sustainability within the organisation, a distinction must be made between the practices adopted to guarantee the safety and physical integrity of employees and the practices that encourage their professional development. The former can be assessed through the measurement of results, such as the number of accidents recorded during a certain time interval, and through indicators of prevention efforts, as the number of accident-prevention procedures, the frequency of inspections or the investment in accident-prevention equipment. Policies on safety at work are particularly crucial in industrial companies where a significant number of staff is employed in production activities and the results achieved in this regard are often considered to be an expression of the management quality of the operations in a wider sense. Measuring the effectiveness of personnel management practices, in contrast, means checking the conditions that guarantee the respect of the specific conditions and demands of individuals, as well as their professional growth. This can be monitored, for example, by checking compliance with the regulations on the protection of child labour or gender discrimination and by verifying the existence of ways of developing professional skills – primarily consisting of training and career development programmes.

The social sustainability of company activities promoted in relation to parties outside the company can, on the contrary, be monitored by observing the initiatives undertaken by the organisation to support the communities in the region in which its premises are located, on the one hand, and the programmes specifically aimed at specific categories of external stakeholders, typically suppliers and customers, on the other hand. In the first case, the investments made and the number and type of projects financed, which may concern the development of infrastructures, the expansion of schools, sponsoring and so on, are measured. With regard to the second perspective, the measurement appears to be more complex as it is linked to the specific initiatives undertaken in order to encourage the development of the partner, even if the most frequent forms of support in this regard are linked to training programmes.

8.4.2 Reference Models

The large number of KPIs that can be used to monitor environmental and social sustainability performance leads to dealing with the problem of an effective selection and logical structure of the indicators required to support the management in the identification of potential improvement areas and related corrective actions. Therefore, proposals have also been put forward in this regard in relation to possible reporting models for environmental and social sustainability, capable of ensuring that the phenomenon can be effectivelly assessed. Furthermore, with specific reference to production and logistics processes, in recent years many contributions have highlighted the need to develop reporting systems that are specifically aimed at assessing the impact of operations on company sustainability levels, often proposing an adaptation of frameworks that already exist (Koh et al., 2013; Reefke and Trocchi, 2013; Yakovleva et al., 2012; Cetinkaya et al., 2011; Hervani et al., 2005). In particular, Cetinkaya et al. (2011) proposed the use of a Sustainable Supply Chain (SSC) Scorecard, which is characterised by an attempt to explain the links of cause and effect between supply chain management practices, environmental and social sustainability performance and the economic and financial results of the company. In this regard, the four perspectives that characterise the framework of Kaplan and Norton (1992) would need to be remodelled in order to take the following considerations into account:

- *Financial perspective*: in the assessment of this perspective, indicators aimed at quantifying the economic advantages deriving from greater environmental and social sustainability must be used in addition to the KPIs peculiar to the standard version of the balanced scorecard (e.g. return on equity, return on investment, economic value added, CAGR revenues etc.). These advantages always come from the implementation of ad hoc projects, which require an initial investment and generate economic results over time. Therefore, it is possible to adopt the usual financial investment assessment tools, such as Net Present Value, Payback Period or Internal Rate of Return. This, obviously, applies more immediately to projects concerning the improvement of environmental performance and (even if somewhat more complex) also to those focused on the topics of social sustainability within the company. Furthermore, it is to be noted that the initiatives aimed at improving the eco-sustainability of production activities often translate into improvements in the economic performance such as lower production costs and working capital. Think, for example, about lean management projects that, by decreasing the various types of waste that can be found in a factory, help to reduce the consumption of resources and improve production efficiency (see Chapter 5). From the perspective of the SSC Scorecard, the following synthetic indicator of social or eco-efficiency could be used (World Business Council for Sustainable Development, 2005):

$$\frac{Value\ of\ the\ product\ or\ service}{Environmental\ impact\ (or\ Social\ impact)}$$

For example, if one of the main resources used in the production process is energy, as is the case in iron mills, the eco-efficiency of the process can be assessed by relating the value of the production, in a given time interval, with the quantity of kilowatts consumed.

- *Sustainability perspective*: the set of indicators to be used in this section of the SSC Scorecard (which ideally corresponds with the customer perspective in the classic formulation of the balanced scorecard) must be based on the observation that nowadays the degree of customer satisfaction in relation to what the company offers does not depend exclusively on the traditionally considered characteristics of the products/services (aesthetic and functional aspects, after-sales assistance, price etc.), but also on the environmental and social performance of the company, which increasingly has an influence on its image and therefore on customer choices. This section of the SSC Scorecard must therefore contain indicators that express a certain causal link. To this end, not only indicators – as customer satisfaction, customer retention, market share measurements and so on, need to be monitored, but also the more 'technical' KPIs that express the environmental and social sustainability of the company (tonnes of CO_2 produced, kilowatts consumed, percentage of recyclable materials etc.). These latter aspects, moreover, have an influence not only on the brand image of the company, but also directly on economic and financial performance, which is highlighted in the first section of the SSC Scorecard.

- *Supply chain perspective*: the set of indicators to be used in this section of the SSC Scorecard (which would correspond to the perspective of the internal processes in the version proposed by Kaplan and Norton, 1992) must be selected by identifying the main production and logistics processes that determine the levels of sustainability highlighted in the customer perspective. This modus operandi leads to the measurement of the impact of specific supply chain design choices (Gallmann and Belvedere, 2011). For example, the tonnes of CO_2 produced in a certain time interval (recorded in the Sustainability perspective) can be explained also in the quantity of kilometres travelled to deliver the goods. The distance to be covered during delivery phases, in turn, depends on multiple factors, among which the level of logistic service agreed with customers, the number of the warehouses and distribution centres, the maximum loading capacity by the means of transport used and so on. A further critical aspect related to this perspective of the SSC Scorecard is the need to also include parties outside the company in the assessment, and in particular subcontractors and suppliers, who may have a significant influence on the sustainability performance in terms of the management of their own production and logistics activities (Schneider and Wallenburg, 2012).

- *Learning and Growth perspective*: in the original proposal of Kaplan and Norton (1992), this perspective ought to contain indicators that measure the adequacy of the resources used in the key processes of the company, and in particular human resources and information technology. The need to quantify these aspects is also emphasised in the SSC Scorecard, and special reference is made to the resources used in the production and logistics processes, underlining, once again, the need to also extend the measurement to the main partners along the supply chain. For example, in the food industry, where tracking systems are one of the primary guarantees of the origin and quality of the product, it would be unreasonable to consider measuring technological adequacy by focusing exclusively on a company and omitting the other players along the supply chain (Beske et al., 2014).

Even if proposals like the ones mentioned in this section are reasonable from a logical point of view, in recent years company choices regarding sustainability reporting have gone in the direction of the adoption of international standards, drawn up by bodies and institutions that aim to promote the dissemination of sustainability reporting, on the one hand, and to facilitate benchmarking between companies as a useful tool for supporting improvement, on the other hand. The next part of this chapter will illustrate two of these standards in particular, namely the standards proposed by the Global Reporting Initiative and the Dow-Jones Sustainability Index.

8.4.2.1   *Global Reporting Initiative*

According to a survey conducted by KPMG on company practices regarding sustainability measurement (KPMG, 2013), 76% of companies that draw up sustainability reports refer to the model proposed by the Global Reporting Initiative (GRI).

GRI is a non-profit organisation aimed at promoting the use of sustainability reporting in companies as a useful tool for pursuing goals that are compatible with the improvement of environmental and social performance. In this regard, GRI drew up a reference model that highlights the most important assessment profiles and the individual indicators for quantifying them. Furthermore, the methods that companies ought to use to record the achieved results are also illustrated, using not only quantitative, but also qualitative information in relation to initiatives undertaken or planned for the future. The degree of detail with which GRI describes its framework and the related methods of application makes reading easy, as well as the comparison of reports in particular, especially for benchmarking purposes. Furthermore, the companies that adopt this framework to draw up their sustainability report can also voluntarily publish them on the GRI website, which, consequently, acts as a repository for the benefit of organisations interested in comparing their achievements with the ones of other companies. There are obviously many benefits linked to the use of this model, including the simplification of the report design process. If the report, in fact, is drafted according to the guidelines drawn up by GRI, it must replicate a standard structure, which can be used as a reference by all types of companies (GRI, 2013a).

The structure of the GRI framework highlights three 'categories' of performance to be assessed, namely economic, social and environmental performance, in line with the theory of the Triple Bottom Line, which has already been discussed (Elkington, 1997). Furthermore, each of these categories is further divided into a series of 'subcategories' and 'aspects' that correspond with the appropriate performance indicators. With regard to the production and logistics processes, a section specifically dedicated to the supply chain was introduced to the latest version of the model (GRI, 2013a; GRI, 2013b) with the aim of pointing out how managerial choices concerning the aforesaid processes may have an impact on specific aspects already present in the framework. The list that follows here reports the categories and sub-categories that, according to GRI, are most affected by supply chain management, as well as some of the indicators proposed to quantify these aspects:

- *Economic*:
  - ○ *Procurement practices indicators* (examples): percentage of the budget for purchases used to buy goods produced locally (providing a definition of 'local').
- *Environmental*:
  - ○ *Energy indicators* (examples): total consumption of kilowatts and its breakdown (per geographical area, phase of the production and logistics process etc.).
  - ○ *Emissions indicators* (examples): tonnes of CO_2 emitted and its breakdown (per geographical area, phase of the production, logistics process etc.).
  - ○ *Supplier Environmental Assessment indicators* (examples): percentage of new suppliers assessed using environmental sustainability criteria; number of suppliers subject to environmental impact assessment.
- *Social*:
  - ○ *Labour practices and decent work indicators* (examples): percentage of new suppliers assessed on the basis of the Labour Practices used; number of suppliers with whom relations have ended due to a negative assessment of their Labour Practices.
  - ○ *Human rights indicators* (examples): percentage of new suppliers assessed on the basis of the degree of their compliance with human rights; percentage of suppliers with whom improvement goals regarding compliance with human rights have been agreed following an assessment process.
- *Society*:
  - ○ *Supplier Assessment for Impact on Society indicators* (examples): percentage of new suppliers assessed on the basis of the type of impact produced on the community; number of suppliers with whom relationships have ended due to the negative assessment of impact on the community.

It must be considered that, for each of these indicators, the GRI Implementation Manual (GRI, 2013b) provides an in-depth description of the data and information that the companies must collect in order to give real meaning to some of the most vague concepts, such as the impact of company activities on the community (i.e. 'Impact on Society'), thus effectively quantifying and disclosing its performance.

8.4.2.2 Dow Jones Sustainability Index The Dow Jones Sustainability Indices were launched in 1999 with the aim of recording the financial returns of listed companies characterised by high standards of sustainability and risk management. The identification of the best-in-class to be included in the indices is based on an assessment process (the Corporate Sustainability Assessment – CSA) conducted by the Dow Jones Indices in collaboration with RobecoSam, in which the first 2500 listed companies are invited to participate each year on an international basis (RobecoSam, 2014).

The participation in the CSA, which is voluntary, requires the company to fill in a questionnaire specific for the sector to which it belongs (the CSA identifies

59 sectors in total) and, depending on the sector, the questionnaire is divided into a minimum of 80 and a maximum of 120 questions, which cover aspects concerning the economic, social and environmental sustainability of the company. The data collected through the questionnaire, complemented with public information regarding the sustainability practices of the company, are used to compute a score between 0 and 100 for each participant, through which it is possible to identify the best-in-class in the sector. Figure 8.2 illustrates the structure of the questionnaire, which is divided into a series of criteria for each area of sustainability (economic, social and environmental), which in turn are assessed through a set of questions.

One peculiar aspect of this process is the fact that the criteria of the CSA have been weighted to take the importance that each one of them has in specific sectorial contexts into account. For example, the importance assigned to the subject of Occupational Health and Safety is 5% in the banking sector, 4% in the electric utilities sector and 2% in the pharmaceutical sector. Furthermore, certain criteria may not even be included in some versions of the questionnaire. For example, 'Climate strategy' is important (and therefore present) in the assessment of environmental

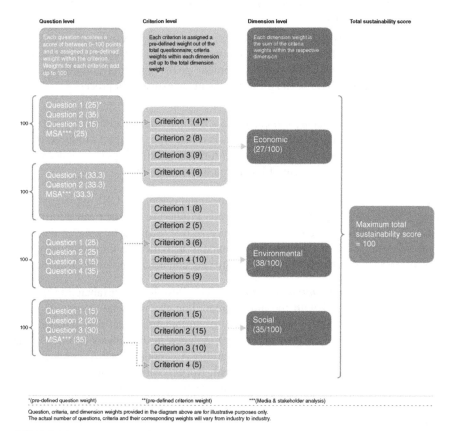

*(pre-defined question weight)   **(pre-defined criterion weight)   ***(Media & stakeholder analysis)

Question, criteria, and dimension weights provided in the diagram above are for illustrative purposes only.
The actual number of questions, criteria and their corresponding weights will vary from industry to industry.

FIGURE 8.2 Structure of the Corporate Sustainability Assessment. *Source:* RobecoSam 2014. Reproduced with permission of RobecoSam.

Question	Please indicate your company's approaches to improve accessibility of drugs in both developing and developed countries. Please provide supporting documents.
Question Points	0–100
Question weight within criterion	50%
Criterion	Strategy to improve access to drugs or products
Dimension	Social
RobecoSAM Rationale	Underprivileged patients are often unable to buy medicine to treat or cure their diseases due to financial constraints. This is often the case in developing countries, and is now becoming a growing concern in developed countries. As a serious social challenge that requires attention from healthcare providers, some pharmaceutical companies are tackling this issue by implementing programs to provide these patients with improved access to medicine. Such initiatives help to improve the company's credibility, build corporate and product brands and increase market penetration of their products and services.

FIGURE 8.3 Example of a question for the pharmaceutical sector. *Source:* RobecoSam 2014. Reproduced with permission of RobecoSam.

sustainability in the electric utilities and pharmaceutical sectors, whereas it is absent from the questionnaire directed at the banking sector.

The score assigned to a company for each individual question is based on an assessment on the degree of its awareness of the subjects of sustainability, the policies adopted, the results achieved and also the quality of the reporting. Given the complexity of the subjects being assessed, the questions are worded broadly, in order to obtain in-depth and documented information from the company. In this regard, see the example in Figure 8.3, which shows a question found on the questionnaire for the pharmaceutical sector.

REFERENCES

Abernathy, W.J. (1978), The productivity dilemma, Baltimore, MD: John Hopkins University Press.

Adler, P.S., Benner, M., Brunner, D.J., MacDuffie, J.P., Osono, E., Staats, B.R., Takeuchi, H., Tushman, M.L., and Winter, S.G. (2009), Perspectives on the productivity dilemma, *Journal of Operations Management*, 27 (2), pp. 99–113.

Ahmed, S., Hassan, M. H., Kalam, M. A., Ashrafur Rahman, S. M., Abedin, M. J., and Shahir, A. (2014), An experimental investigation of biodiesel production, characterization, engine performance, emission and noise of Brassica juncea methyl ester and its blends, *Journal of Cleaner Production*, 79, pp. 7974–7981.

Alston, F., and Millikin, E.J. (2015), *Guide to environmental safety & health management*, CRC Press, Taylor & Francis Group.

Amjed, T.W., and Harrison, N.J. (2013), *A Model for sustainable warehousing: From theory to best practices.* Macquarie University ResearchOnline.

Arvidsson, N., Woxenius, J., and Lammgård, C. (2013), Review of road hauliers' measures for increasing transport efficiency and sustainability in urban freight distribution, *Transport Reviews*, 33 (1), pp. 107–127.

Auernhammer, H. (2001), Precision farming: The environmental challenge, *Computer and Electronics in Agriculture*, 30, pp. 31–43.

Aynsley R. (2011), Estimates of winter de-stratification energy savings in large warehouses, *Architectural Science Review*, 48 (3), pp. 257–264.

Baglieri, E., and Karmakar, U., eds. (2014), *Managing consumer service*, Berlin: Springer.

Baker, P. (2006), Designing distribution centres for agile supply chains, *International Journal of Logistics*, 9 (3), pp. 207–221.

Barilla (2015), *Buono per te buono per il pianeta*, rapporto annuale, 2015.

Bartezzaghi, E., and Turco, F. (1989), The impact of just-in-time on production system performance: An analytical framework, *International Journal of Operations & Production Management*, 9 (8), pp. 40–62.

Bastein, T, Roelofs, E., Rietveld, E., and Hoogendoorn A. (2013), Opportunity for a circular economy in the Netherlands, TNO, Behavioural and Societal Sciences, Delft, The Netherlands.

BCFN – Barilla Center for Food & Nutrition (2012), *Eating planet. Nutrirsi oggi: Una sfida per l'uomo e per il pianeta*, Edizioni Ambiente.

BCFN – Barilla Center for Food & Nutrition (2016), *Eating Planet. Cibo e sostenibilità: costruire il nostro futuro*, Edizioni Ambiente.

Beamon, B.M. (1998), Supply chain design and analysis: Models and methods, *International Journal of Production Economics*, 55 (3), pp. 281–294.

Beamon, B.M. (1999), Designing the green supply chain, *Logistics information management*, 12 (4), pp. 332–342.

Belvedere, V. (2015), *La misura delle prestazioni produttive e logistiche nelle aziende industriali*, Milano, EGEA.

Benn, S., Dunphy, D., and Griffits, A. (2014), *Organizational change for corporate sustainability*, third edition, New York: Routledge.

Berger, S.M., and Ludwig, T.D. (2007), Reducing warehouse employee errors using voice-assisted technology that provided immediate feedback, *Journal of Organizational Behavior Management*, 27 (1), pp. 1–31.

Bernardes, E.S., and Hanna, M.D. (2009), A theoretical review of flexibility, agility and responsiveness in the operations management literature: Toward a conceptual definition of customer responsiveness, *International Journal of Operations & Production Management*, 29 (1), pp. 30–53.

Beske, P., Land, A., and Seuring, S. (2014), Sustainable supply chain management practices and dynamic capabilities in the food industry: A critical analysis of the literature, *International Journal of Production Economics*, 152, pp. 131–143.

Beuren, F.H., Ferreira, M.G.G., and Cauchick Miguel, P.A. (2013), Product-service systems: A literature review on integrated products and services, *Journal of Cleaner Production*, 47, pp. 222–231.

Bevilacqua, M., Ciarapica, F.E., and Giacchetta, G. (2012), *Design for Environment as a tool for the development of a sustainable supply chain*, London: Springer Verlag.

Blackburn, J.D. (1991), Time-based competition: The next battleground in American manufacturing, New York: Irwin Professional Pub.

Blackburn, J. D., Guide, Jr. V. D. R., Souza, G. C., and van Wassenhove, L. N. (2004), Reverse supply chains for commercial returns, *California Management Review*, 46 (2), pp. 6–22.

Blanchflower, D.G., and Oswald, A.J. (2004), Well-being over time in Britain and the USA, *Journal of Public Economics*, 88, pp. 1359–1386.

Bodin, T., Björk, J., Ardö, J., and Albin, M. (2015), Annoyance, sleep and concentration problems due to combined traffic noise and the benefit of quiet side, *International Journal of Environmental Research and Public Health*, 12(2), pp. 1612–1628.

Bolt, K., Matete, M., and Clemens, M. (2002), *Manual for Calculating Adjusted Net Savings, Environment Department*, World Bank.

Bouchery, Y., Ghaffari, A., Jemai, Z., and Dallery, Y. (2012), Including sustainability criteria into inventory models, *European Journal of Operational Research*, 222 (2), pp. 229–240.

Braungart, M., McDonough, W., and Bollinger, A. (2007), Cradle-to-cradle design: creating healthy emissions – a strategy for eco-effective product and system design, *Journal of Cleaner Production*, 15 (13–14), pp. 1337–1348.

Brettel, M., Friederichsen, N., Keller, M., and Rosenberg, M. (2014), How virtualization, decentralization and network building change the manufacturing landscape: An Industry 4.0 Perspective, *International Journal of Mechanical, Aerospace, Industrial, Mechatronic and Manufacturing Engineering*, 8 (1), pp. 37–44.

Brundtland, G.B. (1987) Editor, *Our common future: World Commission on Environment and Development*, Oxford: Oxford University Press,.

BS 8887 (2006), British Standard Institution, www.bsigroup.com.

Calabriso, A., Cedola, L., Del Zotto, L., Rispoli, F., and Santori, S.G. (2015), Performance investigation of Passive Direct Methanol Fuel Cell in different structural configurations, *Journal of Cleaner Production*, 88, pp. 8823–8828.

CAPS Research (2014), *Cross-industry report of standard benchmarks*, Tempe, AZ, Arizona State University Press.

Carbon Trust (2002), *Good practice guide 319: Managing energy in warehouses*, London: HMSO.

Carr, A.S., and Pearson, J.N. (2002), The impact of purchasing and supplier involvement on strategic purchasing and its impact on firm's performance, *International Journal of Operations & Production Management*, 22 (9), pp. 1032–1053.

Carter, C.R., and Carter, J.R. (1998), Interorganizational determinants of environmental purchasing: Initial evidence from the consumer products industries, *Decision Sciences*, 29 (3), pp. 659–684.

Carter, C.R., and Ellram, L.M. (1998), Reverse Logistics: A review of the literature and a framework for future investigation, *Journal of Business Logistics*, 19 (1), p. 85–102.

Carter, C.R., and Rogers, D.S. (2008), A framework of sustainable supply chain management theory, *International Journal of Physical Distribution & Logistics Management*, 38 (5), pp. 360–387.

Cetinkaya, B., Cuthbertson, R., Ewer, G., Klaas-Wissing, T., Piotrowicz, W., and Tyssen, C. (2011), *Sustainable supply chain management: Practical ideas for moving towards best practice*, Berlin: Springer.

Chiu, M.C., and Okudan Kremer, G.E. (2011), Investigation of the applicability of design for X tools during design concept evolution: A literature review, *International Journal of Product development*, 13 (2), pp. 132–167.

Chopra, S., and Meindl, P. (2007), *Supply chain management: Strategy, planning and operations*, Upper Saddle River, NJ: Prentice-Hall.

Christopher, M. (1998), *Logistics and supply chain management*, second edition, London:: Financial Times – Pitman Publishing.

Christopher, M. (2000). The agile supply chain: Competing in volatile markets, *Industrial marketing management*, 29 (1), 37–44.

Christopher, M. (2005). *Logistics and supply chain management: Creating value-added networks*. Pearson education.

Christopher, M. (2010). *Logistics & supply chain management*, fourth edition, Upper Saddle River, NJ: Prentice-Hall.

Church, J.A., and White, N.J. (2006), A 20th century acceleration in global sea level rise, *Geophysical Research Letters*, 33, L01602, doi:10.1029/2005GL024826.

Cigolini, R., and Grando, A. (2009), Modelling plant capacity and productivity: The multi-machine case, *Production Planning and Control*, 20 (1), pp. 30–39.

CIPS (2002), *Environmental purchasing in practice – Guidance for Organisations*, available at www.cips.org, viewed on 9 January 2016.

CIPS (2013), *CIPS code of conduct*, available at www.cips.org, viewed on 15 March 2016.

Cobb, C., and Cobb, J. (1994), *The green national product*, Lanham, MD: University Press of America.

Coman, A., and Ronen, B. (2010), Icarus' predicament: Managing the pathologies of overspecification and overdesign, *International Journal of Project Management*, 28 (3), pp. 237–244.

Cooper, M.C., Lambert, D.M., and Pagh, J.D. (1997), Supply Chain Management: More than a new name for logistics, *International Journal of Logistics Management*, 8 (1), pp. 1–14.

Cooper, R.G. (1975), Why industrial new products fail, *Industrial Marketing Management*, 4, pp. 315–326.

Copacino, W.C. (1997), *Supply chain management*, Boca Raton, FL: St. Lucie Press, APICS.

Corbett, L.M. (2009), Sustainable operations management: A typological approach, *Journal of Industrial Engineering and Management*, 2 (1), pp. 10–30.

Council of Logistics Management (1986), *What is it all about?* Oak Brook, IL: Council of Logistics Management.

Court, D., and Narasimhan, L. (2010), Capturing the world's emerging middle class, *McKinsey Quarterly*, 3, pp. 12–17.

Cox, A., Sanderson, J., and Watson, G. (2001), Supply chains and power regimes: Toward an analytic framework for managing extended networks of buyer and supplier relationship, *Journal of Supply Chain Management*, 37 (2), pp. 28–35.

Craig Smith, N., and Lenssen, G. (eds.). (2009), *Mainstreaming corporate responsibility*, Hoboken, NJ: John Wiley & Sons.

Crosby, P.B. (1979), *Quality is Free*, New York: McGraw-Hill.

Crosby, P.B. (1984a), *Quality without tears: The art of hassle-free management*, New York: McGraw-Hill.

Crosby, P.B. (1984b), *Quality is still free: Making Quality Certain in Uncertain Times*, New York: McGraw-Hill.

Crowther, P. (1999) *Design for disassembly*, Royal Australian Institute of Architecture, Environmental Design Guide, November.

CSCMP – Council of Supply Chain Management Professionals (2012), *Supply chain management terms and glossary*, available at https://cscmp.org/supply-chain-management-definitions, viewed on 15 March 2015.

CSCMP – Council of Supply Chain Management Professionals (2013), *Supply chain management terms and glossary – August 2013*, available at https://cscmp.org/supply-chain-management-definitions, viewed on 3 August 2016.

Da Villa, F. (2000), *La logistica dei sistemi manifatturieri*, Milan: Etas Libri.

Dale, B.G., Van Der Wiele, T., and Van Iwaarden, J. (2013), *Managing quality*, Hoboken, NJ: John Wiley & Sons.

Dale, S.R., Lambert D.M., Croxton K.L., and Garcia Dastugue S.J (2002), The returns management process, *International Journal of Logistics Management*, 13 (2), pp. 1–18.

Day, M. (2002). *Gower handbook of purchasing management*, third edition, Aldershot, UK, Gower Publishing, Ltd.

De Brito, M.P., and Dekker, R. (2010), *A Framework for reverse logistics*, in Dekker, R., Fleishmann, M., Inderfurth, K. Van Wassenhove, L.N. (2010) *Reverse logistics: Quantitative methods for closed-loop supply chains*, Springer, pp. 3–27.

de Koster R., Le-Duc T., and Roodbergen K.J. (2007), Design and control of warehouse order picking: A literature review, *European Journal of Operational Research*, 182, pp. 481–501.

de Meyer, A., and Ferdows, K. (1990), Influence of manufacturing improvement programmes on performance, *International Journal of Operations & Production Management*, 10(2), 120–131.

de Ron, A.J. (1998), Sustainable production: The ultimate result of a continuous improvement, *International Journal of Production Economics*, 56, pp. 99–110.

De Toni, A., & Tonchia, S. (1998), Manufacturing flexibility: A literature review, *International Journal of Production Research*, 36 (6), 1587–1617.

Deasi, A., and Mital, A. (2003), Review of literature on disassembly algorithms and design for disassembly guidelines for product design, *International Journal of Industrial Engineering: Applications and Practice*, 10 (3), pp. 244–255.

Defra (2013a), *Government conversion factors for company reporting*, London, UK: Defra.

Defra (2013b), *Guidelines to Defra/DECC's GHG Conversion Factors for Company Reporting*, London, UK: Defra.

Dekker, R. Bloemhof-Ruwaard, J., Fleischmann, M., Van Nunen, J., Van der Laan, E., and Van Wassenhove, L.N. (1998), Operational research in reverse logistics: Some recent contributions, *International Journal of Logistics: Research and Applications*, 1 (2), pp. 141–155.

Dekker, R., Fleishmann, M., Inderfurth, K., and van Wassenhove, L.N. (2010), *Reverse logistics: Quantitative models for closed-loop supply chains*, Springer.

Deming, W.E. (1986), *Out of crisis*, Cambridge, MA: MIT Center of Advanced Engineering Study.

Denis D., St-Vincent M., Imbeau, D. and Trudeau D.I. (2006), Stock management influence on materials handling in two warehouse superstores, *International Journal of Industrial Ergonomics*, 36, pp. 191–201

Dicken, P. (2003), *Global shift: Reshaping the global economy map in the 21st century*, London: Sage Publications Ltd.

Dicken, P. (2012), *Global shift: Mapping the changing contours of the world economy*, sixth edition, New York: The Guilford Press.

Drake, D.F., and Spinler, S. (2013). OM Forum-Sustainable Operations Management: An enduring stream or a passing fancy?, *Manufacturing & Service Operations Management*, 15 (4), pp. 689–700.

Driussi, C., and Jansz, J. (2006). Technological options for waste minimisation in the mining industry, *Journal of Cleaner Production*, 14 (8), pp. 682–688.

Eagar, R., Boulton, C., and Demyttenaere, C. (2014), *The trends in megatrends: The most important megatrends and how to monitor them*, PRISM, vol. 2, Cambridge, MA: Arthur D. Little, pp. 12–23,

Easterlin, R.A. (1974), *Does economic growth improve the human lot? Some empirical evidence, Nations and Households in Economic Growth*, 89, pp. 89–125.

Easterlin, R.A. (1995), Will raising the incomes of all increase the happiness of all?, *Journal of Economic Behavior and Organization*, 27, pp. 35–47.

Easterlin, R.A. (2001), Income and happiness: Towards a unified theory, *Economic Journal*, 111, pp. 465–484.

EC – European Commission (2001), *Green paper: Promoting a European framework for corporate social responsibility*, available at http://eur-lex.europa.eu/legal-content/EN/TXT/?uri=celex:52001DC0366, viewed on 16 April 2015.

EC – European Commission (2011), *Communication from the Commission to the European Parliament, the Council, the European Economic and Social Committee and the Committee of the Regions: A renewed EU strategy 2011–14 for Corporate Social Responsibility*, available at http://eur-lex.europa.eu/legal-content/EN/TXT/?uri=CELEX:52011DC0681, viewed on 16 April 2016.

EAA – European Environment Agency (2013), *Land take*, http://www.eea.europa.eu/data-and-maps/indicators/land-take-2/assessment-2.

EAA – European Environmental Agency (2014a). *Noise in Europe 2014*, Report No.10, Copenhagen: EEA.

EAA – European Environmental Agency (2014b). *Progress in management of contaminated soil*, Copenhagen: EEA.

EEA – European Environmental Agency (2009), *Water resources across Europe — Confronting water scarcity and drought*, Report No.2, Luxembourg: Office for Official Publications of the European Communities.

EEA – European Environment Agency (2011), *Revealing the costs of air pollution from industrial facilities in Europe*, Publication office of the European Union, Luxembourg.

EEA – European Environmental Agency (2012), *Greenhouse gas emission trends and projections in Europe 2011 Tracking progress towards Kyoto and 2020 targets*, Report No.6, Copenhagen: EEA.

EEA – European Environment Agency (2014), *Exposure to and annoyance by traffic noise*, (TERM 005), European Union.

Elkington, J. (1994), Towards the sustainable corporation: Win-win-win business strategies for sustainable development, *California Management Review*, 36 (2), pp. 90–100.

Elkington, J. (1997), *Cannibals with forks: The Triple Bottom Line of 21st century business*, Oxford: Capstone Publishing Ltd.

Elkington, J. (1998). Partnerships from cannibals with forks: The triple bottom line of 21st-century business. *Environmental Quality Management*, 8(1), 37–51.

Ellen MacArthur Foundation (2012), *Towards the circular economy: Economic and business rationale for an accelerated transition*, January, available at ellenmacarthurfoundation.org, viewed on 10 April 2013.

Ellen MacArthur Foundation (2013), *Towards the circular economy: Opportunities for the consumer goods sector*, January, available at ellenmacarthurfoundation.org, viewed on 12 September 2014.

Eltantawy, R.A., Fox, G.L., and Giunipero, L. (2009), Supply management ethical responsibility: Reputation and performance impacts, *Supply Chain Management: An International Journal*, 14 (2), pp. 99–108.

Emmett, S., and Sood, V. (2010), *Green supply chains: An action manifesto*, Chichester, UK, John Wiley & Sons.

EPA – Environmental Protection Agency (1992), Office of Research and Development, *Facility pollution prevention guide*, Washington, DC.

European Union Road Federation (2013), *ERF 2013 European road statistics*, Brussels: European Union Road Federation.

Ewing B., D. Moore, S. Goldfinger, A. Oursler, A. Reed, and M. Wackernagel. 2010. The Ecological Footprint Atlas 2010. Oakland: Global Footprint Network.

FAO – Food and Agriculture Organization (2011), *Global food losses and food waste: Extent, causes and prevention*, available at http://www.fao.org/docrep/014/mb060e/mb060e.pdf, viewed on 10 May 2014.

FAO – Food and Agriculture Organization (2012), *The state of food insecurity in the world*, available at http://www.fao.org/docrep/016/i3027e/i3027e.pdf, viewed on 2 May, 2014.

FAO – Food and Agriculture Organization (2013), Food wastage footprint: Impact on natural resources, available at http://www.fao.org/docrep/018/i3347e/i3347e.pdf, viewed on 22 January 2014.

Feigenbaum, A.V. (1991), *Total quality control*, third edition, New York: McGraw-Hill.

Ferdows, K., and De Meyer, A. (1990), Lasting improvements in manufacturing performance: in search of a new theory, *Journal of Operations Management*, 9 (2), pp. 168–184.

Fiksel, J. (1996), Achieving eco-efficiency through design for environment, *Total Quality Environmental Management*, 5 (4), 47–54.

Fiksel, J., (2012), *Design for Environment*, second edition, New York: McGraw-Hill.

Fleischmann, M., Bloembof-Ruwand, J.M, Dekker, R., van der Laan, E., van Nune, J., and van Wassenhove L.N. (1997), Quantitative models for reverse logistics: A review, *European Journal of Operational Research*, 103 (1), pp. 1–17.

Fleurbaey, M., and Gaulier, G. (2007), *International comparisons of living standards by equivalent incomes*, Working Paper CEPII, 2007-3.

Florida, R. (2008). *Who is your city: How the creative economy is making where to live the most important decision of your life*, New York: Perseus Books.

Flynn, B.B., Schroeder, R.G., and Sakakibara, S. (1994), A framework for quality management research and an associated measurement instrument, *Journal of Operations Management*, 11 (4), pp. 339–366.

Frazelle, E. (2002). *Supply chain strategy: The logistics of supply chain management*. New York: McGraw-Hill.

Fuller, D.A., and Allen, J. (1995), A typology of reverse channel systems for post-consumers recyclable, in Polonsky, J. and Mintu-Winsatt, A.T. (eds.), *Environmental marketing: Strategies, practice, theory and research*, Binghamton, NY: Haword Press, pp. 241–266.

Gallmann, F., and Belvedere, V. (2011), Linking service level, inventory management and warehousing practices: A case-based managerial analysis, *Operations Management Research*, 4 (1–2), pp. 28–38.

Gasson, C. (2014), A world without water, *Financial Times*, 15 July, 2014, available at http://www.ft.com/intl/cms/s/2/8e42bdc8-0838-11e4-9afc-00144feab7de.html#slide0, viewed on 4 July 2015.

Gatenby, D.A., and Foo, G. (1990), Design for X: Key to competitive, profitable market, *AT&T Technical Journal*, 69 (3), pp. 2–13.

Gauthier, C. (2005), Measuring corporate social and environmental performance: The extended lifecycle assessment, *Journal of Business Ethics*, 59 (1–2), pp. 199–206.

Gerwin, D. (1987), An agenda of research on the flexibility of manufacturing processes, *International Journal of Operations & Production Management*, 7 (1), pp. 38–49.

Gimenez, C., Sierra, V., and Rodon, J. (2012). Sustainable operations: Their impact on the triple bottom line, *International Journal of Production Economics*, 140 (1), pp. 149–159.

Gimenez, C., and Tachizawa, E.M. (2012), Extending sustainability to suppliers: A systematic literature review, *Supply Chain Management: An International Journal*, 17 (5), pp. 531–543.

Goldratt, E., and Cox, J. (1984), *The goal: A process of ongoing improvement*, Aldershot, UK: Gower.

González-Benito, J. and González-Benito, Ó. (2005), Environmental proactivity and business performance: An empirical analysis, *Omega*, 33 (1), pp. 1–15.

Goodship, V., and Stevels, A. (2012), *Waste electrical and electronic equipment (WEEE) handbook*, Cambridge: Philips WP Woodhead Publishing.

Grando, A. (1995), *Organizzazione e gestione della produzione industriale*, Milan: Egea.

Grando, A., and Turco, F. (2005), Modelling plant capacity and productivity: conceptual framework in a single-machine case, *Production Planning & Control*, 16 (3), pp. 309–322.

Grando, A., Verona, G., and Vicari, S. (2010), *Tecnologia, innovazione, operations*, Milan: Egea.

Grant, R. (1991), The resource-based theory of competitive advantage, *California Management Review*, 33 (3), pp. 114–134.

Grant, D.B., Trautrims, A., and Wong, C.Y. (2013), *Sustainable logistics and supply chain management*, London: Koganpage.

Grant, R. (2013), *Contemporary strategy analysis*, eight editions, Hoboken, NJ: John Wiley & Sons.

Greasley, A. (2006), *Operations management*, Hoboken, NJ: John Wiley & Sons.

Green, K., Morton, B., and New, S. (1996), Purchasing and environmental management: Interactions, policies and opportunities, *Business Strategy and the Environment*, 5 (3), pp. 188–197.

GRI – Global Reporting Initiative (2013a), *Sustainability reporting guidelines: Reporting principles and standard disclosure*, available at https://www.globalreporting.org/, viewed on 8 August 2016.

GRI – Global Reporting Initiative (2013b), *Sustainability reporting guidelines: Implementation manual*, available at https://www.globalreporting.org/, viewed on 8 August 2016.

GRI – Global Reporting Initiate (2015), G4 – Sustainability reporting guidelines, available at https://www.globalreporting.org/standards/g4/Pages/default.aspx, viewed on 12 September 2015.

Grolleaud, M., (2002), *Post-harvest losses: Discovering the full story, Overview of the phenomenon of losses during the post-harvest system*. Rome: FAO, Agro Industries and Post-Harvest Management Service.

Gu J., Goetschalckx M., and McGinnis L.F. (2007), Research on warehouse operation: A comprehensive review, *European Journal of Operational Research*, 177, pp. 1–21

Guide, V.D. Jr., Jayarman, V., and Linton, J.D. (2003), Building contingency planning for closed-loop supply chains with product recovery, *Journal of Operations Management*, 21 (3), pp. 259–279.

Guide, V.D., Jr., and van Wassenhove, L.N. (2002), The reverse supply chain, *Harvard Business Review*, 80 (2), February, pp. 25–26.

Guide, V.D., Jr., and van Wassenhove, L.N. (2009), The evolution of closed-loop supply chain research, *Operations Research*, 57 (1), pp. 10–18.

Hanley, P. (2014), *Eleven*, Victoria, Canada: Friesen Press.

Hassini, E., Surti, C., and Searcy, C. (2012), A literature review and a case study of sustainable supply chains with a focus on metrics, *International Journal of Production Economics*, 140 (1), pp. 69–82.

Hatcher, G.D., Ijomaha, W.L., and Windmill, J.F.C. (2011), Design for remanufacture: A literature review and future research needs, *Journal of Cleaner Production*, 19 (17–18), pp. 2004–2014.

Hayes, R.H., and Clark, K.B. (1985), Explaining observed productivity differentials between plants: Implications for operations research, *Interfaces*, 15 (6), pp. 3–14.

Hayes R.H., Wheelwright S.C., and Clark K.B. (1988), *Dynamic manufacturing: Creating the learning organisation*, New York: Free Press.

Hervani, A.A., Helms, M.M., and Sarkis, J. (2005), Performance measurement for green supply chain management, *Benchmarking: An International Journal*, 12 (4), pp. 330–353.

Heskett, J.L., Glaskowsky, N.A., and Ivie, R.M. (1973), *Business logistics: Physical distribution and materials management*, New York: Ronald Press Company.

Hill, C.W. (2007), *International business*, sixth edition, New York: McGraw-Hill.

Hill, T. (2005), Operations management, second edition, Palgrave Macmillan.

Hines, T. (2004), *Supply chain strategies: Customer-driven and customer-focused*, Oxford: Elsevier Butterworth-Heinemann.

Holweg, M. (2007), The genealogy of lean production, *Journal of Operations Management*, 25 (2), pp. 420–437.

Hua, G., Cheng, T.C.E., and Wang, S. (2011), Managing carbon footprints in inventory management, *International Journal of Production Economics*, 132 (2), pp. 178–185.

Hvolby, H.-H., and Steger-Jensen, K. (2010), Technical and industrial issues of Advanced Planning and Scheduling (APS) systems, *Computers in Industry*, 61 (9), pp. 845–851.

Hvolby, H.H., and Trienekens, J.H. (2010), Challenges in business systems integration, *Computers in Industry*, 61 (9), pp. 808–812.

IFPSM (2007). Developing a Code of Ethical Behaviour for Supply Management Professionals – A guidance document for Member Associations of the International Federation of Purchasing and Supply Management (IFPSM), available at www.ifpsm.org, viewed on 15 March 2016.

Igarashi, M., de Boer, L., and Fet, A. M. (2013), What is required for greener supplier selection? A literature review and conceptual model development, *Journal of Purchasing and Supply Management*, 19 (4), pp. 247–263.

illycaffè (2014), Sustainable value report 2014, available at http://valuereport.illy.com/assets/download/isvr_IT_2014.pdf, viewed on 1 March 2016.

INFRAS (2014), *Handbook of emissions factors for road transport 3.1/3.2 quick reference*, Geneva, INFRAS.

Ishikawa, K. (1985), *What is total quality control?: the Japanese way*, Englewood Cliffs, NJ, Prentice-Hall.

Islam, S., and Olsen, T. (2014), Truck-sharing challenges for hinterland trucking companies: A case of the empty container truck trips problem, *Business Process Management Journal*, 20 (2), pp. 290–334.

Johnson, E. (2008), Disagreement over carbon footprints: A comparison of electric and LPG forklifts, *Energy Policy*, 36 (4), pp. 1569–1573.

Johnson, G., Scholes, K., and Whittington, R. (2008), *Exploring corporate strategy: Text and cases*, eighth edition, Upper Saddle River, NJ: Prentice-Hall.

Johnson, H.T., and Kaplan, R.S. (1987), *Relevance lost – The rise and fall of management accounting*, Boston: Harvard Business School Press.

Johnson, P.F., Leenders, M.R., and Flynn, A.E. (2011), *Purchasing and supply management*, 14th edition, New York: McGraw-Hill.

Johnstone, M.L., and Tang, L.P. (2014), Exploring the gap between consumer's green rhetoric and purchasing behaviour, *Journal of Business Ethics*, 132 (2), 311–328.

Juran, J.M. (1988), *Juran's quality control handbook*, New York, McGraw-Hill.

Kaplan, R.S., and Norton, D.P. (1992), The balanced scorecard – measures that drive performance, *Harvard Business Review*, 70 (1), pp. 71–79.

Kaplan, R.S., and Norton, D.P. (1996), Linking the Balanced Scorecard to strategy, *California Management Journal*, 39 (1), pp. 53–79.

Kaplan, R.S., and Norton, D.P. (2001), *The strategy-focused organization: How balanced scorecard companies thrive in the new business environment*, Boston: Harvard Business School Press.

Kathawala, Y.K., and Abdou, K. (2003), Supply chain evaluation in the service industry: A framework development compared to manufacturing, *Managerial Auditing Journal*, 18 (2), pp. 140–149.

Klassen, R.D. (2001), Plant-level environmental management orientation: The influence of management views and plant characteristics, *Production and Operations Management*, 10 (3), pp. 257–275.

Klassen, R.D., and Johnson, R.F. (2004), *The green supply chain*, in New S., Westbrook R. (eds.), *Understanding supply chains: Concepts, critiques and future*, Oxford: Oxford University Press.

Klassen, R.D., and McLaughlin, C.P. (1996), The impact of environmental management on firm performance, *Management Science*, 42 (8), pp. 1199–1214.

Klassen, R.D., and Whybark, D.C. (1999), Environmental management in operations: The selection of environmental technologies, *Decision Sciences*, 30 (3), pp. 601–631.

Kleindorfer, P.R., Singhal, K., and Van Wassenhove, L.N. (2005), Sustainable Operations Management, *Production and Operations Management*, 14 (4), pp. 482–492.

Koh, S., Genovese, A., Acquaye, A. A., Barratt, P., Rana, N., Kuylenstierna, J., and Gibbs, D. (2013), Decarbonising product supply chains: Design and development of an integrated evidence-based decision support system – The supply chain environmental analysis tool (SCEnAT), *International Journal of Production Research*, 51 (7), pp. 2092–2109.

Kopicki, R., Berg, M.J., Legg, L., Dasappa, V., and Maggioni, C. (1993), *Reuse and recycling – Reverse logistics opportunities*, Oak Book, IL, Council of Logistics Management.

KPMG (2013), *The KPMG Survey of Corporate Responsibility Reporting 2013*, kpmg.com/sustainability.

Krause, D.R., Vachon, S., and Klassen, R.D. (2009), Special topic forum on sustainable supply chain management: Introduction and reflections on the role of purchasing management, *Journal of Supply Chain Management: A Global Review of Purchasing & Supply*, 45 (4), pp. 18–25.

Lambert, D.M., and Burduroglu, R. (2000), Measuring and selling the value of logistics, *International Journal of Logistics Management*, 11 (1), pp. 1–18.

Lambert, D.M., Croxton, K.L., Garcia-Gastugue S.J., Knemeyer M., and Rogers D.S. (2006), Supply chain management processes, partnership, performance, second edition, Jacksonville, FL: Hartley Press. Inc.

Lay, G., ed. (2015), *Servitization in industry* Switzerland: Springer.

Lee, J., Lapira, E., Bagheri, B., and Kao, K. (2013), Recent advances and trends in predictive manufacturing systems in big data environment, *Manufacturing Letters*, 1 (1), pp. 38–41.

Lee, S.G., and Xu, X. (2005), Design for the environment: Life cycle assessment and sustainable packaging issues, *International Journal of Environmental Technology and Management*, 5 (1), pp. 14–41.

Leong, G.K, Snyder, D.L., and Ward, P.T. (1990), Research in the process and content of manufacturing strategy, *OMEGA*, 18 (1), pp. 109–122.

Lewis, H., Gertsakis, J., and Grant, T. (2001), Design and Environment: A global guide to designing greener goods, Sheffield, UK: Greenleaf Publishing Limited.

Linton, J.D., Klassen, R., and Jayaraman, V. (2007), Sustainable supply chain: An introduction, *Journal of Operations Management*, 24, pp. 1075–1082.

Luttropp, C., and Lagerstedt, J. (2006), Ecodesign and The Ten Golden Rules: Generic advice for merging environmental aspects into product development, *Journal of Cleaner Production*, 14, pp. 1396–1408.

Lynch, R., and Cross, K. (1991), *Measure up! Yardsticks for continuous improvement*, Cambridge, MA: Basil Blackwell Inc.

Malnight, T.W., and Keys, T.S. (2013), *Global trends report 2013: Towards a Distributed Future*, Strategy Dynamics Global SA.

Manenti, P. (2014), *The Digital factory: Game-changing technologies that will transform manufacturing industry*, London: SCM World.

Mangan, J., Lalwani, C., Butcher, T., and Javadpour, R. (2012), *Global Logistics & Supply Chain management*, John Wiley & Sons.

McDonough, W., and Braungart, M. (2002), *Cradle to cradle: Remaking the way we make things*, New York: North Point Press.

McKinnon, A.C., Browne, M., Piercyk, M., and Whiteing, A. (2015), *Green Logistics: Improving the environmental sustainability of logistics*, third edition, London: Kogan Page.

McKinnon, A.C., and Ge, Y. (2006), The potential for reducing empty running by trucks: A retrospective analysis, *International Journal of Physical Distribution & Logistics Management*, 36 (5), pp. 391–410.

McKinnon, A.C., and Woodburn, A., (1993), A logistical perspective on the growth of lorry traffic. *Traffic Engineering and Control*, 34 (10), pp. 466–471.

McKinnon, A.C., and Woodburn, A., (1996), Logistical restructuring and road freight traffic growth: An empirical assessment, *Transportation*, 23 (2), pp. 141–161.

McKinsey Global Institute (2010), *Global forces shaping the future of business and society*, November, available at http://www.mckinsey.com/insights/strategy/global_forces_shaping_the_future_of_business_and_society, viewed on 20 July 2015.

McKinsey Global Institute (2011), *Urban world: Mapping the economic power of cities*, March, available at http://www.mckinsey.com/insights/urbanization/urban_world, viewed on 22 June 2014.

McWilliams, A., and Siegel, D. (2000), Corporate Social Responsibility and Financial performance: Correlation or misspecification?, *Strategic Management Journal*, 21 (5), pp. 603–609.

Meller, R. D., and Gue, K.R. (2009), The application of new aisle designs for unit-load ware-houses, In *Proceedings of the 2009 NSF Engineering Research and Innovation Conference*, Honolulu, HI.

Mentzer, J.T. (2000), *Supply chain management*, Thousand Oaks, CA: Sage Publications.

Mentzer, J.T. (2004), *Fundamentals of supply chain management: Twelve drivers of competitive advantage*, Thousand Oaks, CA: Sage Publications.

Mentzer, J.T., DeWitt W., Keebler J.S., Min S., Nix N.W., Smith C.D. and Zacharia Z.G. (2001), Defining Supply Chain Management, *Journal of Business Logistics*, 22 (2), pp. 1–25.

Miemczyk, J., Johnsen, T.E., and Macquet, M. (2012), Sustainable purchasing and supply management: A structured literature review of definitions and measures at the dyad, chain and network levels, *Supply Chain Management: An International Journal*, 17 (5), pp. 478–496.

Mintzberg, H., and, Waters, J.A. (1985), Of strategies, deliberate and emergent, *Strategic Management Journal*, July–September, 6 (3), pp. 257–272.

Mollenkopf, D. (2006), *Environmental sustainability: Exploring the case for environmentally-sustainable supply chains, CSCMP Explores*, 3 (3), pp. 1–15.

Monastersky, R. (2015), Antropocene: The human age, *Nature*, 519 (7542), pp. 144–147.

Monczka, R., Trent, R. and Handfield, R. (1998), *Purchasing and supply chain management*, Cincinnati, OH: South-Western College Publishing.

Morana, J. (2013), *Sustainable supply chain management*, Hoboken, NJ: John Wiley & Sons.

Muchiri, P., and Pintelon, L. (2008), Performance measurement using overall equipment effectiveness (OEE): Literature review and practical application discussion, *International Journal of Production Research*, 46 (13), pp. 3517–3535.

Muchiri, P., Pintelon, L., Gelders, L. and Martin, H. (2011), Development of maintenance function performance measurement framework and indicators, *International Journal of Production Economics*, 131 (1), pp. 295–302.

Naisbitt, J. (1982), *Megatrends: The new directions transforming our lives*, Warner Books.

Naisbitt, J., and Aburdene, P. (1990), *Megatrends 2000: The new directions fort the 1990s*, New York: William & Morrow Co.

Nakajima, S. (1988), *Introduction to TPM: Total Productive Maintenance*, Productivity Press.

Narasimhan, R., and Schoenherr, T. (2012), The effects of integrated supply management practices and environmental management practices on relative competitive quality advantage, *International Journal of Production Research*, 50 (4), pp. 1185–1201.

NASA – National Aeronautics and Space Administration (2015), Global Climate Change: Vital signs of the Planet, available at http://climate.nasa.gov/evidence/, viewed on 12 August 2015.

Naslund, D., and Williamson, S. (2010), What is management in supply chain management? A critical review of definitions, frameworks and terminology, *Journal of Management Policy and Practice*, 11 (4), pp. 11–28.

National Center for Design (1997), *A guide to EcoReDesign—Improving the Environmental Performance of Manufactured Products*, RMIT – Melbourne, Australia: Royal Melbourne Institute of Technology.

Neely, A., Gregory, M. and Platts, K. (1995), Performance measurement system design: A literature review and research agenda, *International Journal of Operations & Production Management*, 15 (4), pp. 80–116.

Nguyen, H., Stuchtey, M. and Zils, M. (2014), Remaking the industrial economy, in shaping the future of manufacturing, *McKinsey Quarterly*, 1, pp. 47–63.

Nicodeme, C., Diamandouros, K., Díez, J., Durso, C., Brecx, C. and Metushi, S. (2012), *ERF 2012 European road statistics*, Brussels: European Union Road Federation.

Nordhaus, W., and Tobin, J. (1973), "Is growth obsolete ?", The measurement of economic and social performance, *National Bureau of Economic Research.*

NRC – National Research Center (1991), *Improving engineering design: Designing for competitive advantage*, Washington DC: National Academy Press.

Nussbaum, M. (2011), *Creating capabilities: The human development approach*, Cambridge, MA: Harvard University Press.

Oakland, J.S. (2008), *Statistical process control*, sixth edition, Oxford: Butterworth-Heinemann.

OECD – Organization for Economic Co-operation and Development (2001), *Extended producer responsibility: A guidance manual for governments*, Paris: OECD.

OECD – Organization for Economic Co-operation and Development, (2002), *The Polluter pays principle: Definition, analysis, implementation*, Paris: OECD.

OECD – Organization for Economic Co-operation and Development, (2012), *Environmental outlook to 2050: The consequences of inaction*, available at http://www.oecd.org/env/indicators-modelling-outlooks/oecdenvironmentaloutlookto2050theconsequencesofinaction.htm, viewed on 28 April 2014.

Olson, E. (2010), *Better green business: Handbook for environmentally responsible and profitable business practices*, Upper Saddle River, NJ: Pearson Prentice Hall.

Pagell, M., and Wu, Z. (2009), Building a more complete theory of sustainable supply chain management using case studies of 10 exemplars, *Journal of Supply Chain Management*, 45 (2), 37–56.

Pagell, M., Wu, Z., and Wasserman, M.E., (2010), Thinking differently about purchasing portfolios: An assessment of sustainable sourcing, *Journal of Supply Chain Management*, 46 (1), pp. 57–73.

Pahl, G., and Beitz, W. (1996). *Engineering Design – A Systematic Approach*, second edition, London: Springer.

Pande, P.S., Neuman, R.P. and Cavanagh, R. (2000), *The Six Sigma way: How GE, Motorola, and other top companies are honing their performance*, New York: McGraw-Hill Professional.

Parfitt, J., Barthel, M. and Macnaughton, S. (2010), Food waste within food supply chains: Quantification and potential for change to 2050, *Philosophical Transactions of the Royal Society*, 365, pp. 3065–3081.

Pauli, G. (1998), Upsizing: The road to zero emissions; more jobs, more income and no pollution, Greenleaf.

Peelman, N., Ragaert, P., De Meulenaer, B., Adons, D., Peeters, R., Cardon, L., van Impte, F. and Devlieghere, F. (2013), Application of bioplastics for food packaging, *Trends in Food Science & Technology*, 32 (2), pp. 128–141.

Perrini, F., Pogutz, S. and Tencati, A. (2006), *Developing corporate social responsibility: A European perspective*, Edgar Publishing.

Perrini, F., and Russo, A. (2008), Illycaffe: Value creation through responsible supplier relationships, *Journal of Business Ethics Education*, 5, pp. 139–170.

Phillips, A.J., Newlands, N.K, Liang, S.H., and Ellert, B.H. (2014), Integrated sensing of soil moisture at the field-scale: Measuring, modeling and sharing for improved agricultural decision support, *Computer Electronic Agriculture*, 107, pp. 73–88.

Piecyk, M.I., & McKinnon, A. C. (2010). Forecasting the carbon footprint of road freight transport in 2020, *International Journal of Production Economics*, 128 (1), 31–42.

Pohlen, T.L., and Farris, M. (1992), Reverse logistics in plastic recycling, *International Journal of Physical Distribution and Logistics Management*, 22 (7), pp. 35–47.

Porter, M.E. (1991), America's green strategy, *Scientific American*, 264, (4), p. 96.

Porter, M.E. and Kramer, M.R. (2002), The competitive advantage of corporate philanthropy *Harvard Business Review*, 80 (12), pp. 56–68.

Porter, M.E., and Kramer, M.R. (2006), Strategy & society: The link between competitive advantage and corporate social responsibility, *Harvard Business Review*, 84 (12), pp. 78–92.

Porter, M.E., and Kramer, M.R. (2011), Creating shared value, *Harvard Business Review*, 89 (1/2), pp. 62–77.

Prahalad, C.K., and Hammond, A. (2002a), Serving the world's poor profitably, *Harvard Business Review*, 80 (9), pp. 48–57.

Prahalad, C.K., and Hart, S.L. (2002), The fortune at the bottom of the Pyramid, *Strategy and Business*, 26, pp. 2–14.

Prahinski, C. and Kocabasoglu, C. (2006), Empirical research opportunities in reverse supply chain, *Omega: The International Journal of Management Science*, 34, pp. 519–532.

Pusavec, F., Krajnik, P., and Kopac, J. (2010a), Transitioning to sustainable production – Part I: Application on machining technologies, *Journal of Cleaner Production*, 18 (2), pp. 174–184.

Pusavec, F., Kramar, D., Krajnik, P. and Kopac, J. (2010b), Transitioning to sustainable production – Part II: Evaluation of sustainable machining technologies, *Journal of Cleaner Production*, 18 (12), pp. 1211–1221.

Quayle, M. (2003), A study of supply chain management practices in the UK industrial SMEs, *Supply Chain Management*, 8 (1), pp. 79–86.

Rahman, S. (2012), Reverse Logistics, in Mangan, J., Lalwani C., Butcher T., Javadpour R., *Global Logistics & Supply Chain management*, Hoboken, NJ: John Wiley & Sons.

Reefke, H., and Trocchi, M. (2013), Balanced scorecard for sustainable supply chains: Design and development guidelines, *International Journal of Productivity & Performance Management*, 62 (8), pp. 805–826.

Reichhart, A., and Holweg, M. (2007), Creating the customer-responsive supply chain: A reconciliation of concepts, *International Journal of Operations & Production Management*, 27 (11), pp. 1144–1172.

Reverse Logistics Association (2002), available at http://www.reverselogisticstrends.com/reverse-logistics.php, Viewed on 10 February 2015.

Reyes, P.M., and Meade, L.M. (2006), Improving reverse supply chain operational performance: A transshipment application study for not-for-profit organizations, *Journal of Supply Chain Management*, 43 (1), pp. 38–48.

Rizet, C., Cruz, C., and Mbacké, M. (2012), Reducing freight transport CO_2 emissions by increasing the load factor, *Procedia-Social and Behavioral Sciences*, 48, pp. 184–195.

RobecoSam (2014), CSA Guide – RobecoSAM's Corporate Sustainability Assessment Methodology, version 1.0, March 12.

Rockström, J., Steffen, W., Noone, K., Persson, Å., Stuart Chapin, F., Lambin, E.F., Lenton, T.M., Scheffer, M., Folke1, C., Schellnhuber, H.J., Nykvist, B., de Wit, C.A., Hughes, T., van der Leeuw S., Rodhe H., Sörlin S., Snyder P.K., Costanza R., Svedin U., Falkenmark, M., Karlberg, L., Corell, R.W., Fabry, V.J., Hansen, J., Walker, B., Liverman, D., Richardson, K.,

Crutzen, P. and Foley, J.A. (2009), A safe operating space for humanity, *Nature*, 461, pp. 72–475.

Rogers, D.S., Lambert, D.M., Croxton, K.L., and Garcia-Dastugue, S.J. (2002), The return management process, *International Journal of Logistics Management*, 13 (2), pp. 1–18.

Rogers, D.S., and Tibben-Lembke, R.S. (1998), *Going backwards: Reverse Logistics trends and practices*, Pittsburgh, PA: Reverse Logistics Council.

Rogers, D.S., and Tibben-Lembke, R.S. (1999), Reverse Logistics: Stratégies et techniques, *Logistique & Management*, 7 (2), pp. 15–26.

Rogers, D.S., and Tibben-Lembke, R.S. (2001), An Examination of Reverse Logistics practices, *Journal of Business Logistics*, 2001, 22 (2), 129–148.

Rother, M., and Shook, J. (1999), *Learning to see: Value stream mapping to add value and eliminate muda*, Lean Enterprise Institute.

Rushton, A., Croucher, P., and Baker, P. (2014), *The handbook of logistics & distribution management*, fifth edition. London: Kogan Page.

Salzmann, O., Ionescu-Somers, A., and Steger, U. (2005), The business case for corporate sustainability: Literature review and research options, *European Management Journal*, 23 (1), pp. 27–36.

Sander, A. (2012), Report BCG in Harvard Business Review Italia, June, pp. 10–11.

Sanders N.R. (2012), *Supply Chain Management: A global perspective*, Hoboken, NJ: John Wiley & Sons.

Sanders, N.R., and Wood, J.D. (2015), *Foundations of sustainable business: Theory, function and strategy*, Hoboken, NJ: John Wiley & Sons.

Sarkis, J. (2001), Manufacturing's role in corporate environmental sustainability: Concerns for the new millennium, *International Journal of Operations & Production Management*, 21 (5–6), pp. 666 –686.

Schmidheiny, S., and WBCSD – Business Council for Sustainable Development (1992), *Changing course: A global business perspective on development and the environment*, Cambridge, MA: MIT Press.

Schneider, L., and Wallenburg, C. (2012), Implementing sustainable sourcing—Does purchasing need to change?, *Journal of Purchasing & Supply Management*, 18 (4), pp. 243–257.

Schonberger, R. (1982). *Japanese manufacturing techniques: Nine hidden lessons in simplicity*. New York: Simon and Schuster.

Schonberger, R.J. (1986), *World Class Manufacturing: The lessons of simplicity applied*, New York: The Free Press.

Secchi, R. (2012), *Supply chain management e Made in Italy*, Milan: Egea.

Segré, A. (2015), Food waste reduction: An ethical or financial issue? Food saving workshop, Bocconi University, Italy, 20 May, 2015.

Sen, A. (1992), *Inequality reexamined*, Oxford: Oxford University Press.

Sen, A. (1999), *Development as freedom*, Oxford: Oxford University Press.

Shewhart, W.A. (1931), *Economic control of quality of manufactured product*, New York: Van Nostrand.

Shin, H, Collier, D.A., and Wilson, D.D. (2000), Supply Chain Orientation and supplier/buyer performance, *Journal of Operations Management*, 183, pp. 317–333.

Shrivastava, P. (1995), Environmental technologies and competitive advantage, *Strategic Management Journal*, 16, pp. 183–200.

Silvestri, A., De Felice, F. and Petrillo, A., (2012), Multi-criteria risk analysis to improve safety in manufacturing systems, *International Journal of Production Research*, 50 (17), pp. 4806–4821.

Simanis, E. (2012), Reality check at the bottom of the pyramid, *Harvard Business Review*, 90 (6), pp. 120–125.

Simchi-Levi, D., Kaminsky, P., and Simchi-Levi, E. (2003), *Designing and managing the supply chain*, second edition, New York: McGraw-Hill, Irwin.

Singh, S. (2012), *New mega trends: Implications for our future lives*, New York: Palgrave Macmillan.

Skinner, W. (1969), Manufacturing – missing link in corporate strategy, *Harvard Business Review*, 47 (3), pp. 136–145.

Skinner, W. (1974), The focused factory, *Harvard Business Review*, 52 (3), pp. 113–121.

Skinner, W. (1986), The productivity paradox, *Management Review*, 75 (9), pp. 41–45.

Skjott-Larsen, T., Schary, P. B., Mikkola, J. H. and Kotzab, H., (2007), *Managing the global supply chain*, third edition, Copenhagen: Copenhagen Business School Press.

Seuring, S., and Müller, M. (2008), From a literature review to a conceptual framework for sustainable supply chain management, *Journal of Cleaner Production*, 16 (15), pp. 1699–1710.

Slack, N. (2005), The changing nature of operations flexibility, *International Journal of Operations & Production Management*, 25 (12), pp. 1201–1210.

Slack, N., Chambers, S., and Johnson, R. (2007), *Operations management*, fifth edition, Upper Saddle River, NJ: Prentice-Hall.

Souza, G.C. (2012), *Sustainable Operations and Closed-Loop Supply Chains*, New York: Business Expert Press.

Spangenberg, J.H., Fuad-Luke, A., and Blincoe, K. (2010), Design for Sustainability (DfS): The interface of sustainable production and consumption, *Journal of Cleaner Production*, 18 (15), pp. 1485–1493.

Sprague, L.G. (2007), Evolution of the field of operations management, *Journal of Operations Management*, 25 (2), pp. 219–238.

Srivastava, S.K. (2007), Green Supply-chain management: A state-of-the-art literature review, *International Journal of management Review*, 9 (1), pp. 53–80.

Stafford, J.V. (2000), Implementing precision agriculture in the 21st century, *Journal of Agriculture Engineering Research*, 76 (3), pp. 267–275.

Stahel, W.R. (2010), *The performance economy*, second edition, Basingstoke, Hampshire: Palgrave Macmillan.

Stalk, J.G. (1988), Time: The next source of competitive advantage, *Harvard Business Review*, 66 (4), pp. 41–51.

Steffen, W., Richardson, K., Rockström, J., Cornell, S.E., Fetzer, I., Bennett, E.-M., Biggs, R., Carpenter, S.K., de Vries, W., de Wit, C.A., Folke, C., Gerten, D., Heinke, J., Mace, G.M., Persson, L.M., Ramanathan, V., Reyers, B., and Sörlin, S. (2015), Planetary boundaries: Guiding human development on a changing planet, *Science*, 34 (6223), p. 736.

Stiglitz, J.E., Sen, A., and Fitoussi, J.P. (2010), *Mismeasuring our lives, Why GDP doesn't add up: The Report by the Commission on the Measurement of Economic Performance and Social Progress*, New York: The New Press.

Stock, J.R. (1992), *Reverse Logistics*, Oak Brook, IL: Council of Logistics Management.

Stock, J.R. (1998), *Development and implementation of reverse logistics programs*, Oak Book, IL: Council of Logistics Management.

Stock, J.R., and Boyer S. (2009), Developing a consensus definition of a supply chain management: A qualitative study, *International Journal of Physical Distribution & Logistics Management*, 39 (8), pp. 690–711.

Stroufe, R., and Melnyk, S. (2013), *Developing Sustainable Supply Chains to drive value: Management issues, insights, concepts and tools*, New York: Business Expert Press.

Stuart, T. (2009), *Waste: Uncovering the global food scandal*, London: Penguin.

Svanes, E., Vold, M., Møller, H., Pettersen, M.K., Larsen, H., and Hanssen, O. J. (2010), Sustainable packaging design: A holistic methodology for packaging design, *Packaging Technology and Science*, 23 (3), pp. 161–175.

Sygna, K., Aasvang, G.M., Aamodt, G., Oftedal, B. and Krog, N.H. (2014), Road traffic noise, sleep and mental health, *Environmental research*, 131, pp. 17–24.

Taguchi, G. (1986), *Introduction to quality engineering: Designing quality into products and processes*, Tokyo: Asian Productivity Organization.

Taguchi, G., and Clausing, D. (1990), Robust quality, *Harvard Business Review*, 68 (1), pp. 65–75.

Talberth, J., Cobb, C., and Slattery, N. (2006), *The Genuine Progress Indicator 2006: A tool for sustainable development*, Oakland, CA: Redefining Progress.

Telenko, C., Seepersad, C.C., and, Webber, M.E. (2008), *A compilation of design for environment principles and guidelines*, New York: ASME DETC Design for Manufacturing and the Life Cycle Conference, 2008.

Tencati, A., and Perrini, F., eds. (2011), Business ethics and corporate sustainability, Edward Elgar Publishing.

Tencati, A., and Pogutz, S. (2015), Recognizing the limits: Sustainable Development, Corporate Sustainability and the need for innovative business paradigms, *Sinergie: Italian Journal of Management*, 33 (96), pp. 37–55.

Thierry, M., Salomon, M, Nunen, J., and van Wassenhove, L. (1995), Strategic issues in product recovery management, *California Management Review*, 37 (2), pp. 114–134.

Tibben-Lembke, R. (1998), The impact of Reverse Logistics on Total Cost of Ownership, *Journal of Marketing Theory and Practice*, 6 (4), pp. 51–60.

Tibben-Lembke, R. (2002), Life after death: Reverse Logistics and the Product Life Cycle, *International Journal of Physical Distribution and Logistics Management*, 32 (3), pp. 223–244.

Tibben-Lembke, R. (2004), Strategic use of the secondary market for retail consumer goods, *California Management Review*, 46 (2), pp. 90–104.

Tibben-Lembke, R., and Rogers D.S. (2002), Differences between forward and reverse logistics in a retail environment, *Supply Chain Management: An International Journal*, 7 (5), pp. 271–282.

Tukker, A. (2004), Eight types of product-service system: Eight ways to sustainability? Experiences from Suspronet, *Business Strategy and the Environment*, 13, pp. 246–260.

Ulrich, K.T., and Eppinger, S.D. (2012), *Product design and development*, fifth edition, New York: McGraw-Hill.

UN – United Nations (1998), Kyoto Protocol to the United Nations framework convention on climate change, available at http://unfccc.int/resource/docs/convkp/kpeng.pdf, viewed on 8 August 2016.

UN – United Nations (2007), *Indicators of sustainable development: Guidelines and methodologies*, third edition. New York.

UN – United Nations (2013), *Human development report – Technical notes*, New York.

UN Habitat (2006), *State of the world's cities, 2006/7*, available at http://mirror.unhabitat.org/pmss/listItemDetails.aspx?publicationID=2101&AspxAutoDetectCookieSupport=1, viewed on 4 June, 2014.

UNDESA – United Nations Department of Economic and Social Affairs (2015), Population facts: Youth population trends and sustainable development, United Nations Department of Economic and Social Affairs – Populations Divisions, n. 1, May 2015, available at http://www.un.org/en/development/desa/population/publications/pdf/popfacts/PopFacts_2015-1.pdf, viewed on 11 November 2015.

UNEP – United Nations Environment Programme (2004), *Guidance manual: How to establish and operate cleaner production centers*, UNIDO – United Nations Industrial Development Organization, Vienna.

UNEP – United Nations Environment Programme (2010), *Assessing the environmental impacts of consumption and production: Priority products and materials*, UNIDO – United Nations Industrial Development Organization, Paris.

UNEP – United Nations Environment Programme (2011), *Decoupling natural resource use and environmental impacts from economic growth*. Report of the Working Group on Decoupling to the International Resource Panel, available at www.unep.org/resourcepanel/decoupling/files/pdf/Decoupling_Report_English.pdf, viewed on 15 December 2015.

UN FAO – Food and Agriculture Organization (2012), *The state of food insecurity in the world 2012*, United Nations, Rome.

UNFCCC – United Nations Framework Convention on Climate Change (2010), *Cancun Climate Change Conference, November*, available at http://unfccc.int/meetings/cancun_nov_2010/meeting/6266.php, viewed on 28 April 2014.

UNFCCC – United Nations Framework Convention on Climate Change (2011), *Report of the UNFCCC Conference*, Cancun, December, 2010, Bonn Germany: UNFCCC.

UN GC – United Nations Global Compact (2013), The value driver model: A tool for communicating the business value of sustainability, available at https://www.unglobalcompact.org/docs/issues_doc/Financial_markets/Value_Driver_Model/VDM_Report.pdf, viewed on the 6 July 2015.

UNPD – United Nations Population Division (2014), *World urbanization prospect: The 2014 revision*, available at http://esa.un.org/unpd/wup/, viewed on 25 September 2014.

UNPD – United Nations Population Division (2015), *World population prospect: The 2015 revision*, available at http://esa.un.org/unpd/wpp/DVD/, viewed on 28 August, 2015.

USGBC – U.S. Green Building Council (2015), LEED – Leadership in energy and environmental design certification, LEED V.4, available at http//www.usgbc.org, viewed on 15 July 2015.

Vachon, S., Classen, R.D. and Johnson, P.F. (2001), *Customers as green suppliers: Managing the complexity of the reverse supply chain*, in Sarkis J. (ed.), *Greener manufacturing and operations: From design to delivery and back*, Sheffield, UK: Goenleaf Publishing, pp. 136–149.

Van Audenhove, F.G., Komichuk, C., Shoenmakers, A., and Lammens, L. (2014), The future of urban mobility: Opportunities within extended mobility ecosystems, *PRISM*, 1, Arthur D. Little, pp. 12–31.

Van Kempen, E.E., Kruize, H., Boshuizen, H.C., Ameling, C.B., Staatsen, B.A. and de Hollander, A.E. (2002), The association between noise exposure and blood pressure and ischemic heart disease: A meta-analysis, *Environmental Health Perspectives*, 110 (3), pp. 307–317.

Van Weele, A.J. (2009), *Purchasing and supply chain management: Analysis, strategy, planning and practice*, London: Cengage-Thomson.

Vandermerwe S., and Rada J. (1988), Servitization of business: Adding value by adding service, *European Management Journal*, 6(49), pp. 314–324.

Veleva, V. and Ellenbecker, M. (2001), Indicators of sustainable production: framework and methodology, *Journal of Cleaner Production*, 9 (6), pp. 519–549.

Verghese, K.L., Horne, R. and Carre, A. (2010), PIQET: The design and development of an online "streamlined" LCA tool for sustainable packaging design decision support, *International Journal of Life Cycle Assessment*, 15 (6), pp. 608–620.

Vezzoli, C., and Sciama, D. (2006), Life Cycle Design: From general methods to product type specific guidelines and checklists: A method adopted to develop a set of guidelines/checklist handbook for the eco-efficient design of NECTA vending machines, *Journal of Cleaner Production*, 14 (15–16), pp. 1319–1325.

Vezzoli, C., and, Manzini E. (2008), *Design and innovation for sustainability*, Milan: Springer.

Wackernagel, M., and Rees, W. (1995), *Our ecological footprint: Reducing human impact on the earth*,The New Catalyst Bioregional Series, Gabriola Island, BC: New Society Publishers.

Walker, H., and Brammer, S. (2009), Sustainable procurement in the United Kingdom public sector, *Supply Chain Management: An International Journal*, 14 (2), pp. 128–137.

Walker, H., Di Sisto, L., and McBain, D. (2008), Drivers and barriers to environmental supply chain management practices: Lessons from the public and private sectors, *Journal of Purchasing and Supply Management*, 14 (1), pp. 69–85.

Walker, H., Mayo, J., Brammer, S., Touboulic, A., and Lynch, J. (2012), Sustainable procurement: An international policy analysis of 30 OECD countries. Fifth International Public Procurement Conference, August, Seattle, WA, pp. 17–19.

Walker, P.H., Seuring, P., Sarkis, P.J., and Klassen, P.R. (2014), *Sustainable operations management: Recent trends and future directions*, International Journal of Operations & Production Management, 34 (5), pp. 1–11.

WB – The World Bank (2010), World Development Indicators 2010, available at http://data.worldbank.org/sites/default/files/section2.pdf, pp. 91–92, viewed on 12 July 2015.

WB – The World Bank, (2012), *What a waste: A global review of solid waste management*, Urban Development Series – Knowledge Papers, N. 15. March, Washington, DC.

WBCSD – World Business Council for Sustainable Development (1992), *Cleaner production and eco-efficiency*, Geneva: WBCSD.

WBCSD – World Business Council for Sustainable Development (1999), Corporate Social Responsibility: Meeting changing expectations, Geneva: WBCSD.

WBCSD – World Business Council for Sustainable Development (2005), Eco-efficiency: Learning module, Geneva: WBCSD.

WBCSD/WRI – World Business Council for Sustainable Development/World Resource Institute (2004). *The Greenhouse Gas Protocol: A corporate accounting and reporting standard*, revised edition, Washington, DC: Geneva and World Resource Institute.

WCED – The World Commission on Environmental and Development (1987), *Our common future*, New York: Oxford University Press.

Wills B. (2009), *Green intentions: Creating a green value stream to compete and win*, New York: CRC Press.

Wise, R., and Baumgartner, P. (1999), Go downstream: The new profit imperative in manufacturing, *Harvard Business Review*, 77 (5), pp. 133–141.

Womack, J.P., Jones, D.T. and Roos, D. (1990), *The machine that changed the world*, New York: Free Press.

World Business Forum (2014), *Towards the circular economy: Accelerating the scale-up across global supply chain*, January.

Yang, M.G.M., Hong, P. and Modi, S.B. (2011), Impact of lean manufacturing and environmental management on business performance: An empirical study of manufacturing firms, *International Journal of Production Economics*, 129 (2), pp. 251–261.

Yakovleva, N., Sarkis, J., and Sloan, T. (2012), Sustainable benchmarking of supply chains: The case of the food industry, *International Journal of Production Research*, 50 (5), pp. 1297–1317.

Zhuo, C., and Levendis, Y. (2014), Upcycling waste plastics into carbon nanomaterials: A review, *Journal of Applied Polymer Science*, 131 (4), pp. 1–14.

Zokaei K., Lovins H., Wood A., and Hines P. (2013), *Creating a lean and green business system: Techniques for improving profits and sustainability*, New York: CRC Press.

Zolotas, X. (1981), *Economic growth and declining social welfare*, New York: New York University Press.

INDEX

Sustainable Operations and Supply Chain Management, First Edition. Valeria Belvedere and Alberto Grando.
© 2017 John Wiley & Sons Ltd. Published 2017 by John Wiley & Sons Ltd.

Wiley Series in
Operations Research and Management Science

Operations Research and Management Science (ORMS) is a broad, interdisciplinary branch of applied mathematics concerned with improving the quality of decisions and processes and is a major component of the global modern movement towards the use of advanced analytics in industry and scientific research. The *Wiley Series in Operations Research and Management Science* features a broad collection of books that meet the varied needs of researchers, practitioners, policy makers, and students who use or need to improve their use of analytics. Reflecting the wide range of current research within the ORMS community, the Series encompasses application, methodology, and theory and provides coverage of both classical and cutting edge ORMS concepts and developments. Written by recognized international experts in the field, this collection is appropriate for students as well as professionals from private and public sectors including industry, government, and nonprofit organization who are interested in ORMS at a technical level. The Series is comprised of four sections: Analytics; Decision and Risk Analysis; Optimization Models; and Stochastic Models.

Advisory Editors • Analytics
Jennifer Bachner, Johns Hopkins University
Khim Yong Goh, National University of Singapore

Founding Series Editor
James J. Cochran, University of Alabama

Printed and bound by CPI Group (UK) Ltd, Croydon, CR0 4YY

23/04/2025

14660952-0001